SPECIAL MESSAGE TO READERS

This book is published under the auspices of

THE ULVERSCROFT FOUNDATION
(registered charity No. 264873 UK)

Established in 1972 to provide funds for research, diagnosis and treatment of eye diseases. Examples of contributions made are: —

A new Children's Assessment Unit at Moorfield's Hospital, London.

•

Twin operating theatres at the Western Ophthalmic Hospital, London.

•

A Chair of Ophthalmology at the University of Leicester.

•

The establishment of a Royal Australian College of Ophthalmologists "Fellowship".

You can help further the work of the Foundation by making a donation or leaving a legacy. Every contribution, no matter how small, is received with gratitude. Please write for details to:

THE ULVERSCROFT FOUNDATION,
The Green, Bradgate Road, Anstey,
Leicester LE7 7FU, England.
Telephone: (0116) 236 4325

In Australia write to:
THE ULVERSCROFT FOUNDATION,
c/o The Royal Australian College of
Ophthalmologists,
27, Commonwealth Street, Sydney
N.S.W. 2010.

D0184344

I've travelled the world twice over,
Met the famous: saints and sinners,
Poets and artists, kings and queens,
Old stars and hopeful beginners,
I've been where no-one's been before,
Learned secrets from writers and cooks
All with one library ticket
To the wonderful world of books.

© Janice James.

The wisdom of the ages
Is there for you and me,
The wisdom of the ages,
In your local library.

There's large print books
And talking books,
For those who cannot see,
The wisdom of the ages,
It's fantastic, and it's free.

Written by Sam Wood, aged 92

THE SPICE ISLANDS VOYAGE

This is a book about a journey and a quest: a journey among the Spice Islands of equatorial Indonesia aboard a traditional native sailing vessel; a quest to rediscover a remarkable Englishman — Alfred Russel Wallace. This brilliant and intrepid naturalist's research and travels founded the science of zoo-geography and provided Charles Darwin with vital clues in developing the theory of evolution by natural selection, which Wallace had worked out independently. Tim Severin set out to restore Wallace's reputation by retracing the explorer's journeys through the exotic islands.

Books by Tim Severin
Published by The House of Ulverscroft:

THE JASON VOYAGE
THE CHINA VOYAGE

TIM SEVERIN

THE SPICE ISLANDS VOYAGE

In Search of Wallace

Photographs by
Joe Beynon and Paul Harris

Illustrations by
Leonard Sheil

Complete and Unabridged

CHARNWOOD
Leicester

First published in Great Britain in 1997 by
Little, Brown and Company
London

First Charnwood Edition
published 1998
by arrangement with
Little, Brown and Company (UK)
London

British Library CIP Data

Severin, Tim, *1940 –*
The Spice Islands voyage: in search of Wallace.
—Large print ed.—
Charnwood library series
1. Severin, Timothy, *1940 –* —Journeys—Indonesia
2. Wallace, Alfred Russel, *1823 – 1913.*
Malay Archipelago 3 Large type books
4. Indonesia—Description and travel
I. Title II. Beynon, Joe III. Harris, Paul
IV. Sheil, Leonard
915.9′8′0439

ISBN 0–7089–9011–8

Published by
F. A. Thorpe (Publishing) Ltd.
Anstey, Leicestershire
Set by Words & Graphics Ltd.
Anstey, Leicestershire
Printed and bound in Great Britain by
T. J. International Ltd., Padstow, Cornwall

This book is printed on acid-free paper

'That you have returned alive is wonderful after all your risk from illness and sea voyages, especially that most interesting one to Waigiou and back. Of all the impressions which I have received from your book, the strongest is that your perseverance in the cause of science was heroic.'

Charles Darwin after reading *The Malay Archipelago* writing to Alfred Wallace

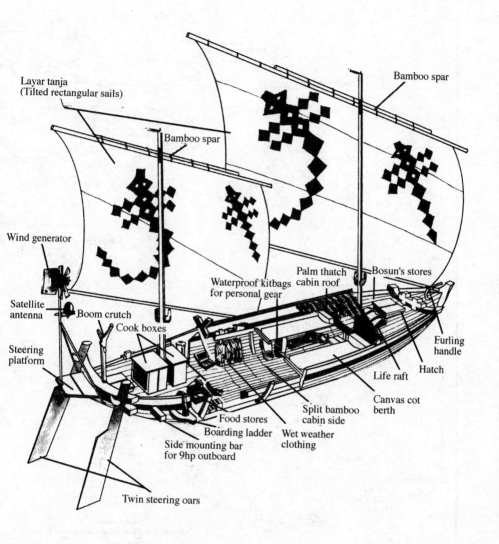

Layar tanja
(Tilted rectangular sails)

Bamboo spar

Bamboo spar

Wind generator

Satellite
antenna

Boom crutch

Cook boxes

Steering
platform

Waterproof kitbags
for personal gear

Palm thatch
cabin roof

Bosun's stores

Furling
handle

Hatch

Life raft

Canvas cot
berth

Food stores

Split bamboo
cabin side

Boarding ladder

Wet weather
clothing

Side mounting bar
for 9hp outboard

Twin steering oars

PRAHU KALULIS *ALFRED WALLACE*

Length: *14.3 metres* Beam: *2.4 metres* Draught: *45cm*

Sail area: *Mainsail 27 sq. metres   Mizzen 18 sq. metres*

BUNAKEN
MARINE RESERVE

Manado   TANGKOKO RESERVE

MINAHASA

Langowen

Labi Labi

P

Ternate   Sidangoli
Tidore

HALMAHERA
(GILOLO)

Makian

Sabatang

Baciam
(BACON)

Gandasoli

0°

SULAWESI
(CELEBES)

M
A

S e r a n

L

BOURU
(BURU)

U

S E R
(CERAM)

Wah

MANUSEL
NATUR
RESERV

Ambon

C

C

U

K

U

5°S

B a n d a   S

S e a

TIMOR

( )   Placenames in brackets refer
     to former names.

10°

Nautical Miles

0   50   100   150   200

0   100   200   300

Kilometres

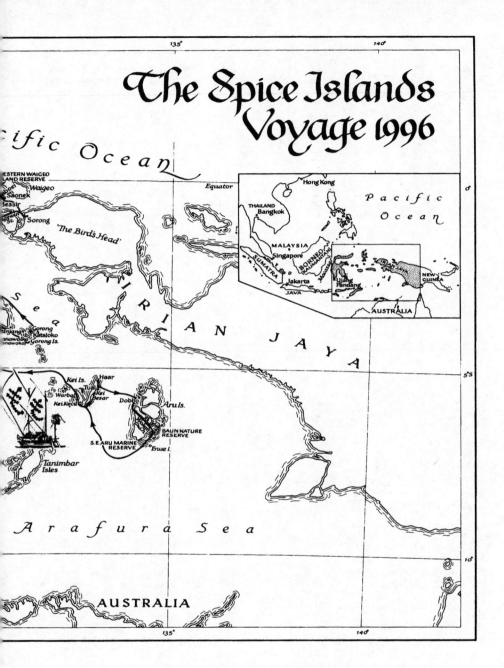

The Spice Islands
Voyage 1996

Map by Alec Herzer

1

The Fever Victim

IN a palm-thatched house a gaunt and impoverished white man lay on a cot, stoically sweating and shivering through an attack of fever. It was late February or early March 1858, the precise date lost because the invalid had made so many field trips that his diary had become vague, and he may have been confused by the fever. For three and a half years he had been exploring some of the remotest islands on earth. Besides contracting malaria, he had endured bouts of semi-starvation and occasionally been so badly crippled by tropical ulcers on his legs and feet that he could move only by crawling on all-fours.

The results of his wanderings lay scattered about him: waterproof storage boxes, locally made of woven and lacquered palm leaves, contained thousands of dead insects. They were mostly beetles, but there were also samples of the region's vivid and spectacular butterflies. The majority of the specimens were already pinned, with detailed notes written rather untidily beside them. There were also the dried skins and skeletons of exotic birds, and a few bones of small mammals. Fresh specimens — which the sick man had not yet had time to scrape and dry — hung dangling by strings from the rafters or were carefully marooned on saucers of water to save them from the columns of ants which regularly pillaged his makeshift work table and carried off bits of flesh and feathers. These unskinned specimens gave the invalid's room a distinct smell of tropical decay, but he was so accustomed to the odour that he scarcely noticed it any longer.

An Englishman in his mid-thirties, the malaria victim was in the Spice Islands or Moluccas, in what is today the Republic of Indonesia, and he was a naturalist of a new kind. He financed his work by sending rare zoological specimens to an agent in London, who sold them to museums and wealthy collectors and remitted the funds to the Moluccas. The wanderer kept a notebook, with lists of just how many beetles and other insects he had shipped, sometimes using discarded gin cases, along with the pressed corpses of unknown bats and even a desiccated tree kangaroo. Occasionally he made a note,

2

calculating how much the shipment might earn him if it sold well. On the inside front cover he wrote himself a reminder, estimating the money he would need to save to provide a worthwhile annuity. The skins of the more beautiful and rare birds earned him most, though few could bring in the money he had made two years earlier when he packed up and shipped back five orang-utan hides (pickled in arrack) and 16 of their skulls from the Sumatran rainforest. He insured the orang skins for £50 and expected to get five times that price if his agent managed to find the right clients. Paying his field expenses in this way, so that he could continue with his scientific research, placed him among the world's first professional naturalists.

The invalid knew he should stay on his cot until the alternating hot and cold fits were over. As he lay there, he kept his mind busy by turning over a puzzle which had intrigued him for more than ten years: how had the world come to be populated by such an extraordinary variety of animals and plants? Was there any way to explain the striking differences between the species, or a universal rule to help understand their individual characteristics? It should be a theory which could be applied equally from the smallest to the largest creature. It should be just as valid for, say, the lumbering Javan rhinoceros or the tiny, round-eyed furry tarsier, the smallest of primates, both of which lived in the rainforests of Indonesia.

The best solution to the puzzle so far had been put forward early in the century by a French naturalist, Jean-Baptiste Lamarck, who had proposed that natural conditions had moulded the development of animals into their present forms. The most conspicuous example Lamarck cited was the giraffe; he claimed that it had grown its long neck over the course of many centuries because the animal had been constantly stretching upward to browse on tall trees. The idea was attractive, but inadequate. It did not properly explain, for instance, why Nature could produce such elaborate creatures as the gorgeous Birds of Paradise which the sick man had seen for himself in those tropical islands the previous year. Nor did Lamarck's theory explain why the Bird of Paradise grew plumage which was often more like twisted wire than feathers, or why the creature danced high in the trees in the morning or evening in a blaze of colour.

As the sick man mulled over the problem of the immense diversity of Nature, he remembered the gloomy theory devised by his countryman, the economist Thomas Malthus, who believed that less-advanced human populations would always be kept under control by 'positive checks'. Disease, accident, war and famine would repeatedly cut back numbers to a sustainable level. The naturalist tried to imagine how this same bleak picture might also apply to the animal world in general, and what would result from such regular, massive threats to the members of any species. 'Why do some live and some die?' he asked himself. 'And the answer was clearly that on the whole the best fitted live. From the effects of disease the most healthy escaped; from enemies, the strongest, the swiftest, or the most cunning; from famine, the best hunters or those with the best digestion; and so on. Then it suddenly flashed upon me that this self-acting process would necessarily *improve the race*, because in every generation the inferior would inevitably be killed off and the superior would remain — that is, *the fittest would survive.*'

As soon as he felt well enough, the naturalist went to his makeshift desk, put on the spectacles he wore for his weak eyes and wrote down his revolutionary theory before the next bout of delirium swept it away. The following evening, and the evening after that, he reworked his phrases until he had the idea lucidly explained. For one of the most profound concepts of the modern scientific age, his essay was surprisingly brief; its exposition ran to a little more than 4,000 words, including examples and explanations. It started by describing what he called 'the struggle for existence' among animals, and then showed mathematically that their rates of reproduction far exceeded the growth in food supply, and therefore the vast majority would die. Of the remainder, the essay concluded, 'those that prolong their existence can only be the most perfect in health and vigour; . . . the weakest and least perfectly organised must always succumb.' 'The more I thought over it,' the lone naturalist recalled, 'the more I became convinced that I had at length found the long-sought-for law of nature that solved the problem of the origin of species.'

Satisfied with his synopsis, he wrote a covering letter asking whether the idea was worth publishing in a learned journal, and signed his name — Alfred Russel Wallace.

Then he sent the package by mail steamer to England, where it was delivered to a country house in Kent whose solid prosperity was a complete contrast to the humble palm-thatch house where Alfred Wallace had worked out his theory. Here, with 15 household servants, a wife who was the daughter of the wealthy pottery manufacturer Josiah Wedgwood, and a private income which would make him the equivalent of a modern millionaire, lived Charles Darwin . . . and at that point the story of the genesis of the 'Darwinian' theory of natural selection becomes murky and contentious.

For most of the previous 20 years, Darwin had been working diligently on the question of how the animal species came to be different. He had not made any public pronouncement of his ideas, though he had put a smattering of his thoughts into letters which he sent to his eminent scientific friends for their comment. This was enough for them to expect that if anyone would crack the 'Species Question', Darwin was the person to do it. From talent and heredity, much was expected of him. His grandfather, the poet and scientist Erasmus Darwin, had already written on the topic of evolution, and the grandson had added to the family's reputation as natural scientists with his superb description of his voyage aboard the exploring ship *Beagle*. During that voyage the sailors had nicknamed him 'FlyCatcher' from his habit of littering the decks with insect specimens. Now the leading savants in England were waiting impatiently for Darwin, who was approaching his fiftieth birthday, to publish his *magnum opus*.

No one knew quite how far Darwin had progressed, for he had become a semi-recluse. He was reading everything that had been written on the subject, building up an extensive private library of books which might throw light on the matter, making margin notes in volume after volume. He had painstakingly written several volumes of his own, collections of learned monographs on fossils and barnacles which he considered held a clue to the way all animals had developed. He was also conducting experiments with the cross-breeding of pigeons, pigs and horses. He spent hour after hour walking in his garden, thinking. His head gardener observed that Darwin would sometimes stand stock still for ten minutes at a time, in a reverie gazing at a single flower. Above all, he was keeping up a voracious correspondence with his fellow savants, seeking their ideas and opinions and asking them for data. But very rarely did he mention how his own work was coming along, though everyone presumed it to be close to publication.

Now arrived Wallace's essay from the Spice Islands: it had taken three months to get to England, and was a bombshell. The effect on Darwin was 'almost paralysing', Wallace later found out. Darwin read the new essay, and was dumbfounded. In a few pages Wallace set out the key elements of the theory of evolution over which Darwin had been labouring for so long. His language was lucid and clear. 'I never saw a more striking coincidence,' Darwin wrote in amazement, 'if Wallace had my ms. sketch written out in 1842, he could not have made a better short abstract. Even his terms now stand as heads of my chapters.'

Darwin knew enough about this lone wanderer at the far side of the world to realise that he was a man to be taken seriously. Zoological journals had been publishing a number of contributions about beetles and tropical birds sent in from south-east Asia, and the author's opinions were invariably perceptive and sound. Indeed Darwin himself had already sent two letters to Wallace asking him to submit interesting specimens, particularly of any unusual native poultry,[1] and encouraging Wallace to pursue ideas on evolution. In his letters, though, Darwin had been deliberately vague about his own work and more interested in learning from Wallace's field observations. Yet in the elite circle of Darwin's scientific confidants, the distant insect hunter was a nobody, a complete outsider. Wallace had never been to a university, and rarely attended the scientific gatherings of which the Victorian savants were so fond, for the very good reason that he was a field naturalist and

---

[1] Later Wallace obliged by sending him a Javanese chicken.

above all because he was extremely shy.

Darwin was racked by conflicting emotions. On the one hand he had to applaud the brilliant thinking of this impecunious collector, a man 14 years his junior, who had been tackling the 'Species Question' alone in the equatorial jungle. On the other hand, Darwin was alarmed that his life's major work would be overtaken at a stroke. Uncertain what to do, he forwarded Wallace's brilliant essay to his friend Sir Charles Lyell, a renowned geologist and leading light of the scientific establishment, and asked for his advice. In turn, Lyell consulted with Dr Joseph Hooker, the eminent botanist and later the Director of Kew Gardens. Lyell and Hooker were among the two most powerful and respected men in British science at the time, and both knew Darwin had long been working on the problem of evolution. But, despite their pleading, he had never published anything.

So they hatched what seemed at first glance to be a fair solution. They came up with the notion that the best way of protecting Darwin's years of meticulous work was for his ideas and Wallace's essay to be placed before the scientific community simultaneously. Luckily Darwin had written down some of his ideas on evolution in 1842, and again in 1844 in letters to his friends. Lyell and Hooker arranged for these extracts to be read out on 1 July to a meeting of the Fellows and Guests of the Linnean Society, the premier learned society for those interested in natural history. Brief sections from Darwin's early letters were read out first, then Wallace's essay which said much the same thing, only more elegantly and much more fully, was 'communicated to the Society'. Neither Darwin nor Wallace was actually present, Darwin because one of his children had died of scarlet fever a few days earlier, and Wallace because he was then in New Guinea, one of the first Europeans to spend any length of time in that huge distant island, collecting more birds and beetles and totally unaware of the stir he had caused.

On the face of it, Lyell and Hooker had come up with a judgement of Solomon. It appeared that they had given an even-handed chance for both men to be recognised as co-authors of the new idea. But the truth of the matter was that the joint announcement gave Darwin his chance to seize the initiative, just as long as Wallace stayed safely out of the way in the tropical rainforest. Darwin's advantage was further improved by the fact that the content of the two papers made very little impact at the Linnean meeting itself. Hardly anyone seems to have realised that Darwin and Wallace had altered the science of evolutionary biology for ever.

Darwin now acted swiftly. He took great care to distance himself from the Lyell-Hooker stratagem, since he realised that Wallace had never been consulted about the announcement, and in a sense he had betrayed his colleague's trust. Badly jolted by Wallace's letter, Darwin rushed into print. Working flat out on his long-delayed manuscript, Darwin completed it in only 17 months by producing a much shorter version of his original planned volume. He gave it the title *On The Origin of Species by Means of Natural Selection or the Preservation of Favoured Races in the Struggle for Life*, and it was published in the year after he received the shattering letter from the Spice Islands.

Darwin's book was a huge success, running through six editions in the next 13 years, and it earned for him the lion's share of the credit. In his book he acknowledged Wallace's pioneer work, but as the years went by he was to make fewer and fewer references to his co-discoverer, instead referring to 'my doctrines'. Soon, only Darwin's name was immediately linked with the theory of the evolution by natural selection, or 'survival of the fittest' as it was paraphrased by the philosopher Herbert Spencer six years later. The impact of this theory was to be one of the most profound scientific developments of the modern age. Darwin's *Origins* would be referred to as 'the book that shook the world', and the main thrust of its argument that all living creatures have developed slowly over time and that all related organisms have a common ancestor would ultimately find general acceptance, though for decades it was contested, criticised and sometimes reviled. Supported by the research of geneticists and molecular biologists, the idea of slow, inexorable evolution now dominates the way we look at the world around us. Yet scarcely anyone recalls that it

11

was originally introduced to a small scientific gathering in Victorian London who would have thought of it as the Darwin-Wallace theory.

Typically, Wallace saw no injustice in the circumstances. His generosity was astounding, even naïve. 'I shall always maintain (the idea) was yours and yours only,' he wrote to Darwin, who naturally worried how Wallace would react when he eventually discovered what had been done in his name and without his permission. He need not have been concerned, for Wallace was even to argue that the theory had required someone of Darwin's eminence to publish it. No one, he said, would have paid any attention if it had come from an insignificant scientist like himself. In fact when Wallace eventually did bring out his own book on evolutionary theory, he went so far as to call it *Darwinism*. When Wallace finally came home nearly three years later, all he wanted to do was to get on with cataloguing and describing his beloved insects and bird skins. Only after that was well advanced did he turn to writing the story of his adventures as a naturalist in south-east Asia, and make public his ideas about animal distribution and diversity which he drew from his experiences. To ensure that no one mistook even that remarkable and fascinating book as a bid for rivalry with Darwin, he dedicated the volume to Darwin with the words 'Not Only as a Token of Personal Esteem and Friendship, but also to express my deep appreciation for His Genius and His Works'.

12

Photo of Wallace in Singapore

In short, Wallace came back from south-east Asia and stepped into Darwin's shadow, deliberately and courteously. His book, *The Malay Archipelago*, was the monument he preferred, and it reveals a truly extraordinary man.

Wallace confounds the usual image of the Victorian explorer which is based largely on the African model. He did not go forward, rifle in one hand, bible in the other, on the lookout for big game or souls to save. Nor did he seek to map the source of great rivers or to climb the peaks of the highest mountains. Africa, of course, was a very different proposition from south-east Asia: the former a huge continental land mass with a little-known interior, while Indonesia is a vast array of islands, more than 13,000 of them spread along the Equator, in seas that had been criss-crossed for centuries by ships from China, South Asia and, more recent to Wallace's arrival, from Europe and North America. Some Indonesian islands like Borneo and New Guinea were of immense size. Their hinterlands presented such barriers that they would not be properly explored until the modern era. Other islands were scarcely larger than a single English county, yet supported rich cities and brilliant civilisations and had been well known to foreign traders and settlers since the time of Christ. Perhaps the most striking characteristic of this huge and sprawling archipelago of archipelagos was its cultural variety. Some island populations were very highly evolved, while others remained in the

Stone Age. And though most of Indonesia was already under Dutch colonial rule by the time Wallace arrived there, this control was only nominal in many regions. Wallace visited places where he was the first European ever to spend any length of time, and he lived for months among the local peoples who had never had a white man stay with them before.

Here, even allowing for the differences between Africa and Asia, Wallace still was an explorer of a different style. He did not advance at the head of a long line of porters, one of them perhaps carrying a tin bath on his head. Wallace worried more about his supply of pins to stick into insect specimens than about bath supplies. He recruited only a handful of local helpers when he needed them, and his only regular companion was Ali, a Malay assistant whom he trained to shoot and skin birds or net butterflies, while Ali taught him to speak Malay. A telling contrast is with his contemporary Henry Stanley, the African explorer. When Stanley needed a boat, he organised his men to haul one in kit form across the veldt. In a similar situation, Wallace purchased himself a small second-hand native vessel for a few shillings, took off his jacket, pulled out his own chisels and wood saw, and adapted the cabin to his own specifications because he knew how to work timber. As for the bible and rifle, Wallace had no revealed religion and made no attempt to be a missionary. The gun he normally carried was a shotgun[1] loaded with bird-shot so that he could knock down specimens and study them. The only time he hunted what might be called big game was in Borneo when he shot the orang-utan. He killed the harmless, slow-moving animals with genuine regret. Discovering that one of the animals he killed was a nursing mother, he retrieved the baby from the mud where it had fallen and tried to rear the orphan. He fed it milk from a dropper, wrapped it in swaddling clothes, cleaned and washed it regularly and even found it a tame monkey as a companion. To his sorrow, the baby orang-utan died of dysentery after a few weeks, but not before it had grown used to cuddling against Wallace's chest, probably mistaking his bushy Victorian beard for the body hair of its mother.

It was Wallace's view of himself which is so strikingly untypical of a Victorian explorer. He saw himself as a bespectacled, ungainly figure, groping his way short-sightedly through the undergrowth, not looking at anything but his insect prey, stumbling into mudholes and

---

[1] With typical generosity, when Wallace finally left for England, he gave both his double-barrelled shotguns plus all his surplus stores to Ali, 'which made him quite rich'. By then Ali had travelled with him nearly seven years, and had found himself a wife at Ternate.

running his nose into cobwebs patrolled by fist-sized spiders while his native companions looked on bemused or laughing, wondering what on earth he was doing. This shy, gentle man was so *decent*. He wandered through the islands of south-east Asia with good humour and incredible fortitude; he did no harm, and he left no bad taste. Today Indonesia is an independent, post-colonial country. Yet Wallace, who lived at the height of the colonial era, is a figure now viewed with affection and respect by those Indonesians who have ever heard of him. And a surprising number do know his name, because another of Wallace's theories is still taught in Indonesian schools, a theory which demonstrates how Indonesia is the meeting ground between the varieties of animal which spread from Asia and the animal species which arrived from Australia. By contrast few Westerners have any idea of who Wallace was, or what he achieved.

So the first purpose of making the Spice Islands Voyage was to rediscover Wallace. His name had long been familiar to me, but mainly in the context of the 'Wallace Line', named in his honour as the division between the fauna of Asia and Australasia. It was only after I had checked the map of Indonesia that I realised how comprehensive had been his travels. This realisation brought me to read *The Malay Archipelago*, and within a few pages I began to appreciate what an extraordinarily likeable person he must have been. I felt that here was someone who was so genuine and so humane that he should not be forgotten. On a personal level, his qualities of quiet humour, self-depreciation and frankness would make him worth all the effort of an expedition that would need at least two years of research followed by several months of potentially arduous field work. The backbone of my plan was to retrace Wallace's wanderings through the islands where he had done his major pioneering work, and to do so using a prahu, a small native sailing boat. Travelling in the same sort of native boat which he used for some of his journeys would help to bridge the gap between our own time and the high Victorian era, so that I could appreciate the conditions under which Wallace had made his journeys and thus bring the gentle itinerant collector into sharper focus.

For authenticity, my prahu should be the same type which would have been available to Wallace 140 years ago. At the start of the project, I would go to the remotest parts of the Indonesian archipelago and track down isolated boatbuilding communities to find out if any of them still made the same prahus as in the mid-nineteenth century. If they did, I would order the correct size of vessel, supervise its construction and, when it was nearly ready for sea, assemble the other members of the expedition to learn how to sail a prahu. Our teachers would be the islanders themselves, and if I could find the right man I would also invite one islander to join us for the trip. It would be sensible if as many as possible of the arriving team were already experienced small-boat sailors, though each would also have his or her own speciality. The team should include a doctor in case anyone had an accident in an out-of-the-way place, or we succumbed to the same sort of fevers which Wallace had suffered. There should also be a photographer and an artist to record our experiences, and — above all — I wanted to recruit at least one trained biologist and an environmental expert to accompany us. The scientists would be in a position to comprehend Wallace's achievement as a naturalist-explorer. They would identify the animals we saw, in particular the rich bird-life which had fascinated Wallace so much, and try to judge how conditions might have changed since Wallace's day. Here the perspective of a 140-year gap would be useful. Wallace had described some of the most interesting natural habitats in the tropical world with a very discerning eye. He had written about the fauna and flora of remote and beautiful islands at a time when they were little exploited by man. Nearly one and a half centuries later we would visit those same places, look again at the environment, and see what had changed and what had not. On the basis of that evaluation we might also gain some insight into what was being done to protect and preserve those unique habitats, and whether those protective measures were effective.

Here too we would be following Wallace's lead. He was acutely aware that the magical places he described were under threat from the moment when he brought them to the attention of the outside world. Passionately he asked his readers to remember that the rare creatures he discovered, particularly the rich bird-life, had lived undisturbed for countless generations. He pleaded that careful thought should be given to the preservation of these marvellous creatures; he strenuously urged the protection of the tropical environment for the benefit of its peoples and animals. In this, as in so many ideas, he was far ahead of his time.

So our trail started with his book, which opens with a typically self-deprecating apology for being so late in publication. 'My readers will naturally ask why I have delayed writing this book for six years after my return,' Wallace begins, 'and I feel bound to give them full satisfaction on this point. When I reached England in the spring of 1862, I found myself surrounded by a room full of packing cases containing the collections I had from time to time sent home for my private use. These comprised nearly three thousand bird-skins, of about a thousand species; and at least twenty thousand beetles and butterflies, of about seven thousand species; besides some quadrupeds and land shells. A large proportion of these I had not seen for years; and in my then weak state of health, the unpacking, sorting and arranging of such a mass of specimens occupied a long time.' He went on to explain that he felt he had to do something towards naming and describing the most important groups in his collections, and making sense of his discoveries in natural history, so that he could include his ideas in his travel book when he came to publish it. Just to tackle the main points meant that he wrote 30 learned articles for various zoological journals, and was obliged to farm out huge chunks of his collections to colleagues for them to classify and describe.

Wallace also decided that his travels were so complicated that if he described them in strict chronological order, they would confuse the reader. He had spent the first couple of years, 1854 – 56, in the western part of Indonesia, visiting Sumatra, Java, Borneo and Sarawak. Then he had gone on to the centre and east of Indonesia, and for the next four years had travelled back and forth between Sulawesi (then called Celebes), the Moluccas, and the many island clusters to the south of New Guinea, before working his way back again to Java, and on homeward to England. In all this time, he calculated, he had made between 60 and 70 separate journeys, frequently doubling back and forth on his track, visiting the same island two or three different times, staying in some localities for a month, then coming back to the same spot maybe two years later to do some more collecting at a different season of the year, and so on. To simplify all this zig-zagging, he would organise his story by regions, generally moving west to east as he described each island he had visited, his adventures there, and the natural history of the region .

It seemed sensible to adopt the same approach as Wallace. The Spice Islands Voyage would make better sense of his story if we travelled along a single, comprehensible route, which would go from island to island, linking together the most significant places he had described. At each landfall, our team would go ashore to assess the changes since Wallace's day. There was no difficulty in deciding where our route should be. Wallace travelled across the width of Indonesia, from Borneo to New Guinea. But the focus of his activities, and the places where he did his most original work — and found the most satisfaction as a naturalist — lay in the farthest east, much closer to Australia than to mainland Asia, and in a broad swathe running roughly south-east to north-west. So we would start among the small island clusters off Irian Jaya, the Indonesian portion of New Guinea. From there our track would take us to the large and densely forested island of Seram and then northward to the area called the Bird's Head at the tip of Irian Jaya. Turning westward we would sail to Ternate and Halmahera, where Wallace had his 'flash of inspiration' about the process of evolution and drafted his 'paralysing' letter to Darwin. We would end our journey on the spider-shaped island of Sulawesi, a living laboratory of nature where Wallace had formulated his equally original ideas about the distribution of the world's animal species. Suitably, much of the territory we would cover is now known to scientists as 'Wallacea', in honour of the pioneer who first described its biology in detail.

The islands of Wallacea are remote and widely scattered. They stand in relation to Jakarta and the heavily populated areas of Indonesia as the outer Hebrides do to London and the Home Counties. Islands on the outermost fringes are difficult to reach. Wild corners have been left undisturbed long enough to have been designated as nature reserves by the government of Indonesia, and here our expedition would have the best chance of finding those same conditions described by Wallace. My first reconnaissance trip to the Spice Islands to prepare the expedition revealed just how distant this region still is for most Indonesians. I went in search of the descendants of the people who, in Wallace's day, had the reputation of being the best boatbuilders in the islands. Wallace had written that the finest shipwrights came from a small archipelago called the Kai Islands off southern New Guinea. 'Ke', wrote Wallace helpfully, was pronounced like the letter K in English. This pronunciation, I found, was still true in Kai and throughout the Moluccas — but not in Java and the capital Jakarta where I had to apply for official permission for the Spice Islands Voyage. On the government map Kai was written Kei, and in official circles the name was pronounced to rhyme with 'Eye', so that at first no one understood where I was intending to travel, and hardly anyone I met in the capital had ever been there. It took three more days' travel, moving across two time zones and using smaller and smaller aircraft which landed on increasingly modest airstrips, before I reached Tual, the administrative capital of the Kei Archipelago, to look for boatbuilders.

Even if the aircraft had not been described as being on a 'Frontier Flight', it was obvious that I had landed in some sort of fringe zone. My fellow passengers were mainly petty civil servants posted to this remote place, or they were returning emigrants. Four were slightly flashy businessmen who appeared much attached to their briefcases. This was explained when I accepted the invitation of one friendly businessman to call at his office that evening. I walked in to find his briefcase open on the table and full to the brim with wads of bank-notes. These he was distributing by the handful to a small band of locals, some of whom seemed to be his direct employees, but others looked remarkably like government officials. It required no imagination to guess what was going on: the only major resource in the Kei Islands was sea products, notably large fish caught on the reefs and exported live to Singapore and Hong Kong where they were status symbols served at banquets. To protect over-exploitation of the fishing there were government regulations about the method of fishing, the size of catches and so forth. But a briefcase full of cash was more powerful than any regulation ordained by distant Jakarta.

A young entrepreneur invited me to visit his fishing station on a remote atoll and was very instructive about what was going on. Philip, let us call him, was charming, well educated and energetic. His current home was in Bangkok, though his family was Singaporean and engaged in the reptile skin trade. They imported and

24

Coastal village scene

exported the skins of snakes, crocodiles and the like by the container load. Sometimes they merely handled the paperwork, and the goods never even passed through their warehouses. The family sat in the centre of a complex web of trade. They knew the producers in

India and Thailand who would send the reptile skins air-dried, in salt or semi-finished. They knew the sweatshop leather workers wherever they were needed to stitch belts or handbags or shoes, and they had customers among the high-fashion retailers in Europe, North America and Hong Kong who sold the finished products. The family kept track of every change in the international trade regulations and quickly devised ways of evading them. Philip was as familiar as the most expert environmentalist with the animals listed in the Convention on the Trade of Endangered Species. He could rattle off the Latin names of different species of snakes and describe their habitats with the competence of a university herpetologist. He had gone into the live fish business, he told me, not because the reptile skin trade had been closed down by international conventions; on the contrary, he had switched because trading in reptile skins was too predictable and dull and there was no room for expansion. He wanted to develop his own commerce, and sending live fish to Hong Kong offered the necessary combination of bravado and fat profits. So he had come to Kei, as had several entrepreneurs like him, and they competed in setting up their fish camps dotted around the coast.

Officially these foreign businessmen supplied the local Kei people with the money to buy small boats, hooks and lines, and they built the bamboo cages where the live fish were kept until they were shipped to Hong Kong. The local fishermen caught the fish on hooks, carefully removed the hooks so as not to damage the fish, and brought the catch to the middlemen. That was the official story. In reality the entrepreneurs supplied the villagers with diving apparatus and brought in experienced divers to show them how to pillage the reefs, using cyanide. The divers would scour the reef face, tracking down every large fish that lived there. Cornering a fish, the diver would squirt cyanide in the animal's gills so that it was stunned and helpless, then simply scoop it up and take it to the catch boat. In this way the reef was stripped of every large fish, many of which had taken 20 or more years to grow to full size, and huge patches of coral were killed by the cyanide. 'I won't let my divers use cyanide. I like diving on the reefs myself. They're so beautiful,' announced Philip righteously. Then he spoiled the effect by adding, 'There's a new acid which I've heard has been developed. It stuns the fish but doesn't damage the coral.'

Philip was the first in a series of interpreters who helped in my initial search. The natives of Kei spoke their own dialect among themselves, but thanks to modern primary education nearly everyone also spoke bahasa Indonesia, the national language based on Malay. The language was gratifyingly simple to learn to an elementary level. Plurals, for example, were made by doubling the noun, so that a hat was a topi and hats were topi topi, and many words in the vocabulary were borrowed from Arabic, Dutch and English. But to negotiate the price of a new boat or discuss her building schedule needed more linguistic skill than I possessed, and a series of friends and chance acquaintances were on hand at the right moment to assist. Besides Philip the exotic fish dealer, there was a young German doctor touring the outer islands while his Javanese wife visited her relatives in Jakarta, and a young American anthropologist studying for his Ph.D. among the villages of the remotest corner of the Kai archipelago, and — at a crucial meeting — I was joined by Julia, an English biologist who would join the team as the environmentalist. Julia was already working in Indonesia and spoke the language well.

Very quickly I felt there was an Alice in Wonderland atmosphere to the Spice Islands, even during those first brief visits. I had gone to find boatbuilders, and on the little island of Warbal in the Kei archipelago I quickly found them — a community of 125 households living on an island that could have come from an advertising company's image of a tropical idyll: gently rustling coconut palms, a long beach of dazzling white sand and a sea of translucent blues and greens. Virtually every family in Warbal's single village could build boats, and built them very well indeed. They specialised in making their own traditional vessel, a light-weight elegant sailing hull which they used for sailing to the main island and back. Technically it was known as a prahu kalulis, and I walked along the beach at Warbal to inspect all the boats drawn up on the sand until I found the one which I judged to be the best made.

'Can I speak to the person who built this

boat?' I asked, with Philip to help as an interpreter. After a half-hour delay, a man appeared hesitantly, almost hiding among the coconut palms. He was barefoot, extremely thin and wore only a pair of shorts. Most Warbal islanders were Papuan-looking, stockily built with dark skins, broad noses and frizzled hair, but this boatbuilder looked as if he came from Southern India. He had a narrow, very bony face, straight black hair, long thin limbs, and walked with a gangling stride. For a moment I thought he also had some sort of speech difficulty. Every time I asked him a question, however gently, he looked over my shoulder or down at his hands, and his face took on an expression of anguish. There was a long, embarrassing silence. Then I would ask another question and again receive no answer. Eventually I understood that Johnny, as he was called, was shy to the point of paralysis. In fact he had come to see me out of politeness and, the moment he could do so, he fled back into the trees and was not seen again for the rest of the afternoon. Nevertheless it was clear from the boats I had seen that he was among the best craftsmen on Warbal, and I still wanted him to build me a traditional Kei Island boat.

It took two visits to Warbal to persuade Johnny to take on the work, and the key negotiations were channelled through two of his cousins, Frans and Salmon, who were members of his boatbuilding team. Could they build me a 14-metre-long prahu kalulis, I asked. Yes, they replied confidently, then paused and asked 'How

Boat on Warbal beach

long is a 14-metre kalulis?' I pointed to a boat drawn up on the beach. About half as long again as that one, I said. The two men looked relieved. To make doubly sure, I asked them to measure the sample boat. They were nonplussed. No one measured boats, and they did not have a tape measure. Well, I suggested, we could measure the boat by using outstretched arms as a rough guide. Hans and Salmon walked over to the beached kalulis, spread out their arms and began to measure the boat around the outside curve of the hull. No, no, I intervened. When I say a 14-metre kalulis, I mean 14 metres measured down the centre of the vessel from bow to stern, not along the curved edges. Fine, said the two brothers, clearly wondering why I was so unnecessarily precise. Then they asked, did I want a house? A house, I wondered. Then I realised that they meant a cabin on the boat. Yes, I wanted a house, two masts and steering equipment. The sails I would supply myself.

That evening I met Johnny's team in one of the village houses to discuss the price and schedule for building my boat. Johnny himself was there, shifting uncomfortably on his wooden chair. All of my questions appeared to be surprises, because every question was met by a mystified pause. The team would look across at Johnny to take the lead, and he would gaze down at his hands and say nothing. After an exchange of glances among the group, Hans — the most confident of the cousins — would give a very hesitant answer. Ten minutes of this ordeal made Johnny bolt for the door, and he did not come back, leaving the others to sort out the arrangements. How long would it take to build the boat? A long pause. About eight months, came the reply, because the boatbuilders would only work occasionally, perhaps one day every week. The rest of the time they would go fishing or tend their 'gardens' as they called the little clearings of cassava they grew in the interior of the island. Clearly life on Warbal went at its own pace, and nothing would disturb it. Was it possible to have the boat ready to be launched in October? No, I was told, because every Christian in the village had promised to devote the month of September to building a new church. The boatbuilders were all Christians, and they had already promised their labour.

So we agreed on a launch date near Christmas. What about the price of the boat? They quoted me 8 million rupiahs, which seemed an immense figure but was less than the price of a round-trip air fare between Europe and Indonesia. Then I asked how much of a cash deposit they would need before they could begin building. This was a major puzzlement. A deposit? That was an entirely new idea. Normally they built a boat and got paid afterwards. I thought it was remarkably trusting to do all that work for a stranger who lived on the far side of the world, even though I would be visiting the island from time to time to see how the boatbuilding was progressing.

We made the bargain, and I insisted on paying a deposit. Then I returned to Jakarta, where I had already applied for the research visas which would allow my team to stay in Indonesia for the full four or five months' duration of the expedition. I needed visas for myself and for Julia, though she would be prevented by her previous work commitments from joining us until about a month into the trip. Other research visas would also be required for Leonard, who would be joining from Dublin as the expedition artist; and Joe, who was both the expedition doctor and its photographer. Joe, who was from London, had sailed with me three years earlier aboard a bamboo raft on the Pacific Ocean for another expedition, the China Voyage, so he was a seasoned traveller. The team's bird expert, Budi, did not need a visa as he was Indonesian, nor did a last-minute volunteer, Bill. He was an American working in England as a sailmaker and professional yachtsman, and had volunteered to accompany us for the first month, largely for the fun of seeing what it was like to sail a traditional Indonesian prahu. In his early thirties, Bill was the same age as Joe and Leonard and, as he would be staying only a few weeks, a normal two-month tourist visa would be sufficient.

Dutifully, I had submitted the four research visa applications in five copies, as the regulations insisted. But if the Spice Islands had its elements of Alice in Wonderland, then Jakarta's bureaucracy was the Cheshire Cat, smiling and enigmatic, though it was the paperwork which vanished. Over the next 12 months, whenever I enquired about progress the officials were charming, but helpless. The visas would soon be granted, I was assured, but please could I send fresh copies of the applications, plus another batch of passport photographs, as the originals had been mislaid. In the end I sent in no fewer than four consecutive sets of applications, and never heard back about the visas until long after we had begun our expedition, having entered Indonesia on tourist visas.

Fortunately a grandee of Indonesia's business community, Ibnu Sutowo, had taken up the environmental cause, establishing a foundation for the protection of the unique environment of Wallacea. In the tightly woven network of Jakarta government, Ibnu Sutowo could arrange introductions. The Minister of Education was his nephew, and provided me with a letter of approval. Another friend was a retired admiral and an enthusiast for traditional Indonesian sailing craft. He also happened to be Chairman of the Supreme Advisory Council of the Republic, and was held in such awe that whenever I produced his letter of support, I felt I was invoking the Red Queen. Armed with these magic documents, I felt confident that we could press ahead with our plans and follow Wallace.

2

Kei Island Prahu

ALFRED WALLACE first saw the Kei
Islands on the last day of 1856 from
the deck of a large trading prahu. It
was a journey he had been longing to make
ever since he had arrived in the Dutch East
Indies two years earlier. Annually, when the
west monsoon began to blow, a small number of
merchant vessels sailed eastward from Macassar
— now Ujang Pandang — the great port at
the hub of central Indonesia's seaborne trade.
Wallace had managed to obtain passage on a
big prahu which would go first to Kei to pick
up supplies, and then onwards to the even more
remote Aru Islands. Even for the regular sailors,
the voyage was considered to be something of

an adventure. The destination was a region notorious for piracy and inhabited by native tribes who had been known to attack unwary visitors. Among the islands the merchants and prahu crew would trade for pearls, the skins from Birds of Paradise, tortoise shell and trepang, the dried sea slug which the Chinese consider such a gastronomic treat that even today it commands huge prices.

Wallace enjoyed his sea passage immensely. The massive wooden vessel 'shaped something like a Chinese junk' ploughed along steadily in front of the west monsoon, the air was balmy and the sea calm. To Wallace's untutored eye, the dozens of ropes controlling the enormous matting sails seemed to be a complete jumble, tangling here and there in confusion. Management of the vessel appeared equally haphazard. The crew of about thirty Muslims from Sulawesi were mostly young men, broad-faced and good-humoured, each man dressed in loose trousers with a cotton handkerchief tied around the head. They seemed to spend most of their time lounging casually on deck, cooking their meals, praying the required number of times each day, and dozing. Steering was left to two older men, the jurumudis. They squatted by the huge, twin steering oars and kept the vessel on course, measuring the hours by a very simple water clock — half a coconut shell floating in a bucket of water. The coconut shell had a small hole in it, through which the water slowly squirted in a fine jet. When full, it sank with a small gurgling sound, and that was the end of the hour. Wallace checked the accuracy of the device against his watch, and found that the time it took to fill the coconut shell varied only about a minute either way, and was not affected by the sea conditions.

Among the sailors, there was no clear chain of command. When action was needed, everyone seemed willing enough to go to work, but also to give their opinions, so that 'half a dozen voices are heard giving orders, and there is such a shrieking and confusion that it seems wonderful any thing gets done at all'. It was typical of Wallace's tolerant attitude that as far as he was concerned, this was the way in which the Sulawesi people had made the voyage for generations, and 'considering we have fifty men of several tribes and tongues on board, wild half-savage looking fellows, and few of them feeling any of the restraints of morality or education, we get on wonderfully well. There is no fighting or quarrelling, as there would certainly be among the same number of Europeans with as little restraint upon their actions, and there is scarcely any of that noise and excitement which might be expected.' The prahu's half-Dutch, half-Indonesian captain had allocated Wallace a tiny thatched cabin on deck. It was only four feet high to the ridge line, but in it he could keep his gun-case, insect boxes, clothes and books, and still have room to stretch out on the slightly springy floor of split bamboos. It was, he said, 'the snuggest and most comfortable little place I ever enjoyed at sea', and he preferred it to the 'gilded and uncomfortable saloon of a first class steamer'. Instead of the smells of paint, tar, grease and oil which made him feel queasy on a modern vessel, he had only the smells of bamboo and rattan, coir rope and palm thatch, pure vegetable fibres which reminded him of quiet scenes in the green and shady forest.

His reception on Kei Besar came as a shock. Wallace had already spent two and a half years in Indonesia, but had lived mainly among the Malay peoples of the centre and west. He described the Malay character as quiet and reserved. Now, three or four canoes manned by Kei islanders put out from shore and came racing eagerly towards the big prahu. The canoes themselves were spectacular. Bow and stern were raised up in beaks two or three metres high, and were decorated with shells and waving plumes of cassowary hair. They came dashing up at high speed, with the paddlers singing and shouting, and dipping their paddles deep into the water and throwing up a great spray.

Had I been blind [Wallace wrote] I could have been certain that these islanders were not Malays. The loud, rapid, eager tones, the incessant motion, the intense vital activity manifested in speech and action are the very antipodes of the quiet, unimpulsive, unanimated Malays . . . on coming alongside, without asking leave, and without a moment's hesitation, the greater part of them scrambled up on our deck just as if they were come to take possession of a captured vessel.

Then commenced a scene of indescribable confusion. These 40 black, naked, mop-headed savages seemed intoxicated with joy and excitement. Not one could remain still for a moment. Every member of our crew was in turn surrounded and examined, asked for tobacco or arrack, grinned at and deserted for another. All talked at once, and our captain was regularly mobbed by the chief men, who wanted to be employed to tow us in, and who begged vociferously to be paid in advance. A few presents of tobacco made their eyes glisten; they would express their satisfaction by grins and shouts, by rolling on deck, or by a headlong leap overboard . . . Our crew, many of whom had not made the voyage before, seemed quite scandalised. They reminded me of a party of demure and well-behaved children suddenly broken in upon by a lot of wild, romping, riotous boys whose conduct seems most extraordinary and very naughty!

Today the natives of the Kei Islands are nowhere near as distinctive nor exuberant as in Wallace's time. Indonesia has a total population in excess of 180 million, of which the overwhelming majority live in Java and Sumatra. Java, with only 6 per cent of the land, is crammed with 60 per cent of the people so that it has twice the population density of Holland or Japan. By comparison the Moluccas and Irian Jaya, the Indonesian half of the huge island of New Guinea, are empty; they contain just

2 per cent of Indonesia's population, thinly spread across a quarter of the nation's land surface. Not surprisingly, the massive overhang of Javanese population dominates life throughout Indonesia. The peoples of the outlying islands are being moulded into a single national identity by the central government in Jakarta, and the policy has been extremely effective. The process begins early in school. A child in Kei wears exactly the same colour and style of school uniform — maroon, grey or blue according to the class — as another schoolchild of the same age 3,000 miles away in Sumatra, or in any other national school from one end of the huge country to the other. He or she also follows an identical curriculum. Every child has to learn the national language, and they must know by heart the founding principles of the republic established in 1945. The message of a national Indonesian identity is hammered home incessantly by radio and television. Everywhere are visual reminders of Indonesian unity. The red and white flag flies on public and private buildings, there is constant use of red and white in house decoration, the national emblem is repeated on the cap badges of the police or the shoulder flashes of the civil servants. The great multitudes of state apparatus — the large armed forces and the even more enormous bureaucracy — march to a drumbeat set by the central government. In Kei there is a constant arrival of government officials and appointees who are not Kei islanders, but come usually from Java and the larger islands and stay in Kei for a few

years, returning home after their term of office. While they occupy the higher echelons of the government service, they set the standards of behaviour in a community where a government job, however lowly, is the best hope of a secure future.

Nor, for a century, has Kei been as isolated as in Wallace's day. The Kei islanders are notoriously poor businessmen, so the commercial life of Tual, the only place of any size in the islands, is in the hands of outsiders. The town lies in a shallow valley leading up from the harbour in a sprawl of low tin-roofed bungalows and utilitarian concrete buildings. Down near the port is the largest bazaar on Kei. Here the great majority of stalls, as well as the small shops selling cheap clothing, electrical goods and hardware, are owned by traders who have come from Sulawesi. The larger shops in the main street are likely to be run by families of Chinese origin, many of whom have been in Tual for six or seven generations and effectively dominate the retail life of the town. Their competition comes from a small number of Arab Indonesians, whose forebears arrived as shipowners from the Hadramaut in South Arabia three generations ago, and who still organise the commerce with the Muslim communities on the smaller outlying islands. Of the native Kei islanders hardly anyone has become a leading figure in the economic life of the administrative capital, but there has been a great deal of intermarriage so in the streets of Tual there is a complete mixture of physical types from the distinctive Papuan features to the Chinese.

Only when I left the town and headed for Warbal and its boatbuilders did I begin to feel I was among the exuberant islanders whom Wallace met. The journey from Tual to Warbal began with a half-hour ride in a rickety bus, always crammed with market women and villagers who had been on shopping trips in town. The narrow tarmac road ran straight across low undulating country, covered with the straggly vegetation of the type that takes hold after forest has been cut down to make cassaya gardens, and then the cassava fields are abandoned after two or three years when the soil is exhausted. There were no birds or ground animals to be seen as the bus raced along at a breakneck pace, its cassette player blasting out at full volume. The tunes were Indonesian versions of Western songs or crashing instrumental numbers played on electronic guitars and music synthesisers. After a cramped and very noisy half-hour, the bus halted at a little jetty. Most of the disembarking bus passengers climbed aboard the sailing dinghies which operated a short ferry service across an inlet to several villages on the far side. For Warbal, which was much farther out to sea, there was no regular ferry. You had to wait, hoping that some sort of transport would turn up. To pass the time, you could play pool in a small shack beside the jetty, or watch the striped sackcloth sails gliding back and forward across the inlet as the short-haul ferries took their passengers, sometimes with their motorcycles balanced on the thwarts.

The wait at Debut could be for an hour or the best part of a day. Sometimes it was possible to get a lift from a returning shopping group of Warbal people who were heading back to the island on their own boat, or you could also try bargaining with a local ferryman to get you there. However this meant a journey of two to five hours under sail, and the small ferry-boats were not really seaworthy enough to make the 13-kilometre passage safely. The quickest, and wettest, option was to ride to Warbal aboard one of the island's 'Johnsons'. These were long dugout canoes fitted with a powerful outboard motor which raced along at 10 – 15 knots, usually overloaded with a dozen shoppers plus all their purchases. If the sea was moderately rough, waves began to slop inboard, and the passengers started screaming with fright and shouting prayers for survival, while the boatman bailed. Fortunately no one seemed to have drowned on this casual and swift passage.

Landing in Warbal explained why Wallace had been so rapturous about the islands. A cluster of low wooden houses straddled a small promontory. The approach was either down a narrow channel into a large lagoon which dried at low tide and provided a completely safe anchorage for the village boats; or, you turned away to the north and dropped anchor before the beach of dazzling white sand, backed by a dark green line of coconut palms. In either case the final kilometre of the arrival was across a sea of such clarity that you could count every ripple in the sand of the sea floor six metres below, and admire the shadows and colours of the great coral boulders which lay scattered below the surface. To make the scene even more attractive, one approach channel led past a low sandspit where flocks of white pelicans stood solemnly on the sand at low tide. Sharp-tailed frigate birds hovered overhead, and the water was so rich with fish that shoals of tiny bright silver spratlings would come suddenly skipping out of the water. These fish were a couple of centimetres long and they leaped out of the water for a second or two, in thousands upon thousands, making brief fountains and sheets of liquid silver.

A 'Johnson' could run its bow up on the soft sand, while a prahu kalulis with its slightly deeper draught would come to rest with a flap of its sail, in perhaps 30 centimetres of water. There was not a hint of pollution, as you trudged up the soft fine sand into the shade

Lateen rigged canoe

of the coconut palms. Here a footpath led past the graves of the village cemetery under the palm trees. It was a spot so picturesque that in the space of ten metres you could not imagine the dead more peacefully at rest. Beyond the cemetery was one of the half-dozen wells in the village, its concrete tube sunk into the sand, and beyond that again the little houses. They were all much the same, small rectangular buildings of wood frame filled with mud brick, thatched with dark brown palm leaves and divided into one or two rooms with a cement floor. There was no glass in the windows, which had shutters which could be closed against the rain. The exterior walls were either left in their natural colours and patterned beige and brown, or whitewashed. Neat streets of sand ran at right angles to one another, and many of the houses had small front gardens decorated with bougainvillea or large helmet shells. The sandy streets were very clean, and of course there was no traffic, nor was there any electricity nor a telephone. The only machinery, besides the outboard engines for the 'Johnsons', was a single small petrol-driven machine for grating cassava roots and a chainsaw. When either machine started up, the noise was startling. Otherwise the sounds of Warbal were the cries of children, the morning calls of roosters and the massed howling of the dogs which greeted the tolling of the church bell.

The spread of Christianity and Islam was the greatest change to island life since Wallace had been there. When Wallace had come to Kei, the islanders were pagans, with perhaps a few Muslims near the coast where they had met the Sulawesi traders. A century later, every village in the archipelago had become either Muslim or Christian, or both. Warbal was overwhelmingly Christian, with a small Muslim group living round a very discreet mosque near the main landing beach, and Christianity had altered Warbal's village life even more than nationalism. The community was intensely and actively religious. A large church occupied the centre of the village, with 'Immanuel' spelt out in dark purple letters over its front entrance. Foundations were already dug and a first few pillars in place for a second, even more ambitious church on the outskirts. This new church would be huge. From the ground plan it seemed that it would accommodate at least twice the total congregation of Warbal, and the cost of the project must have been prodigious. Although Warbal's Christians had

Warbal Houses

46

pledged to give free labour, thousands of sacks of cement would have to be imported at huge cost to the community. Meanwhile the old church was thriving. It reverberated to prayer meetings and hymn singing; there were matins and evensongs, Sunday-school sessions and special thanksgiving services. And when the Warbal islanders did not go to church to pray, they met in one another's homes; small groups of men and women could be seen entering one of the little houses, prayer books in hand, at almost any time of day.

★ ★ ★

Visitors to Warbal, if they were foreigners, were expected to be guests of Frans and Mima, who possessed the only house with an aluminium corrugated roof and had a spare room. Frans was a relic of the Dutch colonial days soon after the Pacific war with Japan. Just old enough to have been recruited for the Dutch colonial army, like thousands of other Moluccans he had gone to live in Holland when the Dutch withdrew from Indonesia, evacuating their supporters with them. For 30 years Frans had lived in Holland, working in a Phillips factory, before finally coming back home to retire in Warbal. In Holland he had divorced his first wife and married Mima, who also came from Kei and was perhaps 20 years younger than her husband. They had one young son, Tommy, who was extremely spoiled and went to the Warbal primary school. Their other children were older,

47

Street scene, Warbal

and had to live in Tual to continue with their education because there was no secondary school on the island. Frans — short, friendly and losing both his hair and his memory — was the wealthiest man on the island, and a little lonely. The other islanders referred to him as the Belanda, the Hollander, and regarded him as being half-foreign and out of touch. Yet Frans' monthly pension from Holland meant that he owned the newest and largest Johnson, and he could live out his retirement very comfortably in the sunshine, employing a maid and sending men out in his motorised dugout to catch fresh fish for his table. Mima, despite her frequent laugh and constant chatter, hankered after a more modern life in Holland. She admitted that, for all its warm climate and easy lifestyle,

Warbal was a dull place to be a housewife after living in the suburbs of Amsterdam.

On the surface at least, Warbal was tranquillity itself. At dawn the men went off in their small dugouts to fish on the reefs, or paddled away to spend the day on the neighbouring smaller islands which also belonged to the Warbal community, where they had their cassava gardens. The women might go with their men to help with the agricultural work, but usually spent their time near their little houses, watching over the toddlers, cleaning, cooking and endlessly washing clothes. They could earn a little extra money by cleaning seaweed and setting it out to dry in the sunshine. On sunny days, parts of the streets were carpeted with fronds of seaweed which would be collected up by traders and sold in Tual for export to Japan.

The luckiest inhabitants were the island children. Warbal's primary school was on the edge of the village, across a piece of common land which also served as a playground. The children, neat in their maroon and white uniforms, never had to walk more than 400 yards to get to class, wherever they lived. And by early afternoon school was shut. The rest of the day was spent playing under the coconut palms, the girls watching over the smallest children while the boys would spend hour after hour splashing in the shallows, cavorting with small and worn-out dugout canoes until their fathers came sailing home on the evening breeze. It was a way of life which, as we followed Wallace's trail across the Moluccas, we would find in island after island,

49

but in Warbal the setting happened to be more beautiful and picturesque.

The idyll was superficial. Warbal, like many small and isolated communities, seethed with political tension. The village had split into two rival camps, who disliked one another and refused to cooperate. A good village headman, the kapala desa, would have kept the rivalries in check. But Warbal's previous headman had retired and left the island, and the two rival factions were deadlocked in a struggle to choose his successor. Until the deadlock was broken by the arrival of an appointee from the regional government in Tual, the village was run by a temporary kapala desa, a lazy and ingratiating old man who merely sought to line his pocket with meagre bribes.

There were other tensions, too. It emerged that Johnny, even if he was the best craftsman on the island, was not the senior boatbuilder, and he could not accept my commission to build the boat without the approval of the man who had taught him his skills. That master builder was Yanci, and he was brother to Frans the Hollander. Unfortunately, the two brothers had quarrelled bitterly years ago and were not on speaking terms. So while Yanci gave his permission for Johnny to build my prahu, and even took on the role of technical adviser and part-time member of the building team, I could never meet him at Frans' house because he had sworn he would never enter it again. The only place I ever saw Yanci to discuss the progress and design of the boat was at our boatbuilding site under the coconut palms by the landing beach.

With a head boatbuilder too shy to speak his mind and a technical adviser at daggers drawn with my host, it was lucky that I had decided to let the design of my prahu take a natural course. I wanted the vessel to be a true Kei Island craft, made to their traditional design, with as little outside influence as possible. It would be interesting to see whether Johnny's team still built boats in the same way that Wallace had described. I had only specified the length which I calculated had been suitable for Alfred Wallace in his travels, and asked that the vessel should have two masts. Wallace had written:

The forests of Ke produce magnificent timber, tall, straight and durable, of various qualities, some of which are said to be superior to the best Indian teak. To make each pair of planks used in the construction of the larger boats an entire tree is consumed. It is felled, often miles away from the share, cut across to the proper length, and then hewn longitudinally into two equal portions. Each of these forms a plank by cutting down with the axe the uniform thickness of three or four inches, leaving at first a solid block at each end to prevent splitting. Along the centre of each plank a series of projecting pieces are left, standing up three or four inches, about the same width, and a foot long; these are of great importance in the construction of the vessel.

Wallace explained how the raw planks were laboriously hauled through the forest by three or four men to the beach, where the boat is to be built. A stout, curved keel piece was then set up on blocks, and carefully trimmed so that the planks could be fitted each side and gradually built up to form the hull of the vessel. The men used hard wooden pins to join the planks together, and he was so impressed by the precision and neatness of the work that, in his view, 'the best European shipwright can not produce sounder or closer fitting joints.'

Broadly, Johnny's team still followed the system Wallace had seen. They took their timber from the woods on the next-door island of Manir, using their chain-saw to cut down the trees and slice the planks, rather than split them with axes. Then they dragged and floated the pieces of wood to the building site on the main beach. There they set up the keel of the vessel and began to fit the planks in exactly the way Wallace described, by attaching the planks edge to edge with dozens of pencil-size wooden pins. It was very delicate work, and performed without the aid of measuring tool or mechanical device. It was also extremely quick. The team — eight men in total, though usually only five or six showed up at the same time — could shape, bend and fit a plank each side of the hull in a single day, using only hand tools. With a parang or cutlass and an adze, they could work to very fine detail. They calculated that the hull would need only eleven planks on each side, so in theory the shipwrights could have built the boat in a couple of weeks — but this was not how the Warbal islanders worked. Johnny's building team would show up, spring into action and fit a plank in a day. Then they would not reappear at the building site for another fortnight. They simply vanished between work bouts; there seemed to be no plan nor programme to their actions. If, by chance, I came across one of the boatbuilders at the door of his little house in the village, he always seemed on the point of leaving for another island or was too smartly dressed to be doing manual work and probably heading off for a prayer meeting. There was no point in chivvying them. I had to trust that Johnny and his men would finish the job in time for us to sail with the last of the west monsoon in March.

As the work slowly progressed, it was also clear to me that the team had no fixed idea of how high or wide the eventual boat would be. They had no technical drawing to follow, not even a rough sketch. The traditional design of the prahu kalulis, the typical Warbal boat, was obviously held in their heads. But in whose head? Johnny was in charge, yet he always consulted Yanci and usually deferred to his judgement. Meanwhile the other members of the team, right down to Isaac (the youngest at 20 years old), had his input and would be listened to. So the boat grew larger by group consensus, and this included the casual advice given by onlookers who walked by on their way to fishing or gathering coconuts. And even if there had been a fixed plan, it was evident that the size and quality of the wood they cut had its influence. If the builders happened to cut down a thin tree, then they fitted narrow planks. If the tree was short and stout, they fitted short broad planks. In all, I paid five different visits to Warbal to check on progress with the boat, and each time was surprised by an unexpected change in the building style.

Then came the day when I learned not to worry about this apparently haphazard approach. On my third visit, in August, I found that the keel was laid on the sand and the first two planks had been pegged in place. I asked Johnny where he proposed to put the two masts I had requested. He looked even more embarrassed than usual, and said nothing. I persisted with the question, and Johnny finally replied that it was far too early to think about that matter; he would decide on the mast positions when the boat was higher. Three months later, when the hull form was nearly complete, I again asked Johnny where he would set the masts. Again he looked embarrassed, and it seemed to me that he had not given the matter any thought. Once more I pressed him, reminding him what he had said earlier. Reluctantly he climbed into the half-finished boat, and gazed up and down the length of it. Then he walked slowly along, balancing on the keel. At one point he stopped and pointed with his bare toe. 'One mast here,' he mumbled. He moved a little farther along, then nudged again with his toe. 'The other mast here.' I thanked him and, when he had left, I carefully measured the positions he had indicated, and made a drawing of the hull. As soon as possible I sent the data to a professional naval architect. He made his calculations, ran the numbers through his computer, and informed me that the two mast positions were accurate to within an inch.

★ ★ ★

So the boat took shape in fits and starts, agonisingly slowly during the first month of April and on through June, then with increasing urgency as we approached the planned launch date in late November. I had been expecting a scaled-up version of the usual island prahu kalulis, the width and length increased in the same proportion. But that was not the case. Johnny and his team were building a boat of 14 metres length, just as I had ordered, but they made the vessel much narrower and finer and shallower than I had expected. The hull was so lightly built that it quivered each time I climbed aboard. I could see that it was going to be a very fast vessel indeed. In one important respect it differed from the boats Wallace had seen. In his day, the planks and ribs were tied together in the final stage with twisted tree roots, whereas Johnny and his men preferred to use wooden pins which they hammered in with great gusto. After they had built the cabin, using palm fronds for the roof, I could see why they called it the boat's 'house', for it looked exactly like one of their beach-side shacks. They crumpled up dusty sheets of what looked like brown paper,

Warbal beach hut

the skin of the paper-bark tree, and pounded it into any hairline cracks between the planks, and the vessel was nearly ready.

An old friend, Nick Burningham, arrived to stay on Warbal in mid-November during the final phase of building, and to help with the launch and sailing trials. A leading authority on traditional Indonesian boats, Nick was concerned that Johnny and his men had built a vessel that was too fragile. He recommended that four extra ribs should be added in the mid-section to strengthen it. The programme was to launch the boat in less than two weeks when the tides were right, and it seemed impossible that Johnny and his men could cut, shape and fit four complete ribs in that time. But Johnny agreed to do the job, beginning next morning. At 7 o'clock Nick and I arrived at the building site to find no one there, and there was no sign of any tools nor indication that any work had been done. My heart sank. Had I offended Johnny by asking for the extra ribs? Then we heard the sound of the chain-saw and followed it into the nearby woods, where we came across Johnny and four of his team busily cutting down small, crooked trees. They were selecting trees which had the right curves for the extra ribs, and within a couple of hours had got what they wanted. After they had roughly shaped the timbers on the woodland floor, they carried the timbers down to the boat. Then, with one man working on each rib, they began to finalise the shapes, using only hand-axes. Chips flew. Every now and then a man would call on a colleague to help him pick up the half-finished rib, carry it up into the hull and make a trial fitting. Back down to the sand came the rib, and the carpenter again attacked it with blows from his hand-axe. Back and forth, each rib was fitted, re-fitted and re-fitted, checked until it lay flush to the inside of the hull. When it was a perfect fit, holes were drilled, pegs were whittled, and two men hammered home the fastening pins. The speed of work was astonishing; beating home the fastening pegs was like watching two men playing a duet on a kettle-drum. By early afternoon all four new ribs had been cut, trimmed, smoothed and fitted in the space of time — as Nick put it — when a Western carpenter was probably still deciding which power tools he would need for the job.

Ten days before we were due to launch the boat, I had another anxious moment when I learned that five Warbal prahus were going off on an expedition south to the Tanimbar islands 160 kilometres away. The purpose of their journey was to pick up a shipment of *sopi*, palm wine, because Warbal had been without alcohol for several months. I had a vision of all Johnny's building crew with such hangovers that they would not be able to work until the new supply of wine was finished. But the expedition taught a quite different lesson. The five boats were away for a little less than a week; then four of them reappeared, loaded down with their cargo which was distributed through the village. No one, as far as I could see, went on a binge. But what about the missing boat? The entire community was worried when it failed to show up with the others.

Two days later it arrived, the crew looking shame-faced. A sharp discussion took place right beside us as we worked on the finishing touches for our boat, an elderly fisherman questioning the captain of the missing prahu. What happened, enquired the fisherman, why were you so late? The skipper growled something, and the other man laughed at him. Apparently the skipper of the missing prahu had sailed slightly off his correct track during the night on the way back from Tanimbar. At dawn he and his crew had seen an island on the horizon, and mistaken its identity. Thinking they were farther south than their real position, they had sailed onwards instead of changing course, and had sailed right past Warbal. Eventually realising their mistake, they had tried to turn back, but the current had been against them and they had taken two extra days to get into port. Listening to this was an instant lesson in native navigation techniques. It was clear that native boats did not navigate with a compass or charts, but by line of sight. They simply sailed from one island to the next, and in those waters there was usually an island on the horizon to serve as a guide post. But you had to identify them correctly, and the currents were so strong that if you made a mistake, you could be carried past your destination and out of control.

The launch of the *Alfred Wallace* came at the end of November, just a week behind schedule, and the event was as casual as anything else that the islanders did except when it came to church services and political discussions. It was a perfect morning with a few patches of high cloud in the tropical blue sky, and a light northerly breeze to cool us as we gathered at the work-site underneath the coconut palms. I had arranged with Mima for enough tea, soft drinks and cakes for the entire community. This was served on the beach beside the boat, which had been decorated with a garland of palm leaves.

The *tuan tanah*, the 'Lord of the Land' appeared. Technically he was a shaman, the man who intervened on behalf of the villagers with the spirits of the land and water, the wind and the forest. The job was hereditary, so the *tuan tanah* on Warbal always came from the same family. However the shaman looked no different from any other villager, and he was dressed in loose shirt and trousers like everyone else; he was blind as a result of an eye disease. As everyone clustered around the boat, he spoke a few sentences blessing the vessel, and I put into his hand a saucer with a small gift of money covered with a cloth. Then, without any ceremony, the crowd laid hold on the ropes and began to pull the boat down to the water's edge. A line of small logs had already been laid on the sand to make a launch ramp. The logs came from a special type of tree with a slippery bark, and so the keel slithered as if on grease. It took no more than three minutes to get the boat to the water. The crowd heaved and pulled, and then trotted alongside the moving boat as she slipped along without fuss. In less than 40 centimetres of water she was afloat. Someone threw an anchor overboard, the new vessel came to a stop — and by the time I turned round to look, the villagers were all sauntering casually back to their houses as if nothing had happened.

Nick and I walked to Mima's house to have lunch, and when we returned to the beach our brand-new prahu was gone! After a moment's panic, I looked to my right and there she was, all sails set, heading towards us, parallel to the beach. In true Warbal style there was no careful checking of mast and rigging for strength. Nobody bothered to look if there were any leaks in the bilge. On the very first day the builders hoisted full sail, pulled up the anchor and set off to see how the vessel performed. In this case I could see that Johnny with his distinctive lanky silhouette was steering, seated nonchalantly on the stern and holding the twin rudders. By his relaxed attitude it did seem that the vessel was going very satisfactorily.

I would have liked someone from the building team to have travelled as permanent crew on our voyage to follow Wallace. But none of Johnny's men was willing to go off for four or five months. They were boatbuilders, not wandering sailors, and they had families to keep them at home. Also my original choice for crew, a fisherman named Beil, had been injured in a freak accident. He had been in his canoe, fishing off the reefs, when a bonefish came hurtling at him. Bonefish are like sword blades, long, thin and sharply pointed. The fish catches its prey by sheer speed, chasing its victim in a series of low flat leaps over the surface of the sea. In this case the bonefish, intent on the hunt, had leaped straight over the dugout and slammed head-first into the fisherman, its sharp head spearing deep into the back of his leg. The wound severed the nerve, and left Beil partially crippled.

Then I remembered a person whom Philip, the Singaporean dealer in live fish, had described — his foreman, Yanis. This man, he said, was from Warbal and was totally reliable and very loyal. Where all Philip's other employees in the fish business had been changed by the opportunity to make quick money, and become more demanding or less enthusiastic, Yanis had remained the same — always ready to work, always cheerful and always modest. By now Philip had left Kei, finding the commercial competition too stiff and abandoning his fishing operation, so Yanis would be out of a job. I enquired for him, and within minutes he showed up on the beach at Warbal. He was exactly as his former employer had described him — a stocky wide-shouldered figure came running cheerfully along the sand, a huge smile on his face.

Yanis was about 40 years old, and looked as if he had not bought a new item of clothing in the past five years. His large, broad feet were bare, his shorts torn, and his grubby tee-shirt had more holes than fabric. Standing slightly bow-legged, with deep chest and powerful arms, he exuded good nature. His face was very dark, with a heavy brow ridge, deeply set brown eyes and tightly curled hair. He waited expectantly, and I noticed quiet smiles appear on the faces of other islanders nearby. They all knew I was looking for a crew member, and it was obvious that they held Yanis in some sort of special affection. It turned out that he was one of the most popular people in the community, and known generally as Om Yanis, 'Uncle Yanis', because he was so good-natured and helpful. He was also, as I was to learn, someone who did not think ahead more than a few hours. Today was good enough for Yanis, and he was as carefree as the legendary grasshopper. He did not mind whether there was rain or sun, whether he was asked to work for 20 hours at a stretch or just to wait patiently on a beach all day long. He was blessed with an open, friendly nature which was to work wonderfully to our advantage during the voyage. He had no hesitation or inhibitions, and would walk straight up to a stranger to ask for a favour or for help. He was also a little simple, and had a habit of scratching his head in puzzlement with a half-smile on his face, which may or may not have been deliberate but certainly won him instant cooperation. The moment the problem was solved, the half-smile burst into a huge, broad grin.

Yanis made up for what he lacked in brain power by sheer energy. He loved to work, and attacked any task with gusto and very little planning. He was also extremely strong and, because he was rather clumsy, it was inevitable

The Alfred Wallace

that his workmanship was very rough and ready. Over the next few months I was to learn that Yanis would break any tool entrusted to him, including a hammer, and that he was never so happy as when trudging off up the beach laden with watercans which he had to fill at a local village well. Within minutes he would have charmed the local ladies and be chatting to them gaily, his cap tipped rakishly over his curly head, the very image of the jaunty sailor. Yanis was to become a major figure in our shipboard lives, for better or worse, and produce some surprises.

Two days after the launch, I left Warbal to travel to Jakarta and make final preparations for the main expedition. Now I did not have to wait to hitch a ride aboard a Johnson or a prahu kalulis; I had my very own boat. The boatbuilding team wanted to go shopping in Tual to spend some of their pay, and they volunteered to act as temporary crew. Nick was waiting nervously on the beach, eyeing a large, sinister thunderstorm which was approaching Warbal from the north. 'If we don't get going now,' he said, 'it will be too dangerous.' Johnny and his builders put in a belated appearance, strolling leisurely along. We hurried everyone on board and set sail.

Alfred Wallace behaved impeccably as we began the 13-kilometre passage to the main island. Soon we were rushing along in swash-buckling style, the new ropes creaking and stretching under pressure. Isaac, the youngest of the team, had taken took over from Johnny at the helm. Halfway to our destination, everything was going splendidly when the cloudburst struck us. A thick curtain of rain enveloped us, and soon we were drenched. Tropical rain hammered down, the wind speed rose, and our brand-new and untried boat leaned flamboyantly to the wind. Nick and I wiped the streaming water from our eyes and looked around. Only Isaac was still on deck. I peered through the little door to the cabin. Down below, the other builders were all sprawled out comfortably on the split bamboo floor and passing around a bottle of palm wine. It was clear that most of them were already tipsy. Sudden gusts of wind made the boat lean over even more steeply, and I wondered if she would capsize.

Our destination was the little jetty at Debut where the bus dropped off passengers from Tual, and it lay at the head of a bay encumbered with shallows. We hurtled into the mouth of the bay at full tilt, just as several of the builders appeared on deck. *Alfred Wallace* was the biggest and most unusual Warbal boat to have been built in years, and Johnny's team were determined that everyone who saw her for the first time would remember the event. Without reducing speed, we raced towards the end of the jetty under full sail. Yanis was with us, standing on the bow holding the anchor and ready to throw it overboard. With exquisite judgement Johnny, who had again taken the helm, brought the *Alfred Wallace* swinging round the end of the jetty as a crowd of longshoremen emerged from the pool-room and watched with keen interest. We were travelling so fast that for a moment I thought Johnny was headed for a catastrophe. If we didn't smash into the end of the jetty, the boat would go careering up the beach or even flatten one of the wooden stages which stood on shaky wooden pilings and projected from the shore. The 'sentry-box' at the end of each staging was a lavatory, and I wondered what its startled occupant might think when the whole structure was swept away by the enthusiastic men of Warbal. But they had timed it nicely. Yanis flung the anchor just at the right moment. The rest of the crew dropped the sails, and *Alfred Wallace* came swinging round on the end of the anchor rope like a pebble in a sling and came to rest gently against the stone side of the jetty.

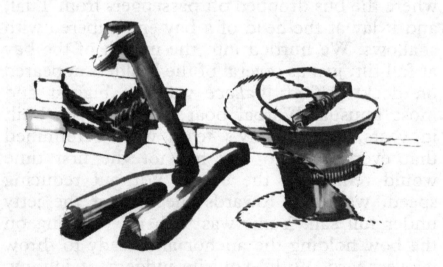

Boarding ladder and bucket

3

Big Kei

ALFRED WALLACE'S career owed
nothing to family connections or financial
advantage. He was the seventh child of
a shabby genteel family whose fortunes were
spiralling inexorably downward. This decline
was caused by his father's total incomprehension
of money matters which, to a degree, Alfred
Wallace shared. Alfred was very inept with
the money he earned from his writings and
the sales of hard-won zoological specimens. He
made bad investments, and had to write book
reviews and give lectures in order to make
ends meet, as well as constantly economise on
his day-to-day expenses. He did not, however,
sink into such difficulties as his father, Thomas

Wallace. Trained as a lawyer, Thomas had a small inheritance so he never really practised the law until it was too late. He failed to foresee that his modest private income, sufficient to keep him as an idle bachelor, was not enough to support a large family. When that family duly expanded, Thomas Wallace was either too timid or too lazy to take up his profession. Instead he dabbled briefly in magazine publishing, and when that venture collapsed — taking most of his inheritance with it — he retreated. He began looking for cheaper and cheaper places to live, accepted various part-time jobs as a schoolteacher and librarian, and took up gardening so that he could save money by growing vegetables for the family table. When Alfred was born in 1823, the family was living temporarily in a small house in Usk in Monmouthshire, and by the time Alfred was five years old the Wallaces would have moved first to Dulwich and then to Hertford.

Alfred Wallace was to say later that the sheer necessity of having to get out into the world from this lackadaisical environment, and learn how to fend for himself, was the real benefit from this upbringing. It was a lesson he started to learn very early. By the time he was 12 years old, his parents could not afford the school fees for Hertford Grammar School, so they made an arrangement with the headmaster that Alfred would stay on as a senior pupil on condition that he helped to teach the youngest children. Alfred was mortified. He was already very tall for his age — he would be almost six feet by the time he was 14 — and felt thoroughly inadequate. He was shy, and hated being singled out. 'Every time I entered the schoolroom I felt ashamed. For at least twenty years after I left, and I think even longer, I was subject to frequently recurring dreams of still haying to go to school in the hybrid position of pupil and teacher, aggravated by feeling myself taller and, at last, a man and yet suffering over again with increased intensity, the shyness and sense of disgrace of my boyhood. In my dreams I hated to go; when I reached the schoolhouse I dreaded to open the door, especially if a few minutes late, for then all eyes would be upon me. The trouble of not always knowing what to do came upon me with exaggerated force, and I used to open my desk and fumble about among its contents so as to hide my face as long as possible.'

Shyness was to stay with Alfred Wallace. For most of his life he would be more at ease when working on his own or in very small teams. The embarrassments of his childhood, with his family sinking further and further into poverty, also made him aware of the shortcomings and insensitivity of Victorian society. One school incident, in particular, would find an echo in his Indonesian experiences. His frugal mother made him a pair of cuffs of black calico to pull up over the sleeves of his school jacket to protect them from wear, but naturally Alfred Wallace was far too embarrassed to use them in school for fear of ridicule. Then came the day when the schoolmaster found the calico sleeves, called

Alfred up in front of the class and made him put them on in public. 'I dare say they did not look so very strange . . . ' Wallace recalled, 'but to me it seemed a cruel disgrace, and I was miserable as long as I wore them.' Years later he was to use this classroom incident to explain the great importance in many Eastern cultures of 'saving face', and how shameful it felt to be humiliated by the insensitive foreigners. 'Those who have suffered . . . can well appreciate the agony of shame endured by the more civilised Eastern peoples, whose feelings are often outraged by the total absence of all respect shown them by their European masters or conquerors.'

Alfred's ordeal at the Grammar School ended when, before his fourteenth birthday, his father made one final house move for reasons of economy, and Alfred was withdrawn from school and sent away to stay with an older brother, John, who had already been apprenticed to a London builder. Effectively Alfred had finished his formal schooling, and the rest of his teenage years would be spent in the care of whichever of his brothers could look after him. On arrival in London, he found that brother John was housed at such low rent that he would have to share the same bed.

Alfred acquired woodworking skills as he helped out with odd jobs for the carpenters in the builder's yard where his brother John worked. But his stay in London had another, more profound result; for just off the Tottenham Court Road was a 'Hall of Science'. In essence, this was a working man's club. Alfred went there with John several evenings a week to play draughts and dominoes, drink coffee and read the free newspapers and periodicals. It also offered a programme of lectures and discussions, and here Alfred came in contact with the powerful doctrines of a garrulous and persuasive Welshman, the social reformer Robert Owen. It was Owen's belief that man's character is formed by circumstances over which he has no control, and so he is not a proper subject for either praise or blame. Such a point of view was to have enormous relevance to Wallace when he was living among peoples of totally different cultures whose behaviour others might have considered barbaric and primitive. Nor did Owen believe in revealed religion. He maintained that it was more relevant to concentrate on progressive education and improvement in working and social conditions. Alfred Wallace agreed with him, and for the rest of his life he was an Owenite. This outlook would colour all his writings, his social conscience, and the way he responded to the eminent and privileged members of Victorian society he encountered, as well as his attitude to the native peoples of his travels.

This influential London interlude lasted just a few months before Alfred Wallace was handed on to yet another brother, William, to be looked after. William was a freelance land surveyor, then based in Bedfordshire, and good at his job. He made maps to suit all sorts of different purposes, whether fixing parish boundaries, preparing for enclosures or siting canals and railways. His contracts took him on field trips all over southern England and into Wales. Helping out as his assistant, Alfred began to sense what he would prefer to do as a career. He loved the open-air life and he enjoyed handling survey instruments — the sextant, thermometers and measuring chains — as well as the satisfaction of doing calculations in trigonometry and mathematics. He was also intrigued to stumble on the fringes of the natural sciences. Finding fossils in the local quarries led him to read his first book on geology. Overhearing a chance remark about the Latin name of a wildflower made him buy a book about botany, and then try his hand at assembling a small herbarium of pressed and dried hedgerow plants and flowers.

Eighteen years later, as the Macassar trading prahu approached the shore of Kei, Wallace still retained that same enthusiasm for the natural landscape. He was entranced. 'The coast of Ke, along which we had passed, was very picturesque. Light-coloured limestone rocks rose abruptly from the water to the height of several hundred feet, everywhere broken into jutting peaks and pinnacles, weather-worn into sharp points and honey-combed surfaces, and clothed throughout with a most varied and luxuriant vegetation . . . Here and there little bays and inlets presented beaches of dazzling whiteness. The water was transparent as crystal, and tinged the rock-strewn slope which plunged steeply into its unfathomable depths with colours varying from emerald to lapis-lazuli. The sea was calm as a lake, and the glorious sun of the tropics threw a flood of golden light over all. The scene was to me inexpressibly delightful.'

Wallace knew that he was on the threshold of unknown territory for any naturalist. As far as he was aware, no other collector had managed to get a close look at the animals and plants of the island. 'I was in a new world', he wrote, 'and could dream of the wonderful productions hid in those rocky forests, and in those azure abysses. But few European feet had ever trodden the shores I gazed upon; its plants, and animals, and men were alike almost unknown, and I could not help speculating on what my wanderings there for a few days might bring to light.'

The captain of Wallace's trading prahu had chosen to call at the northern tip of Kei Besar Island, the most logical place for a stopover as it lay close to the direct route to the Aru Islands. Kei Besar, or 'Big Kei', is very different from Kei Kecil, 'Little Kei', where Tual is situated. Little Kei and its surrounding small islands like Warbal are quite flat, and most of their original forest cover was cut down earlier in this century by a Dutch logging company. Warbal's trees for building *Alfred Wallace* had come from secondary forest. By contrast Big Kei is much less accessible. It is a long, narrow dagger of an island, 80 kilometres long but only eight kilometres wide, with a backbone of steep mountains rising abruptly from the sea. Its timber has been much less exploited, and here and there it is still possible to see immense trees, over 30 metres tall, clinging to the mountain slopes. Budi calculated that about one-third of Kei Besar's forest cover remained as it had been in Wallace's day.

Budi had joined us in Warbal when we were fitting out the *Alfred Wallace*. He was from Kalimantan, formerly known as Borneo, where he had been working as a naturalist at a forest reserve in the interior. He was a university graduate in biology and a specialist on Indonesian bird-life, so his first responsibility on our journey was to observe and identify all the birds we saw so that we might have some comparison with the bird-life which Alfred Wallace had recorded. Budi's grandfather had been a Bugis sailor out of Sulawesi, who had migrated to Kalimantan, and this coincidence rather pleased Budi who was looking forward to re-establishing his family link with the sea by sailing with us. In appearance Budi was quite different from Yanis, and true Malay. He was of medium height, slender and fine-boned, with a gold-brown skin and black, lightly curled hair. He had delicate hands, and all his gestures and movements were very neat and precise. He matched Alfred Wallace's description of the Malay character as being very quiet and reserved, almost diffident. Budi was also a skilled woodsman and enthusiastic naturalist, who kept a python as a pet in his house. He had arrived in Warbal with a rucksack containing his bird-identification book, a very serious looking hunting-knife and a pair of binoculars. He volunteered to sleep on deck, and that night it rained very heavily. In the morning I found Budi hanging like a lemur in his jungle hammock which he had slung under the mainsail. He was as snug under his poncho as if he had been deep in the forest.

Leonard was another recently arrived crew member. He was an Irishman whom I had known since he was a boy accompanying his family on a sailing cruise along the Irish coast. Nearly 20 years later he was working as a professional artist, making his name as a painter and book illustrator. Like Budi, he had a quiet and retiring manner. In fact, when Leonard set foot in Warbal I could not help noticing the physical similarity between him and Alfred Wallace when he travelled to Indonesia. Both men were roughly the same age and build, and both wore very similar round-framed glasses. Alfred Wallace described how he had gone on insect-hunting walks in the forest, so intent on catching beetles and spiders that he was always stumbling over tree roots and rocks and bumping his face into cobwebs. Leonard behaved in similar fashion when he was absorbed in his own artist's world of images and impressions.

On his first day in Warbal, I had asked Leonard to paint sailmarks on the khaki-coloured sails for the boat. These sailmarks were stylised pictures of geckos, the small lizards which are found everywhere in Indonesia, clinging with their special suction-pad feet to walls or crawling across ceilings as they hunt small insects. Indonesians believe that geckos bring good luck, and as a symbol for Alfred Wallace's fascination with the natural world I thought the

75

gecko most suitable. Leonard spread out the sails on the firm sand of the school playground, and cut himself a long stick to which he tied his pencil so that he could draw his pictures while standing up. Naturally the schoolchildren were open-mouthed to see this white-skinned stranger shuffling around barefoot on the spread-out sails, drawing outlines of giant geckos on the cloth, stooped over his extra-long pencil like a thin walking stick.

From time to time Leonard would step back to see the effect, cupping one hand around his eye to check the perspective. To keep off the sun, he was wearing a broad-brimmed hat of the same shape as the hat which Alfred Wallace is shown wearing in a photograph taken in Singapore. And like Alfred Wallace in the field, Leonard was utterly oblivious to his surroundings and to everyone watching him. His lips moved slightly as he talked to himself. The crowd of onlookers increased to 40 or 50 people, including adults, and there was a fascinated hush as they waited for each line to be drawn. Unasked, children scurried to hand Leonard a knife to sharpen his pencil and, when he started painting the sailmark, they kept his brush loaded with black paint. Wallace had recorded something similar when he sat in his little hut in the native villages at the end of his day's walk with his butterfly net, engrossed in his insect collection, the pinning and preservation of tiny beetles and insects, a mysterious occupation for the onlookers.

Geckos were not the only symbols painted on our boat. We had moored our brand-new prahu kalulis in the lagoon behind the village, and were making final preparations, when Johnny the head boatbuilder sent a message asking if I would call at his little house. This request was so unusual that I lost no time in going to meet him. He was as shy as ever, but managed to make me understand that he wanted to add 'eyes' to the boat, saying it was his role as the chief boatbuilder. I was pleasantly surprised. In many maritime cultures, the 'eyes' painted on the bow of a boat allow a vessel to 'see' her way across the water. But as far as I knew, none of the other Warbal boats had eyes painted on them. Perhaps this was because they made only short journeys across to the main island or down to Tanimbar. The farthest voyage that any Warbal prahu kalulis had made in living memory was to the provincial capital at Ambon 480 kilometres away. That trip had been nearly 20 years earlier, and was a voyage which was still talked about. Now Johnny and everyone else on Warbal knew that I intended to take the new boat four or five times that distance.

Next morning Johnny appeared, walking ankle-deep across the shallows where *Alfred Wallace* lay aground on the low tide. In one hand he held a tin of white paint and a small brush, in the other a bright scarlet rag and a knife. With the point of the knife he gouged a small hole in a plank just near the bow, then he produced a small gold ring and used his knife to scrape gold dust on to the scrap of cloth. He prodded the scrap of gold-dusted cloth into the little hole — this made the pupil of the 'eye'. Then he took his paint brush and drew a white circle around the pupil, about six inches in diameter, and from it painted four radiating, curved arms. It was both an 'eye' and a very ancient sun symbol. Johnny drew an identical magic sign on the opposite bow to make the second 'eye'. I was curious. Was there any other traditional magic for the boat? Johnny shifted from one foot to the other in embarrassment. 'Yes,' he said, 'I placed a grain of rice in the main joint of the keel, before we closed it up, also a piece of tree root.' What sort of root? Johnny could not tell me the exact species of tree, only that it had magic properties. The fibres had been taken from a length of root which had grown vertically, straight down into the soil, which meant that the boat would be safely connected with the spirits of the land at all times. Once again, I thought to myself, Warbal was not all it might seem. Johnny, an extremely devout Christian, still practised folk magic.

It took us a day to sail from Warbal to Kei Besar. On board were Yanis, Budi, Joe, Leonard, Bill, myself and another Warbal islander, Bobby, who had been recruited by Yanis as his assistant. At the far northern end of Kei Besar we hoped to pick up Alfred Wallace's track and identify the beautiful landfall he had described 140 years earlier.

It had been an overcast day, and by the time we arrived off the southern tip of Big Kei the light was fading. To navigate an untested boat along an unlit coral coast in pitch-darkness would have been foolhardy, so I decided to look for an overnight anchorage in the shelter of the cape. The jagged profile of the headland was like the tail of a giant crocodile, rising in a series of ridged steps from sea level to join the central mountain ridge. Cliffs fell sheer on each side, and were pockmarked with the dark mouths of sea caves. Along the crest of the ridge the feathery tops of nipa palms waved in the stiff breeze.

We rounded the tip of the land to find a small village which looked like something out of a novel by Joseph Conrad. There was a cluster of grey-brown native houses down by the shore, the white dome of a small mosque which at a distance could have been mistaken for a lighthouse, and a pale sliver of a small beach protected by the steep hillside which rose behind the settlement. The place was very remote. To reach it by land would mean a long walk across the central mountain spine of Kei Besar, and I could see no boats of any size for travellers to arrive by sea. Even compared to out-of-the-way Warbal, it was the end of the world.

We dropped anchor as close to the shore as I dared, and cooked our first shipboard supper on the paraffin stove in its wooden box on the aft deck. Our cook that evening was Bobby. He was a strapping, handsome young man in his early twenties who was always immaculately turned out, even on a small sailing boat. Like all Warbal people, he knew how to handle sails and paddle a canoe. But his cooking skills were limited to boiling rice to a soggy mush and sprinkling dried fish with a dusting of chili powder. Yet, like 'Uncle Yanis', he was so good-natured and likeable that no one complained. Bobby had spent most of the day hovering in the background, waiting to be useful and looking rather puzzled as to what he could do to help. Any time you caught his eye, a wide and slightly embarrassed grin would appear under his beautifully trimmed black moustache.

We had just finished our plates of rice and peppery fish when two small dugouts glided unexpectedly from the darkness and into the circle of light thrown by the hurricane lamp on deck. In each canoe were three men, and for some odd reason they were tiny; not one of them could have been much more than five feet tall. They paddled straight to the side of the boat, talking animatedly amongst themselves, reached up to grab the boat and scrambled aboard without a moment's hesitation. Only then did they look round and see that there were white-skinned people on board. There was a clearly audible gasp from one man, followed by a sudden complete silence. Their eyes widened, and then they looked at one another in amazement. When they began to speak again, it was in whispers exactly like children in the company of adults whom they do not believe can hear them. With his usual friendliness Yanis was soon explaining who we were and what we were doing, and the atmosphere became more relaxed. We ought to move our anchorage, the little men suggested, because we had moored over some rocks which might damage our boat at low tide. If we shifted forward, we would be over a much safer patch of sand. Our visitors stayed for an hour, until they had learned all the gossip, then they left. It was the pattern we would encounter again and again over the ensuing months: the eager arrival of local people to chat and gossip within minutes of our dropping anchor, the boarding without so much as a by-your-leave just as Wallace had described, and the astonishment that foreigners were wandering the islands on board such a small and uncomfortable craft.

To drop anchor off an unknown shore in the half-light, and then to awake next morning to a brilliant dawn and find yourself on the edge of a tropical garden of Eden, is one of the delights of Indonesian sailing. We were roused by a strange sound, being repeated every 20 – 30 seconds. It was a bird call unlike anything any of us had heard before. It was like the hooting of an owl but more strident and with a higher pitch, and it had a strange liquid quality. Going on deck we found that we were floating over clean white sand as our guides had advised us the previous night, and that our slight shift of anchorage in the darkness had also brought us into the entrance to a small, lovely cove. We were perhaps 30 metres from a sandy beach on which the water lapped softly. Behind the semicircle of the sand grew low bushes, from which dozens of coconut palms rose in open plantation. Beyond them the forested hillside climbed to become the lower slope of the mountainous spine of the island. We were anchored just far enough away from the equatorial forest to be able to survey the entire scene, yet we were not so far away as to miss its detail. We could see the shapes of individual branches, the sudden movement of a bird, the sway of leaves. The shape of the hillside made a perfect reflector for sound, and this accounted for the strength and clarity of the strange bird call. During the silences you could hear the cries of other birds. There was a loud bubbling coo from some sort of pigeon, and a short metallic clacking which Budi identified also as a pigeon's call. Occasionally there was the screech of a parakeet. All these sounds came absolutely clearly to us across the calm water. There was no interference from the noise of engines or of aircraft passing overhead or the general background hum of civilisation. It was as if we were sitting in a theatre with perfect acoustics, and watching a three-dimensional panorama of pristine tropical Nature.

Budi was entranced. For half an hour he sat on the cabin roof, binoculars to his eyes, as he searched the branches of the trees for the birds which were making these strange calls. Without leaving the boat he was able to identify seven different species, including a bright blue kingfisher perched on the rocks overlooking the bay, and a magnificent fruit pigeon which flew across the green forest slopes with its characteristic looping flight — rising up, swooping, rising up and then with a short quick glide settling into the crown of a palm tree with a white flash of its wings. The sunlight pierced the clear water and every detail of the sea floor was visible as if through glass, from the white sand underneath our prahu's hull to the green-brown shadows of the sea-grass beds near the shore. The crew rested in the shade or went swimming while Budi made a quick foray ashore to expand his notes. He returned looking very satisfied. In two hours he had identified 15 different species of birds, and — even more remarkably — had come across large numbers of Great Bird-Winged Butterflies.

This was a surprise. In Indonesia Great Bird-Winged Butterflies are famous from the forests

Great Bird-Winged Butterfly

of Irian Jaya. But they have been widely collected for their remarkable beauty and increasing rarity, and their habitat has been so badly degraded that their numbers have fallen drastically. It is feared that several species are on the point of extinction, and they are now listed as protected. But here on the southern tip of Kei Besar, seemingly overlooked, they were still in abundance. Wallace would have been delighted; to him the Great Bird-Winged Butterfly was 'one of the most magnificent insects the world contains'. He recalled that when capturing his first specimen in his butterfly net, 'I trembled with excitement as I saw it coming majestically toward me, and could hardly believe I had really succeeded in my stroke till I had taken it out of the net and was gazing, lost in admiration, at the velvet black and brilliant green of its wings, seven inches across, its golden body and crimson breast. It is true I had seen similar insects in cabinets at home, but it is quite another to capture such one's self — to feel it struggling between one's fingers, and to gaze upon its fresh and living beauty, a bright gem shining out amid the silent gloom of a dark and tangled forest.'

Was all this too good to be true? So often I had read that the natural environment of eastern Indonesia had been destroyed, and that the habitats for its special creatures were gone. Yet here, on our first almost casual landfall on Kei Besar, we had come across rare insects and a remarkable variety of bird-life. Would this be the pattern of our voyage? Or was this an exceptional occurrence? It was highly unlikely that the experts were wrong and that everywhere we would find an unspoiled paradise. But Budi's brief excursion onshore had laid to rest the nagging worry that we were wasting our time in setting out to search for the world that Wallace had described. It was already apparent that in some distant corners of the Moluccas the natural world did survive largely intact.

We headed on northward along the coast, and more of Wallace's descriptions began to unfold before our eyes. The limestone rocks, buff and yellow, rose in bold cliffs along the coast. Occasionally great lumps of rock had torn away and dropped into the ocean to make islets. The vegetation was so luxuriant that it found foothold even on these offshore boulders which sprouted strangely contorted trees hung with lianas and climbing plants. For the first 15 – 25 kilometres there was no human habitation on the coast, and we passed close enough for Budi to be able to watch the tree-tops through his binoculars to identify more birds and for the rest of us to listen to their calls. There were the distinctive cries of mynah birds, another bright blue kingfisher, and the wheeling shape of a large fish eagle. The predator plunged into the water as we watched, and lifted up such a heavy fish in its talons that it had difficulty in getting back to its roosting tree, and was obliged to fly in a series of slow, flat curves to gain altitude. There were a few signs of human activity. Occasionally the dark green of the wild forest was broken by a patch of much lighter green where a cassava plantation had been cleared. Several times we saw a pale grey column of smoke drifting up from the canopy where someone had lit a camp-fire or was clearing the jungle for their crops. It was well into the afternoon before we did see another village, and although it lay only 50 metres from the shore it had turned its back on the sea. Its houses stood on a low shoulder of land, and access was by a flight of stone steps. There were only three small canoes on the beach, each large enough to take two men at most, and we could see the extensive patchwork of cassava fields on the hillside behind the settlement. 'Land people,' said Budi, not people of the sea.

Off the next village, 15 kilometres further on, we stopped again to anchor for the night but decided against going ashore, as it was a dirty and dilapidated place and we were put off by the slovenly appearance of the youths who paddled out to inspect us. Their village must have been less isolated than our previous halting place, because their garish clothes had come more recently from the cheap market stalls, and they were smoking from new packs of cigarettes. But it was certainly a village of sea people, because at least two dozen dugouts left the beach soon after dark. Each canoe was paddled by one man, and they were going to their regular night fishing ground over the fringing reef. Soon a long necklace of bright hurricane lamps glinted on the water to seaward of us, no more than a kilometre away, to attract the fish. Each man sang as he fished, lonely in his dugout canoe and separated by perhaps 100 metres from his nearest comrade. Throughout the night we heard them taking it in turns to follow the song, or to join a chorus. As they paddled ashore in the dawn, we could still hear them singing over the murmur of the swell.

A red sun was coming through the morning clouds as we pushed on north because we had yet to reach the spot where I calculated Wallace must have made his first landfall. We passed three or four more villages, strung close together along the coast, and again these were different from anything we had seen before. They belonged to a people whose ancestors had fled to Kei Besar two centuries earlier when their own islands, the Banda group, had been 'ethnically cleansed' in the vicious campaign for control of the spice trade. The refugees had sailed to Kei Besar and settled on its coast. They still spoke their own dialect rather than the local language of Kei, and their villages recalled photographs of Inca villages in the Andes. Flights of stone steps led up to the houses and, perhaps as a legacy of their early vulnerability, the Bandanese villages had the remains of wall defences and there were wooden palisades down by the beach.

We were now very close to the spot we were seeking: the village where Wallace had gone ashore to examine the natural world of Kei Besar. In the 1850s the place had been called Haar, and the captain of his Macassar prahu had purchased two small half-built boats from the villagers, who were accomplished boatbuilders like all Kei islanders, and waited four days for

Coast of Kei Besar

them to be completed. This stopover had given Wallace enough time to go for walks near the village, and compile a useful inventory of the birds and insects of the region.

A village by the name of Haar was marked on the modern chart, almost at the northern tip of Kei Besar. Yanis blithely said he would be able to point it out to us from the sea because he already knew the coast of Kei Besar from his earlier travels. It was becoming clear that our happy-go-lucky crew member was a real vagabond who had held odd jobs all around the Moluccas. He had first left Warbal as a teenager, getting a berth on a Bugis sailing trader and working long hours for a pittance as the boat zig-zagged among the smallest islands, anchoring off isolated villages to trade small utensils and plastic goods for copra, dried coconut. Then he had done a long stint as a deckhand aboard a Korean-owned fishing vessel cruising wherever there were fish to be had, whether off the Aru Islands or farther west near Ambon. After that he had moved on to a job with a big Indonesian timber company; for them he had loaded and driven trucks, felled timber and sailed aboard a work boat which towed barges loaded with logs. He claimed to have been the first mate of the work boat, but we were not so sure. Yanis seemed much too slapdash and carefree to have been driving a motor vessel without close supervision.

Now we waited for Yanis' call as we scanned the little villages along the coast. But it never came, even after we were approaching the very last point of land and could see the open ocean stretching before us all the way to Irian Jaya. Either we had overshot the correct location of Haar, or Haar no longer existed, or perhaps the village had changed location as often happens in the islands when a village can relocate to a more suitable site. By a stroke of luck when we reached the final headland, we found a Bugis trading vessel at anchor there. In all probability it was moored in exactly the same spot where Wallace's vessel had first stopped, just south of the cape, to get shelter from the prevailing monsoon. We steered close enough under the stern of the Bugis vessel to shout our question — Haar? Where's Haar? The Bugis sailors called back and pointed south. We had to turn back and sail past the next headland; the first large village was the village of Haar.

Yanis cheerily bluffed his way out of the situation. Of course he had recognised Haar when we passed it earlier, he said. It was just that I had not made it clear that I wanted to stop there. So we turned back and, because the anchorage off Haar seemed rather exposed, we nosed our prahu into the protection of a tiny bay which was scarcely more than a nick in the coastline. From there, I calculated, it was no more than an hour's walk to Haar which Alfred Wallace had described rather disparagingly as 'only three or four huts, situated immediately above the beach on an irregular rocky piece of ground overshadowed with coconuts, palms, bananas and other fruit trees. The houses were very rude, black and half rotten.' Going inside, he found them little more than shacks, raised a few feet on posts, with low sides of bamboos or planks and high thatched roofs. They had small doors and no windows; only an opening under the projecting gables let the smoke out and a little light in. The floors were made of strips of bamboo, 'so weak that my feet were in danger of plunging through at every step'. Boxes and mats of pandanus leaves and slabs of palm pith, jars and cooking pots of native pottery, and a few European plates and basins made up the only furniture. 'The interior was throughout dark and smoke-blackened,' he concluded, 'and dismal in the extreme.'

But shabby native huts were not what Wallace had come to see. While the prahu captain supervised the construction of the two small boats, and the prahu sailors bargained for wooden bowls, carved goods, parrots and lories which they would sell on when they got back to Macassar, Wallace and his two Malay assistants, Ali and Baderoon, explored a path leading into the forest surrounding the village. The village children guided them along the narrow track. Almost at once they were puzzled by the sounds of deep booming and sudden clacking which came from the tops of some tall trees. Wallace soon identified the noise as coming from some large pigeons, and after several misses his assistants managed to shoot one for closer inspection. It turned out to be a fruit pigeon, a magnificent specimen 'twenty inches long, of a bluish white colour, with the back wings and tail intense metallic green with gold, blue and violet reflections, the feet coral red, and the eyes golden yellow'.

Wallace noted the bird's remarkably elastic mouth. The beak was quite narrow, but it could stretch its jaws and throat so wide that it could swallow large fruit, including the seeds an inch across. Wallace pronounced it a 'rare species'. It was the same species of fruit pigeon, the Elegant Imperial Pigeon, which Budi had identified on his first shore excursion when its deep coo and strange metallic clacking had immediately caught our attention.

Wallace discovered that walking in the forest of Haar was no easier than treading the treacherously 'thin, slippery, and elastic' bamboo floors of the native huts. The bare red earth of the native path was worn slick, and although the natives managed very well in their bare feet, Wallace slipped and slithered badly in his leather shoes. Worse, the path led to an area where the bare rock was exposed. Here the ground was so rugged and broken, and honey-combed into sharp points and angles, that Wallace's two assistants cut themselves frequently, even though they had gone barefoot all their lives. Their feet soon began to bleed and Wallace's shoes, too thin to give real protection, started to disintegrate. Only the native children guiding them seemed unconcerned. 'They tripped along with the greatest ease and unconcern', and were surprised by the clumsiness and discomfort of their visitors. Wallace abandoned the excursion before his shoes were ruined, and during the rest of his stay at Haar confined himself to exploring near the beach or level areas where there was a covering of soil over the sharp rocks. Here he searched happily for beetles and other insects, pursued little green lizards with heavenly blue tails, and captured an evil-smelling tiger beetle

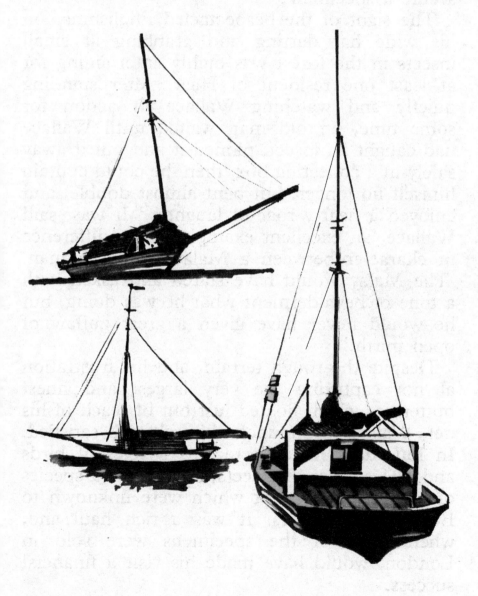

Bugis boat

which resembled 'a very large ant more than an inch long and of a purple black colour'. This tiger beetle tried to evade him by scurrying round the trunk of a tree 'in a spiral direction so that it requires a sudden run and active fingers to secure a specimen'.

The sight of the bespectacled Englishman in his wide hat darting and grabbing at small insects in the forest was highly entertaining for at least one resident of Haar. After standing quietly and watching Wallace in action for some time, an old man waited until Wallace had caught an insect, pinned it and put it away safely in a collecting box, then 'he could contain himself no longer, but bent almost double, and enjoyed a hearty roar of laughter.' It was, said Wallace, an excellent example of the difference in character between a Malay and a Papuan. 'The Malay would have stared and asked with a tone of bewilderment what he was doing, but he would never have given a great guffaw of open mirth.'

Despite the rough terrain, and his frustration at not capturing the very largest and finest butterflies which floated just out of reach of his net, Wallace pronounced himself well satisfied. In four days he collected 15 species of birds and 194 species of insects, including 35 species of butterflies many of which were unknown to European collectors. It was a rich haul and, when some of the specimens were sold in London, would have made his visit a financial success.

But how much of what Wallace had seen still

remained? At half-past two in the afternoon, leaving Bobby to keep watch on the boat, the rest of us went ashore to the little hamlet at the back of the anchorage to investigate.

The headman of the little hamlet, whose name turned out to be Ohoirat, met us on the beach. He was young for his post, perhaps in his mid-forties, and he had an odd quirk of making little snorts through his nostrils to punctuate his sentences, and wagging his eyebrows up and down between each sentence, as if in surprise. He began by apologising for not coming out to see us immediately we had arrived with our boat. He had feared we might be the same two Chinese traders who had come in a small boat the previous winter; they were wanting to buy sea slugs and wild pearls, and had paid such miserable prices and been so demanding that they caused him much trouble. Evidently little had changed in the ways of island trade since Wallace was there. I told the headman that all we wanted to buy were fresh vegetables, and he was equally apologetic for his little settlement was so small that no one had surplus produce for sale. Then, still snorting softly and wiggling his eyebrows, he led us to the edge of the hamlet and pointed out the way to Haar.

It was a narrow footpath which crossed a cassava field and then plunged straight into the forest. The change was instant. One moment you were in the hot sunshine, walking between the shoulder-high cassava plants with their thin stalks and narrow leaves. With the next step you had passed directly into the cool shade of wild forest. Many of the trees were 25 or 30 metres tall. At their feet grew delicate sprays of fern and a thick cover of ground plants. There were small flowers of violet and blue, and a creeping plant like miniature ivy with the elegant almond-shaped leaves in two shades of olive; the outer part of each leaf was pale, and the inner surface dark. These plants spread out beside the footpath as if you were walking through an equatorial greenhouse where the gardeners had deliberately laid out all the most eye-catching vegetation to best effect. Shafts of sunlight found their way down through the forest canopy, and into their beams flew a brilliant variety of butterflies. Wherever you looked, you saw butterflies. Some of them were enormous, and they were the great bird-winged varieties which Budi had reported. Their colours were black and white or black and yellow. Other butterflies were tiny and a bright yellow. The loveliest were pairs of the most exquisite orange and brown butterflies which intertwined as they mated on the olive-green leaves beside the path.

Yanis led the way briskly. To him the forest scene was nothing special, and the only time he veered off the track was when he spotted a rare black orchid hanging half-way up a tree. He briskly swarmed up to collect it and presumably sold it in the next good-sized port we came to; from there the orchid would have gone to the Jakarta market. From time to time Yanis had to stop and wait for the rest of us to catch up because we were wandering along, craning our necks to see the butterflies above our heads.

Budi was a lost cause. He kept plunging off the path into the undergrowth to stalk some bird or other he had glimpsed or heard in the distance. Within half a mile he was totally separated from the rest of us.

Soon after leaving Ohoirat, we had stepped over a low wall of coral that had been built across the footpath to protect the cassava field from the wild pigs which foraged in the forest. Farther on we smelled woodsmoke and came across a patch which was being cleared for plantation. Native women were chopping back the undergrowth and burning the rubbish. Mostly the path was of soft red earth, and only occasionally did we have to cross ribbons of the broken coral rock which Wallace had complained about. But we were wearing strong shoes and were not troubled. Sometimes the track took us through groves of coconut palms, many of which were in the process of losing their older leaves, and here too flights of butterflies circled high among the yellow and gold fronds.

We met villagers along the path — men and women returning from their work, invariably carrying in one hand their work tool, the cutlass that throughout Indonesia is called a parang, and often with a woven basket slung on a tump line round their forehead and dangling on their backs. The basket normally contained a load of firewood and, as we approached, the villagers insisted on giving us priority. They politely stepped aside off the track and waited in the undergrowth, turning stiff-necked under the brow band of their basket strap to watch as

Haar village

we passed. In spite of the human traffic along the trail there were wild birds everywhere. The heavy-set fruit pigeons were so large that they always caught one's eye as they landed in the tall, exposed tree-tops. But there were also wood swallows, sunbirds and coucals. Keeping pace with us, almost as if the bird was tame, was a sleek black drongo with a double fan tail which fluttered through the woods. Occasionally it would pause, hanging upside-down to feed off a bunch of wild red berries, then hurried on to keep level with us again.

After an hour's walk a pair of bright purple bougainvilleas planted beside the path announced the outskirts of Haar, and suddenly we were standing on the edge of a tall cliff, with the sea on our left, and looking across at Haar itself. No longer the squalid little hamlet of four smoke-blackened houses which Wallace had described, Haar was now a well-kept, prosperous and large village. It was superbly situated, overlooking a remarkable double bay divided by a high spur of land. On this promontory stood the Christian church with its spire and white-painted façade, and two or three substantial houses belonging to the wealthier families. The rest of the village spread around the hillsides behind the two bays, and all the neat thatched houses had a magnificent panorama of the sea. About 30 – 40 dugout canoes were drawn up on the beaches, and behind them stood the wooden frames on which the fishermen dried their nets. Several of the older canoes, now abandoned, were huge: as much as 18 metres long and more than a metre across. They gave some idea of the size of giant forest tree which would have been needed to make their hulls. Either the fishermen had given up the labour of hacking out canoe hulls from such enormous trees or there were no more forest giants available, because all the newer canoes were much smaller. Banana trees, sago palms and coconut palms grew along the village paths, and where the footpath descended steeply to the beach someone had planted ornamental cacti and bushes with deep pink leaves. Alfred Wallace would have been amazed and pleased by the transformation.

We paid a courtesy call on the village headman and spent the rest of the afternoon exploring Haar. There was expert boatbuilding in progress, as in Wallace's day. A team of men were constructing a small motor fishing-boat, using exactly the same pegged-plank technique as in Warbal. But in Haar they seemed rather more professionally organised, with a foreman obviously in command and giving orders, where Johnny had been so diffident and his team had worked on a casual basis. A Christian graveyard extended for half a kilometre beside the path running along the shore. The tombs were half hidden by rushes and tall reeds, and the graves were decorated with an eclectic mixture of ornaments. Most had plain white tiles stuck to them in random patterns, but one was embellished with Coca-Cola bottles and another had a display of porcelain insulators from telegraph poles. Here the palm trees were very mature, roughly 25 metres high, and neglected so that they were draped with curtains of lianas. Strung between the trees were great cobwebs with spans of 2.5 metres and more. And once again, high among the palms, were butterflies, dozens and dozens of them, circling and spiralling, always seeming to be ascending until they reached the tree-tops.

It was twilight when we started to walk back along the track to Ohoirat, and I deliberately hung back to accompany Budi so that he could explain the evening flighting of the forest birds. Squadrons of small parrots, red-headed and green, flew overhead towards their roosts, chattering noisily. A pair of brightly coloured lories announced their arrival with remarkable vulgarity, shrieking at the tops of their voices as they approached, and landed brazenly on a bare branch right over our heads. Fruit pigeons settled for the night into the tree-tops, with a booming call which then ended in a slowing tonk-tonk-tonk like a small single-cylinder diesel engine shutting down. We heard the last notes of that strange owl-like bird-call which first woke us two days earlier off the south tip of Kei Besar, and which we never succeeded in identifying. Soon afterwards came the hooting of the true owls. A thunderstorm was brewing away to the north, and against a lurid sky slowly flapped the silhouettes of flying foxes as the giant fruit bats set out for their evening feeding. It was easy to see how Alfred Wallace would have been exhilarated by his visit to 'Big Kei'. Its plant life was so luxurious, and the remarkable diversity of birds and insects seemed to be living together in harmony.

It struck me, also, that the forest of Kei was notable for its friendliness. There was nothing in this jungle which seemed to menace. Its largest animals were two species of slow-moving harmless cuscus, furry marsupials with prehensile tails, relatives to the Australian possums. Among reptiles there were several large species of lizard, small pythons and — though no one was quite sure — one or two species of snakes which may or may not be venomous. But it was the tolerance of the plant life which was really remarkable. Although we were walking along a single-track path, where the bushes grew so close that they constantly brushed one's legs or shoulders, there were no hooked or thorny branches to catch and tear or hold you back. And when Budi led me on sudden brief side forays into the jungle to try to identity the flitting shape of some unknown bird, the vegetation was open enough to push through without difficulty and without fear of getting stung on bare legs and arms. Nor were there tangled ground roots to snag one's feet. The forest seemed so trustworthy, and this was even more striking when night closed in completely and we found ourselves walking fast along the trail in almost complete darkness. Now there was barely enough light to see the line of the track, and the vegetation uprose on each side in black shapes. Sometimes these black shapes converged into a solid wall in front of us, higher than our heads, and the line of the path was lost. Yet, trusting the forest, we walked on briskly, straight into the solid wall of black. It was like throwing ourselves into a well of black water which parted harmlessly. A few strides and we emerged once again into a clearing and could just make out the small green shapes of plants around us.

Right towards the end of our walk was a never-to-be-forgotten sight. We emerged from the wall of blackness and there, slightly to one side of the track, was a small, open tree about the size of a tall holly bush. It was a plant of the bean family, and an attraction for fireflies. Dozens upon dozens of these insects had settled on its branches, outlining the shape and structure of the tree in points of luminous green which pulsed randomly as Nature's electric illuminated Christmas tree. The phenomenon stopped me in amazement, and I stood watching the vivid green specks glow and fade, then glow again, and occasionally shift a detail of their pattern as insects changed position on the branches.

A hundred metres farther on Budi and I stepped across the coral stone wall which protected Ohoirat's gardens from the wild pigs, and five minutes later we were standing on the beach looking across the water at the *Alfred Wallace* against a horizon which flickered with the lightning of the west monsoon.

Some time afterwards, towards the end of our search for Alfred Wallace, I was to ask myself why that initial visit to Kei Besar had left such a strong impression. Was it because this was the first visit ashore, and I had been very susceptible to those original vivid impressions of the tropical forest? Or was there something more? The forest trees of Kei Besar we had seen were not particularly large, nor was the vegetation very unusual. Later in our trip we would go deeper into primary rainforest and camp amongst much taller trees and stranger plants. Yet I remembered there had been something special about the Kei Besar forest: it was the feeling of a harmony between man and nature. On every side we had seen evidence of humans. There were clearings and cassava plantations, villagers walking along the track, the smoke of fires, the sounds of parangs chopping. But the creatures of the forest appeared to be little disturbed. There were thousands of butterflies; the birds came and went, almost ignoring the humans, and Budi had identified 42 different species of birds in a place where Alfred Wallace had collected only 25 species.

The remoteness of the place was one reason for this impression of unspoiled nature. The northern end of Kei Besar is so difficult to reach that it is still isolated from many commercial pressures. But there may well have been another reason. I learned later that the area around Haar came under the authority of a traditional leader, a 'rajah', with strong opinions on the management of the environment. His exact authority was vague. Officially Kei Besar was administered according to standard Indonesian government procedure with a full hierarchy of regions, sub-regions and all the usual civil servant apparatus. But parallel to this formal structure was a much older form of authority. Traditionally, the people of Kei were divided into three social classes which rarely intermarried.

Ostensibly these social ranks no longer existed, yet village heads were almost all chosen from members of the old ruling class. Intermediaries between the people and environment, such as the *tuan tanah* of Warbal who had presided at the launch of our prahu, usually came from the same family. In certain matters, the authority of these tradditional leaders was more respected than the regulations which ultimately came from Jakarta. The rajah or 'king' of Maur Ohoiwut, whose territory included Haar, firmly believed in the age-old methods of resource management. He held that exploitation of the land and sea should be done according to custom. There were specified times and quotas for collecting coconuts, gathering forest crops, cutting timber, taking shellfish, catching certain species of fish. These laws were hallowed by custom and were empirical. When there was a strong advocate like the rajah, these laws were also obeyed. In all likelihood the same customs and controls had existed at the time Alfred Wallace visited Haar, but he was unaware of them. Possibly they had protected the environment of Kei Besar for the following century and a half, until we came to see the place for ourselves. But we had no way of knowing until we had the opportunity to compare the forest and wildlife of Kei Besar with a formal Nature Reserve along our route. That first officially sanctioned Nature Reserve would be our next landfall — on the Aru Islands some 100 kilometres to the east which Wallace had described as 'exceedingly interesting and little known'.

4

Aru

IN 1843 when Alfred Wallace was 20, his
father died and the family disintegrated. His
mother had to find work as a housekeeper.
The only surviving daughter (three others had
died in youth or infancy) emigrated to the United
States where she became a teacher. John stayed
in London as a builder and the youngest boy,
Herbert, was apprenticed to a luggage-maker.
Even William, the competent land surveyor, was
finding work difficult to obtain and his income
was dwindling. So, to ease the financial burden,
Alfred took a job as a school usher in a private
boarding school in Leicester. The post meant
that he had to do some teaching and supervise
the evening homework of the 40 or so boarders,

but it had the great advantage that he lived rent-free in the house of the headmaster, and he had time to read.

Alfred had always enjoyed books. His father, even at his lowest ebb, always had books in the house, either from book clubs or brought home when he worked part-time in a local subscription library. He read aloud to his children and Alfred Wallace, introspective and retiring, had developed a natural preference for reading. There was a subscription library in Leicester, and here he came across two books which were to mould his future. The first was Malthus' *Essay on the Principles of Population*, whose theory of population control through natural disasters would later underpin Wallace's theory of evolution by natural selection. The second book was *A Personal Narrative of Travels in South America* written by the brilliant German naturalist Baron von Humboldt. The latter started Wallace dreaming about the idea of becoming a travelling naturalist in the tropics.

This apparently fanciful notion was encouraged by a chance encounter in the Leicester library with the future discoverer of the principle of animal mimicry, Henry Walter Bates. Twenty years later Bates would bring powerful support to the Darwin-Wallace theory of evolution by demonstrating how some species of animals guarded themselves against predators by developing the same appearance as less edible or more aggressive species. When Alfred Wallace met him, Bates was an apprentice in the Leicester hosiery trade, and the two rather serious-minded young amateur naturalists found that they shared an immediate interest. Both enjoyed rambling in the countryside around the town, collecting. But where Wallace was on the lookout for plants for his nascent herbarium, Bates searched for insects, particularly beetles. When Bates proudly showed Wallace his collection of butterflies and beetles, all of them captured within a ten-mile radius of Leicester, Wallace was amazed. He had no idea that so many different species of insects could exist in such a small area, or that humble insects like the beetle could have such beautiful forms and colours. From that moment onward entomology became his personal preference. He put aside his primitive plant herbarium, bought a large tome on English insects and happily succumbed to beetle-mania. Years later, deep in the Indonesian forests, he would devote as much time to peeling back the bark of rotten logs and searching for beetles, as to looking upward into the tree canopy for new species of birds.

That first meeting in the Leicester Library also marked the start of a striking parallel in their careers. The two men were almost the same age — Wallace a year older than Bates — and they both came from similarly modest backgrounds. Bates, though from 'trade', was actually slightly better off, even if he had been sweeping out the company shop at 7 a.m. each morning. During their lifetimes the two men would travel together, botanise and collect together, both write best-selling books about their particular tropical adventures, both apply for the same jobs and receive similar scientific honours. There were so many similarities that even their contemporaries tended to get them mixed up. Bates was to tell the story how, later in his career, he was walking in the Zoological Gardens near the seal pond when he encountered Sir Charles Lyell the eminent geologist. Lyell, he reported, 'was wriggling about in his usual way, with spy glass raised by fits and starts to the eye, and began, "Mr. Wallace, I believe . . . ah? . . . ah?"' To which Bates had to reply 'My name is Bates.' 'Oh, I beg pardon; said the great man, 'I always confound you two.'

It was with Bates that Wallace first began to discuss the 'Species Question'. Of course the two novice scientists had not the least idea of what was going on in the more advanced world of scientific research in London and Paris. Darwin was already working on the problem, painstakingly collecting his data and writing questionnaires to his circle of expert friends. An assistant schoolmaster and the apprentice hosier in Leicester Library were in an altogether different category, full of enthusiasm but short of information and access to good source material. Wallace and Bates were much impressed, for example, by a popular book by an anonymous writer[1] on evolution who, after postulating

---

[1] He was in fact Robert Chambers, an Edinburgh publisher, after whom *Chambers Encyclopaedia* was subsequently named.

correctly that animals could and did change their forms, went on to propose such odd ideas as that the colour yellow in all animals denoted evil, particularly if their skins were also striped. The tiger, of course, was his prime example, but the Chinese and other yellow skinned peoples were also suspect.

Then, in 1846, yet another family disaster overtook the Wallaces when the eldest son, William the surveyor, died of pneumonia. Ironically, the railways which had provided his main living also killed him. The country was in one of its periodic orgies of railway speculation, and hundreds of projects for new private railways were being proposed, discussed, condemned and advertised. Surveyor William was invited to London to give evidence to a Railway Committee there. On his way back to Wales, where he was surveying, he contracted pneumonia while travelling overnight in February in the open truck that was then a third-class railway carriage. News of his death brought Alfred and brother John to Wales to try to sort out their brother's business affairs. They found that William was owed various sums of money and, though these were small debts, they were important because William had been helping to support their mother. Collecting these petty debts was a task which Alfred Wallace found extremely distasteful. The debtors were reluctant to pay and had to be cajoled and, in one case, threatened with legal proceedings. Unworldly and high-principled, Wallace was disgusted by the level of venality and dishonesty. He began to think of emigrating, like his sister.

He was prevented from doing so by the same railway boom that had ended the life of his brother. Speculation in railway schemes was running out of hand. Railway companies were being floated at such a pace that it was calculated that there was not enough money in circulation in the entire country to make the deposits which had to be sent in to the Board of Trade before actual rail-building could go ahead. Many of the railway companies were, of course, shams and get-rich-quick schemes for the promoters, but to keep up an appearance of authenticity they needed to produce convincing prospectuses and drawings for new railway lines. This in turn meant that they needed maps of the areas where the railways would run. Suddenly there was a huge demand for railway surveyors, at whatever price. To his astonishment Alfred heard that surveyors were being paid two guineas a day, a princely sum for a junior schoolmaster. He had inherited brother William's survey instruments; he had a novice assistant in his brother John, and he had enough experience to do the job himself.

In just a few months of work Wallace managed to save £100, enough for his dream of travelling in the tropics. He wrote a letter to Bates suggesting that the two of them should set off for the river Amazon. There they would travel up-river into the tropical forest and collect rare and unknown plants, insects and animals, particularly the gorgeous and rare birds of the Amazon basin. Some specimens they would keep for themselves; others they would send back to England to be sold, and thus pay their field expenses. But the ultimate goal was something far more ambitious: together they would gather facts to be 'used towards solving the problem of the origin of species'.

Approaching the Aru Islands in eastern Indonesia eight years later, the nagging problem of the origin of species had still not yet been solved, though Wallace was beginning to have a glimmering of the solution. Yet he could be confident that the technique of paying for his research travel by collecting rare animals, which had worked well enough with Bates in Amazonia, was likely to be even better rewarded in the next few weeks. The Aru Islands were an Eldorado for the bird collector; they were known to be a home of the semi-legendary Bird of Paradise, a highly priced rarity. For centuries the skins and feathers of these birds had been appearing in Europe, brought back in small numbers by sailors and travellers. The stunning colours and strange-shaped feathers had led to all sorts of fanciful notions. There was the tale that the birds were not really of this world but were ethereal creatures. It was said that they never came to earth and, lacking even legs on which to stand, either hovered all their lives in the sky on their silky golden wings, or hung upside-down from branches by their extraordinary long and curly tail feathers. This rumour had arisen because few people had ever seen the Birds of Paradise in the wild, and knew only their cured skins which the natives traded, after cutting off the legs in the curing process. Linnaeus, the great pioneering naturalist, had inspected the skins and bones of a few dead Birds of Paradise and, significantly, both the species which he had managed to classify came from Aru.

Now Alfred Wallace had the chance to see for himself how the Bird of Paradise lived and, equally important, he could gather specimens which ought to fetch handsome sums when sold in London. He knew of only one or two French exploring ships which had touched briefly at the islands, and a single naturalist, a Monsieur Payen from Brussels, who had stayed just a few days without doing any significant work. Fewer than 20 specimens of Aru's birds and insects were positively known; the rest were for Wallace to discover.

He landed at Dobbo, the only place which could even remotely be called a settlement in the wild, flat islands covered with vast green mangrove swamps which form the Aru archipelago. He found Dobbo was 'at first sight a most strange and desolate-looking place'. It was inhabited only during the trading season when a migrant population of Chinese merchants and Bugis traders from Sulawesi would arrive on their prahus and come ashore on a low sandspit. They set about cleaning and refurbishing the three rows of weather-beaten bamboo and thatch houses, little more than large sheds, which they kept as their temporary bases on the islands. Here they would spend the next five or six months, while the local natives brought in bird feathers, pearls and dried sea slugs for sale, or

Dobbo, in the trading season
(*taken from* The Malay Archipelago)

the traders sent out collecting parties in small
boats to the even more remote corners of the
archipelago. When Wallace arrived on 8 January
1857, he found that he was a couple of weeks
ahead of the main trading influx. The entire
population of Dobbo amounted to just half
a dozen people, Bugis and Chinese. Even
so, accommodation was hard to find. Every
bamboo shed, however ramshackle, had an
owner who was expected to arrive shortly and
begin trading. All available houses were either
half-built, roofless or too expensive. Eventually,
with the intervention of his prahu captain,
Wallace managed to organise the short-term
rental of a house whose owner was not expected
for a few weeks. Inside, he rigged up a few

115

light planks to serve as table and bookshelves, spread out some mats on the floor, installed a cane chair and his collection boxes, and cut a hole in the palm-leaf wall to let in some light so that he could work at his home-made work bench. He was agog with anticipation. 'Though the place was as gloomy and rough a shed as could be imagined, I felt as contented as if I had obtained a well-furnished mansion, and looked forward to a month's residence in it, with unmixed satisfaction.'

During the five months he spent on the islands, Wallace witnessed an extraordinary transformation overtake Dobbo. Throughout January there was a steady arrival of boats and traders, 15 big prahus from Macassar and up to 100 smaller boats from Kei, the New Guinea coast and outer Aru. They clustered into the anchorage or were pulled up on the beach to be scrubbed and have new coats of anti-fouling, while their crews moved into the bamboo houses. The settlement buzzed with activity, and Wallace marvelled — as he had already done at the well-mannered behaviour of his prahu crew — that this ill-assorted mass of people managed to get on so well without any formal rule of law, courts or police to keep order. Dobbo was full to bursting with a 'motley, ignorant, thievish population' of Chinese, Bugis, half-caste Javanese, men from Seram, with a sprinkling of half-wild Papuans from Timor and the islands to the south. Yet 'they do not cut each other's throats, do not plunder each other day and night, do not fall into the anarchy such a state of things might be supposed to lead to. It is very extraordinary.' It made him wonder that perhaps European countries were over-governed, and that 'the thousands of lawyers and barristers whose whole lives are spent in telling us what the hundred acts of Parliament mean' indicated that 'if Dobbo has too little law, England has too much'.

The reason for the orderliness and good behaviour in Dobbo, he decided, was that every person there had come to trade, and that a peaceful environment for the marketplace was in everyone's interest. So the little sandspit was an amicable parade of regional types and costumes. Chinamen soberly walked down the single street, with their long pigtails hanging down to their heels. Half-naked Aru islanders — wearing nothing but a loin-cloth and with enormous bushes of frizzy hair held in place by gigantic wooden combs — called at every door to offer tradable items and see who would pay the best price. Young sailors from Macassar played a kind of aerial football with a hollow ball made of rattan which they kept in the air with a succession of kicks and knocks from feet, elbow and shoulder.

★ ★ ★

Pale pink lightning was flickering over Dobbo when the *Alfred Wallace* approached the Dobbo anchorage 139 years later. The odd colour of the flashes was from the dawn sun, still hidden below the horizon, which gave a distinctly red

117

tint to the lightning. We had been watching the electrical storm for the past eight hours, ever since we had left Kei Besar and headed south-east, closing the Aru coast. We were now nearly at the extreme south-east limit of our planned itinerary, with the Australian coast lying 650 kilometres to the south, and the Aru Islands tucked under the curve of the great island of New Guinea. In fact, geographically and zoologically, the Arus are an extension of New Guinea, separated by the shallow seas of the Sahul shelf and sharing many of the characteristic fauna and flora — tree kangaroos, brush turkeys and giant ferns. Long considered to be among the most desolate and inaccessible of Indonesia's island clusters, the Arus has only recently acquired its first all-weather airstrip, essential in a region which receives more than 2,000 millimetres of rain every year. The exact population is unknown, because some inland areas are so difficult to reach through their dense mangrove swamps and the tropical lowland deciduous forest. It was calculated that about 60,000 people live on the Arus, mostly on the perimeter of the six main islands, divided by narrow channels, which spread across more than 6,000 square kilometres, and the vast majority of the islanders are concentrated in the regional capital at Dobbo.

Even at eight kilometres' distance we could distinguish almost nothing of the land itself, only a thin line on the horizon, because the Aru coastline was nowhere more than six metres in elevation. As the sun rose further, it climbed behind a thick mass of monsoon cloud, and so it was under a heavy overcast that we entered the wide mouth of the channel.

We might as well have been venturing into a West African river. The air was hot and heavy, mud flats extended away on each side until they merged into mangrove swamp spiked with an occasional coconut palm, and the tidewater which flowed out of the channel was an opaque grey-green. The flatness of the landscape was accentuated by the black silhouette of a single fisherman. He was at least 100 metres from the shore, yet still standing in shallows, up to his waist in the water with a throw net in his arms. Behind him a long sweep of a rather grubby sandy beach appeared on our starboard side, and beyond it were the first few houses, low white blocks roofed with red corrugated-iron or the usual palm-thatch huts. Dobbo was on the south side of the estuary, and in another kilometre we saw the white spire of a church in the middle of the town buildings, the green roofs of what looked like government offices, and a tall radio mast. It was a very modest place and the government offices, four or five stories high, dominated the rest of the settlement. Everywhere the land was so low-lying that a slight rise in water level would drown the entire town of Dobbo.

There was no difficulty in identifying the sandspit where Wallace had set up his base among the warehouses of the Bugis and Chinese traders. Now forming the core of the modern town, it projected out into the harbour and terminated in a battered concrete jetty where the visiting ferry-boats tied up. Extending round the sides of the sandspit and back towards the main shore were long wooden sheds, built on massive wooden pilings sunk in the mud. Most of the sheds were warehouses or workshops, built of the same simple style — long and capacious — as the warehouses which Wallace had described. Together they formed a sombre waterfront of grey-brown wooden pilings under dark brown sheds. Apart from the occasional white concrete building, it could have been the waterfront of any moribund fishing port in the last century.

Dobbo, which Wallace had found so orderly and animated, now proved to have a rather scruffy and desolate atmosphere. Budi and I were the first to go ashore. After we dropped anchor, Yanis paddled us across to the jetty in the dugout we used as a dinghy. Walking to the foot of the jetty, we found that the main commercial street of Dobbo ran down the spine of the sandspit just as in Wallace's time. Where he had strolled between traders' warehouses, we now walked between the shopfronts of the general stores of the local traders. The vast majority of shopkeepers were still Chinese, selling all the usual stock-in-trade we had already seen in Tual: plastic goods, cheap radios, groceries, hardware and shoddy clothes. In just two small, dark shops we found goods which Wallace would have recognised: there were ropes of indifferent cultured pearls, large oyster shells opened to show their glittering mother-of-pearl linings, twisted bangles of reddish coral, and arrangements of dishes of what looked like the polished and shiny talons of giant eagles. The traders called them 'sea cassowary' and explained that this was a certain type of coral, much prized for decorative work. Also for sale were a few eggs of the real cassowary, which were still to be found in the interior, though officially it was forbidden to harm them or collect their eggs. The same disregard for the law seemed to apply to the sea cow or dugong, which was once common in the shallow water to the south of Aru. There were plenty of dugong tusks for sale, drilled and carved to make cigarette holders. Of Birds of Paradise, dead or alive, there was no sign, and this was welcome. The Birds of Paradise of Aru were at severe risk of extinction and strictly protected — or at least that is what I had been told by the government authorities in Jakarta.

Like Tual in the Kei Islands, Dobbo's main function was bureaucratic. It was the administrative centre for the Aru archipelago, and the chief employment was found in the dozens of local government offices strung out behind the town. These were little more than shabby bungalows, each with a peeling notice board stating to which department they belonged. To reach them meant crossing an area of town which in Wallace's day had been mostly swamp. The swamp had not been properly drained, and the fetid canals and drains between the shacks of small residential houses now stank with putrid water. Budi and I walked through this unlovely suburb and on down the road until we reached the offices of the Forestry Department. We were required to contact the local civil servants responsible for administering the Nature Reserve on the far side of Aru; only with their permission could we visit this last significant area on Aru where the Birds of Paradise survived in large numbers.

We were sent from one shabby office to another, and then taken to the house of the deputy unit chief who had not bothered to go to the office that day — as on many others, I surmised. We were meeting very junior civil servants, miserably paid and virtually unsupervised 3,000 kilometres away from Jakarta. They were polite, lazy and disinterested. The deputy unit chief said we had to have a guide to take us to the Reserve, which was a day's journey away by boat. He himself would take on this role; he would prepare his kit that afternoon and come down to the boat next morning to join us — but he needed 100,000 rupiahs in advance to cover his food and expenses. I handed over the money — the equivalent of about two weeks' wages — and was not surprised never to see him again. Instead the next day he sent an underling, a small, bored man who climbed aboard *Alfred Wallace*, looked around for the most comfortable spot on deck and immediately sat down on it, making it clear that we were to transport him and feed him but he was certainly not going to lend a hand.

Dobbo seemed thoroughly dispirited. It was difficult to see what there was to do, apart

Dobbo today

from form-filling bureaucracy. The economic
life of the islands, such as it was in those
broad empty mangrove swamps and forests,
was elsewhere. In the interior there were a few
logging camps, and a sprinkling of plantations
had been started up to absorb immigrant labour
sent from overcrowded Java. We were told that
Japanese investors had tried to start cultured
pearl farms, because Aru's wild pearls had once
been world famous, attracting pearling boats
from Australia, across the shallow Arafura Sea.
But there was something wrong with the water
quality now, and for some unknown reason
the oysters no longer flourished. The Japanese
pearl farms had never been developed. Aru's
main wealth still came from the sea, from the
extensive fisheries of the coastal waters; but the
fish stocks were in decline, and the only thriving
fishing centre was a few miles farther south along
the coast. Here the crews stayed on their boats,

anchored offshore and did not come on land very often.

Dobbo was still the place where almost everyone who arrived or left Aru had to come, because it had the only airport and the ferry terminal. The main ferry came two or three times a month and was quite smart. But the secondary ferry looked more like a refugee ship and its ill-adjusted clattering engine could be heard from five kilometres' distance as it clanked its way up the channel. Upper and lower deck were so crammed with animals, boxes and people that it seemed a few would be squeezed over the rails and into the harbour. Flapping strips of grimy tarpaulin were rigged to offer inadequate shelter to the upper deck, but there was no escape from the discordant bellowing of the tannoy which blared out-of-tune music. After the rusty vessel had tied up, there was a surge of passengers seeking to get off and down the gangplank, hauling their bundles. They somehow vanished into the maw of Dobbo, because in half an hour the main street was as deserted and dull as it had ever been.

Budi and I were stopped on our way back to the boat by an officious sergeant, dressed in the skin-tight brown uniform of the national police force. He wanted to see our identity papers, and when I said they were back on the boat, he demanded we bring them to the police headquarters next morning. There the scene would have done justice to a banana republic. A dozen policemen lounged idly on the benches outside, all belts and pistols and boredom. Their uniform caps were parked on a high shelf behind them, a theatrical outfitter's parade of tall peaks and flashy cap badges. The offices of the police station were like stark schoolrooms, with more benches and walls lined with blackboards marked with out-of-date briefing notes. No one was in a hurry, and clearly visitors were put in their place by being made to wait. In the end a police corporal found time to read my letter of recommendation from the admiral in Jakarta, and the mood abruptly changed to apology and subservience. Our identity papers would not be needed, I was told. Just our names in the ledger would be enough. The ledger was produced; there was no ink in the pen; then there was a problem finding a ruler to draw lines in the ledger. Finally all was ready, and our names were written down. But the paper was so soggy that the ink ran and smudged illegibly. If Wallace had judged Dobbo as a place where minimal government ran smoothly, now it was the exact opposite. It was choking under a burden of civil servants and bureaucracy. Thankfully, as it turned out, our experience in Dobbo was to be the only time in all our travels in Wallace's trail where we were troubled by officialdom.

We hoisted anchor and left Dobbo without regret. It had not been a restful night. The first mosquitoes of our trip had appeared and kept us all awake, and both Joe and Leonard were finding the humidity and heat very exhausting. Joe was characteristically uncomplaining, but he confessed to feeling utterly tired at the end of

125

the day and his skin was coming out in a rash of blotches. Leonard was grey and drawn. Bobby, Yanis' assistant, was lacklustre and lethargic; he seemed to be suffering from a mild fever. Only Yanis was immune. In the early morning he was found curled up inside a large plastic bag and wedged in the tiny anchor hold, to avoid the mosquito attack. Now he bounced around the deck with his usual energy and enthusiasm, looking for work to do.

Our destination was the Baun Nature Reserve at the edge of a region called Kobroor on the far side of the islands. Wallace had never managed to reach this area because it was so distant, but he did meet some of the Kobroor natives who came to see him and offer Birds of Paradise. They were, he said, 'the worst and least civilised of the Aru tribes'. They sported huge wooden combs, horseshoe-shaped, which they wore over their foreheads, touching the temple on each side. Today, with the general mixing of the populations, we could see no regional difference among the visitors to Dobbo, in either dress or features. Everyone looked and dressed much the same in cheap trousers and shirts, their hair cut short or occasionally frizzy, and there was the full range of skin colour from dark black to Budi's golden brown.

The waterways we now had to follow through the islands, however, had not changed at all. Though they look like rivers, the channels are arms of the sea, up to 150 kilometres long, and they are said to be unique hydrographic features. Three main channels cut clear through

Aru, and Wallace used the northern channel to reach a village on its banks where he searched for beetles and paid the natives — usually with bottles of arrack — to bring him Birds of Paradise. His boat journey made a considerable impression on him. The channel had 'the aspect of a river about the width of the Thames at London, winding among low and often hilly country. The scene was exactly such as might be expected in the interior of a continent. The channel continued of a uniform average width, with reaches and sinuous bends, one bank being often precipitous, or even forming vertical cliffs, while the other was flat and apparently alluvial; and it was only the pure salt water, and the absence of any stream but the slight flux and reflux of the tide, that would enable a person to tell that he was navigating a strait and not a river.' Wallace and his boat crew stopped to cook their supper by a small brook where it fell into the river, bathing in the freshwater pools. Then they continued on for a couple of hours, and moored for the night by tying up to the overhanging branch of a convenient tree. Next morning their guide took them down a side branch almost blocked by coral, and they had to get out to lighten the boat, dragging it the last section, crunching over the coral to their destination.

Our shortest way to Baun was through the southern channel and, after we had left Dobbo and headed south, we located its entrance by the smoke plume of a large fish-canning factory and the remarkable numbers of fishing-boats moored there. The place was not so much a fishing port as a fishing camp and fishing graveyard. The working boats came, unloaded their catch and departed, but other vessels were abandoned and stayed there for ever. There must have been at least 70 boats, and their different shapes and states of preservation told the story of the rise and fall of the Aru fishery. First we passed the modern trawlers, still in use. There were only six of them; four were from Taiwan, and their hulls had been painted in gaudy stripes of red, blue and yellow. Next to them were the two new Indonesian boats, built of wood, and their decks piled high with hundreds of bright blue fishing-floats; they looked well maintained and very efficient. Behind them were two sad lines of mothballed trawlers, again from Taiwan but clearly out of work, with their hulls and superstructure rotting away with rust, and not a soul to be seen. Finally, thrown up against the bank, were the local boats which had started the fishery. Small, battered, built of wood to a traditional design, they must have been driven out of business by larger boats, run ashore and simply abandoned. I counted nearly 30 of them, crumbling away as forlorn hulks. Judging from the decline in numbers, I wondered just how much longer the fishery would survive.

We passed out of earshot and smell of the fish-cannery with the roar of its generator and the stench of its fish, and turned into the Wokai channel. Two dolphins escorted us for ten minutes. They were either juveniles or a distinct species living in the channels, because they were smaller than sea dolphins, with dorsal fins set farther back than usual, and a very steeply humped posture as they dived. By the time the dolphins left us, we were well into that strange world — half river, half strait — which Wallace had described. At first the channel was a khaki flood of water with the shore far away and featureless. Then it narrowed until it was no broader than a fair-sized river, and the details of the vegetation along its banks became much more distinct. For mile after mile the shore was lined with a wall of undisturbed mangrove forest, from which we could hear the calls of birds. As we penetrated farther into the heart of Aru, the channel began to twist and turn around small hills which emerged from the mangrove flats. On these hills grew blocks of much taller rainforest trees; and where the channel ran very close, there rose steep bluffs from which these larger trees leaned out, trailing vines and lianas in the water. A few of the trees showed small yellow patches of flowers, and they were very spectacular, standing roughly 20 metres high, their grey trunks rising up from the deep green of the mangroves at their feet. Their dead leaves floated by us in the current, shaped like the ace of spades and 40 centimetres across.

Towards evening, the entire forest landscape changed again. The mangrove wall in the foreground took on a luminous green which contrasted with the darker green of the more distant forest, and flights of small parrots, lories and lorikeets appeared. They were crossing from one bank to the other, moving from their feeding

Through Aru sea canals

grounds to their roosts, and they passed directly over us in groups of six or seven, so we could clearly hear their high-pitched chattering.

This scenery must surely have reminded Wallace of the collecting trips he had already made, with Bates, along the rivers of Amazonia. Yet for some reason he did not make the obvious comparison, though he had spent four years in tropical Brazil. The first two years were with Bates before the two men agreed that it would be more efficient if they went into separate regions to pursue their collections. Bates then stayed on for a total of 11 years compiling a huge collection of birds and insects, while Wallace came back to England in 1852, disheartened by the loss of his youngest brother, Herbert. He had invited Herbert out to Brazil to join him as an assistant, but soon after arriving the young man contracted yellow fever and died. So the Brazilian experience had not been an altogether happy one for Wallace, and though he did write it up in a small volume entitled *Narrative of Travels on Amazon and Rio Negro*, only 750 copies of the book had been printed and it had not sold particularly well. For whatever reason, Wallace was rarely to draw comparisons between Indonesia and Brazil, the two areas of the greatest bio-diversity on the planet.

Still today in central Aru there are no roads, so the sea channels are the only lines of communication. Yet we saw only three other vessels in all our transit. They were little motor boats, shabby and cramped, chugging along the channel and serving as ferries for the half-dozen passengers crouching under tarpaulins to ward off the frequent equatorial downpours. When the worst of these rainstorms hit, the crew of the *Alfred Wallace* stripped off and washed in the drenching rain — much to the disgust of our so-called guide, the unwilling delegate from the Forestry Department. Every time it rained, he scuttled into the shelter of the cabin and stayed there until the rain stopped, picking his teeth and occasionally bobbing up his head through the entrance-way to spit over the side. No one was willing to lend him a waterproof jacket because he had already borrowed Joe's hat without asking and been sucking on the hat-string. When Joe got it back, he found the string covered with bits of half-masticated food. Even good-natured Yanis got irritated with the man. The guide was meant to know his way down the channel and to tell us which direction to take when it braided its way past different islands. But he was sometimes wrong, and he collected a very dirty look from Yanis when he failed entirely to identify the backwater that would lead us to the village where we had planned to spend the night.

So, like Wallace before us, we halted in the channel. Wallace had tied to an overhanging branch, but I hoped to avoid the mosquitoes by anchoring in midstream. There we passed a noisy night, listening to strange sounds. Budi identified the calls of brush turkeys in the forest, and there were frequent rattles and bumps on the hull as flotsam was carried past by the tide. Then came a mysterious series of heavy splashes, approaching down the river, passing us and then fading into the distance. We saw nothing in the pitch-darkness and it may have been a river dolphin, but it sounded exactly like a fat swimmer doing an inexpert backstroke. Joe and Bill sniffed the rotten-eggs smell of the bilge water in the cabin, and preferred to spend the night sleeping on the foredeck. There they were not troubled by mosquitoes but woken several times by a large bat which visited and revisited them, hovering noisily, Bill claimed, like a miniature helicopter.

We reached the Baun Nature Reserve just before noon on the following day. The Reserve is named after the island which it covers, and our guide showed us where we should drop anchor off the only village on the island. As we went ashore in the dugout, I noticed a modern but mistreated motor-boat; built of fibreglass, it bore the markings of the Forestry Department and was lying beached far up on shore, right at the high-water mark. The boat was canted over on one side, there was no propeller, and it had the neglected air of a vessel that had not been afloat for at least half a year, maybe longer. The name of the village was Kobadanga and, though it was a small place with just 70 families, it was far cleaner and in better order than the majority of the villages we had seen. Most villages were lucky to have a single tiny shack serving duty as a shop, and Kobadanga had three shops. There was also a rather flamboyant mosque with a lot of fancy sheet-metal decoration, a row of bungalows which

Natives of Aru shooting the Great Bird of Paradise (taken from The Malay Archipelago)

were apparently accommodation for visitors to the Nature Reserve, a small health clinic and — unique for such a remote place — the central section of the main street was actually paved with a thick slab of concrete.

Budi and I walked the 50 metres to the little house of the Indonesian park ranger, whose job was to oversee the running of the Nature Reserve. He was a man in about his mid-thirties, and it was not clear whether he was exclusively an employee of the Forestry Department or in some way supported by the international wildlife organisations which helped to fund the Reserve. He was affable and, while his chubby, cheerful young wife served us tea, he answered questions about his job and the surviving population of the Bird of Paradise. He had been at the Reserve since 1991, and in that time he claimed that the numbers of Birds of Paradise had increased. They were, however, still hunted by poachers who sneaked on to the Reserve from outlying villages, their method of hunting being the same as Wallace had described. The hunter concealed himself under one of the 'dancing trees' where the birds came early in the morning and at dusk to show off their plumage. These were tall trees, usually protruding well above the forest canopy so that the hunters often had to climb into lower trees to get within shooting range. The Birds of Paradise ran up and down the branches, bowed and bobbed, fluttered from one bough to another, shook their gorgeous feathers and constantly called out. The islanders said the birds were 'playing', though in fact the purpose of this extravagant display was to win over the watching female birds who mated with the most impressive males. During the display the birds were so obsessed with the ritual that they ignored the human hunters, who shot at their prey with special, rather clumsy arrows, tipped with a hard knob or a small wooden cup, which stunned or killed the target without damaging the feathers which were later sold to traders.

Wallace had to wait several days before the first Bird of Paradise was brought to him from the forest, but it was worth all the delay. 'It was a small bird, a little less than a thrush. The greater part of its plumage was of an intense cinnabar red, with a gloss as of spun glass. On the head the feathers were short and velvety and shaded into rich orange. Beneath, from the breast downward, was pure white, with the softness and gloss of silk, and across the breast a band of deep metallic green separated this colour from the red of the throat.' The most remarkable feature of this gorgeous small creature was its display feathers 'about two inches long, and each terminated by a broad band of intense emerald green'. These normally lay concealed under the wings, but in the courtship dance could be raised up as elegant fans. To add to its extraordinary appearance were two tail feathers like slender wires which diverged in a beautiful double curve. 'About half an inch of the end of this wire is webbed on the outer side only, and is coloured of a fine metallic green, and being curved spirally inward, form a pair of elegant glittering buttons, hanging five inches below the body, and the same distance apart.'

This was Wallace's first sight of the King Bird of Paradise — one of the two species identified by Linnaeus from mutilated carcasses — and he was thrilled. To find one of these birds was one of the chief reasons why he had travelled to the Far East. The erectile fans and the glittering buttons of the tail ornament did not occur 'on any other species of the eight thousand different birds that are known to exist upon the earth; and combined with the most exquisite beauty of plumage, render this one of the most perfectly lovely of the many lovely productions of nature'. Yet it was typical of Wallace's self-awareness that, even in moments of triumph, he could see how eccentric and odd his jubilation must

have seemed in the eyes of the local people. His Aru guides, he said, were thoroughly amused by his expressions of admiration and delight. They 'saw nothing more in the "burong rajah" than we do in the robin or the goldfinch'.

The forest ranger at Kobadanga said that the King Bird of Paradise was still to be found on the Baun Reserve, though it was difficult for us to track down. More numerous were Great Birds of Paradise: a larger bird with a magnificent cascade of golden-yellow tail, once much prized by European milliners who used the plumes to adorn extravagant hats for ladies of fashion. He also confirmed that we were too early in the season to see the Great Bird of Paradise in its full mating plumage. This was unavoidable, as our prahu was dependent on using the annual regime of the monsoon winds and we had no choice but to be in Aru before the prevailing wind direction changed. Yet we had come there with the intention of getting some idea of how present conditions in the forest compared with Wallace's description, so we asked the ranger to take us into the Nature Reserve itself.

The visit produced a very different impression from our recent experience in the forest of Kei Besar. The most striking difference was the response of the bird-life. In the Reserve, the creatures were far more easily frightened. During our first walk into the Baun forest Budi identified more species and in greater numbers than in Kei. There were large red parrots, doves, drongos, brush turkeys, flights of white- and sulphur-crested cockatoos screaming raucously as they flew off. When we returned on subsequent visits to the forest, we never again saw birds in such large numbers. Quite simply, they had scattered, as opposed to Kei where the bird-life was at ease with humans. Later on our voyage we would visit forest as wild as Baun, and find that the birds had seen so few humans that they hardly reacted at all to our presence. Baun, by contrast, seemed to be in the uncomfortable middle status: the animals were allegedly in a protected area, but they were highly nervous.

Baun's vegetation was also less hospitable than Kei Besar. Its plants were more prickly or obstructive, and it conformed much more to the popular notion of tropical jungle. In many places the undergrowth was so dense that we had to push aside low palms, rattans and stands of large ferns, or clamber across moss-covered logs covered with a fine tracery of small vines with bright, shiny green leaves. Thick lianas twisted across the ground or looped from one tree to the next at head height. Mushrooms and fungi sprouted everywhere, from the forest floor, logs and the roots of living trees. The buttress roots of the taller trees could extend for more than six metres across the ground, standing up in thin plates that looked more like grey metal barriers than living plants. A few tree-trunks had a rich ochre colour which contrasted with the general russet and green of the vegetation. Spiders had placed broad webs between the branches of small shrubs and waited in the middle of their nets, their bodies spotted with bright orange patches and suspended two or three feet from the nearest plant. Once or twice we skirted muddy backwaters of stagnant yellow water. Here, said our guide, lived a few crocodiles, but they were very shy and vanished at the first hint of intruders. Everywhere the muddy ground had been cut and churned by the snouts of wild pigs, and from time to time we startled the animals and they went charging off, grunting and squealing as they crashed through the undergrowth.[1] We also came across a cuscus, and were reminded that Aru is well inside the zone of animals of Australian origin. The possum-like cuscus with its beautiful silver-grey fur was clinging to the upper trunk of a tall bare tree, and its brown pop-eyes in a round, furry brown face gave it a very startled look as it peered down at us and then very slowly began to climb farther upward.

The forest was also very noisy. There was a constant racket of bird and insect sounds as if we were in some huge tropical aviary. From every direction came chirping and buzzing and

---

[1] In 1865, after his return to England, Wallace was to correspond with Charles Darwin about these Aru pigs. Darwin wanted to know whether they were domestic pigs run wild or a native species, as this might be an example of local evolution. Wallace thought they were a new species; Darwin was doubtful and probably correct.

Cuscus ornatus
(*Taken from* The Malay Archipelago)

screeching. Budi was constantly vanishing from sight. He would hear a particular bird-call, identify it, and then go stalking off into the bushes with his binoculars to locate the bird, confirm the identification and add it to the list of species in his notebook. Some species seemed to be ventriloquists. One little bird, hardly bigger than a sparrow, settled on a branch not three metres away, and we could see it distinctly, puffing up its chest and opening its beak to call. Yet the sound appeared to be coming from a totally different direction. From time to time the background buzz of the tree crickets made a crescendo as if an express train was approaching through the woods. There would be a distant roaring shriek that grew louder and louder and almost painful to hear, until it suddenly collapsed back into its usual murmur.

Wallace had warned about the cry of the Bird of Paradise. Despite such a splendid appearance, it had one of the ugliest voices imaginable. He described the sound as a coarse, repetitive 'wawk-wawk-wawk', and soon we heard it for ourselves. The call could never have been mistaken. The bird was announcing its presence to other members of the same species and in turn they replied, so that soon there was a sequence of distant wawk-wawk-wawks as two or three birds circled and called to one another in the distance. As we paused to rest near a dancing tree, the warden pointed. 'Cendrawasi!' he whispered dramatically. 'Bird of Paradise!' It was a female, and was about as dull and uninteresting as any bird could be. It looked for all the world like a large immature starling. Budi, however, was ecstatic. For the first time in his life he had seen the living Bird of Paradise, and it did not matter that it was not a male, not in plumage, and fluttered above our heads for less than 30 seconds. Like Wallace before him, he had fulfilled one of his voyage ambitions.

This was the only Bird of Paradise that we saw during our visit to Baun, though on four more occasions we sat and waited hopefully under the dancing trees and also under the favourite fruit trees where the cendrawasi fed. It was not the right season to be watching for Birds of Paradise, and we had to be content with a parade of other species ranging from splendid sea eagles to the owl-like bird called a frog mouth. Budi counted 87 different species in all, a tally probably as great as Wallace would have been able to record. Yet, in the end, I was left with a slight feeling of unease. If the claims of the warden were to be believed, the Baun Reserve was a success. He said that the number of Birds of Paradise was increasing, poaching was declining, and that other species of animals were flourishing. What troubled me was that the warden's claims were so much in line with what an interested visitor would like to hear, and I would have preferred to see the proof for myself. Judging from the prosperity of Kobadanga with its three shops and concrete main street, it was clear that the Reserve was very good business for the villagers. Money came from the outside, sent by foreign agencies to protect the wildlife, and had paid for the village improvements. As long as that money continued to arrive, it was evident that the system would continue to work. But I had an uncomfortable feeling that if the outside funds dried up, then the same lethargy and lack of interest that we had seen among the civil servants of Dobbo would seep into Kobadanga, and forest protection would be neglected. The village was already pushing up against the forest boundary, its cassava gardens and tree plantations nibbling into the protected area. Without strict enforcement they would expand into the Reserve and take over. Without any apparent traditional structure to preserve the wildlife resources as in Kei Besar, or indigenous enthusiasm, the Reserve would be destroyed. Perhaps I was being over-pessimistic, but I foresaw an unhappy scenario.

On that memorable day in Aru when Wallace held his first specimen of the King Bird of Paradise in his hand, he had looked into the future and feared for the continued existence of these magnificent creatures.

I thought [he wrote] of the long ages past, during which the successive generations of this little creature had run their course — year by year being born, and living and dying amid these dark and gloomy woods, with no intelligent eye to gaze upon their liveliness — to all appearance such a wanton waste of beauty . . . It seems sad that on the one hand such exquisite creatures should live out their lives and exhibit their charms only in these wild inhospitable regions, doomed for ages yet to come to hopeless barbarism; while on the other hand, should civilised man ever reach these distant lands, and bring moral, intellectual and physical light into these recesses of these virgin forests, we may be sure he will so disturb the nicely-balanced relations of organic and inorganic nature as to cause the disappearance, and finally the extinction, of these very beings whose wonderful structure and beauty he alone is fitted to appreciate and enjoy.

A century and a half later this was to become the most-quoted of all Wallace's observations, and he would be acknowledged as a pioneer of environmental awareness. But this accolade had an apparent contradiction. The King Bird of Paradise, whose uncertain future as a species produced in him 'a feeling of melancholy', had been shot and killed on his instructions. His brilliantly coloured Greater Birds of Paradise, dead, were likely to provide him with a useful sum of cash. 'I have discovered their true attitude when displaying their plumes', he wrote

Coconut root

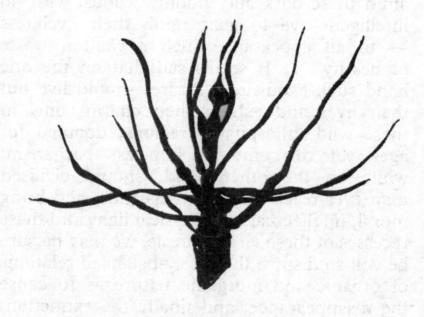

enthusiastically to his agent Samuel Stevens, 'which I believe is quite new information. They are so beautiful and grand that, when mounted to represent it, they will make glorious specimens for show cases, and I am sure will be in demand for stuffers.'

Later, we were to realise that this was not such a contradiction after all, and that a bird in the hand was indeed worth two in the bush, and could lead to species survival.

5

Turtle Beach

AT Kobadanga we left behind our slovenly escort from the Forestry Department in Dobbo, who was happy to take a cash payment and the price of his fare to Dobbo. He would wait at Kobadanga for a day or a week — it did not matter to him — until the next passing motor-boat that could carry him back through the sea channels to his office in Dobbo. We, however, were travelling in the opposite direction, around the Aru coast.

Our destination was the South-East Aru Marine Reserve 50 kilometres to the south. It looked fine on the map; a dotted line enclosed the maze of coral cays, lagoons and small islands which extend off the south-east corner of the main islands. This area was designated as a refuge for protected marine species, particularly sea turtles and dugong or sea cows. These large mammals, something like walruses without tusks, graze on the beds of underwater sea grass and had once been numerous there. Wildlife protection laws passed in Jakarta made it illegal to catch or kill them, though dugong are often trapped in fishing nets and drown. This, at least, was the excuse from the sellers of dugong teeth in Dobbo. When we asked the warden at Kobadanga, it turned out that he was also responsible for patrolling and protecting the Marine Reserve. He claimed that he went there six or seven times each year to check that all was well, but I wondered how he managed to do this. He already had 13,000 hectares of Baun Island to look after, and the Marine Reserve could only be reached by boat. We had already remarked on the decrepit state of the Forestry Department patrol boat on the beach, and it had obviously been out of action for a long time. Nor was there an obvious replacement boat. Once again I found myself wondering if we were being told a version of the truth tailored to make a good impression.

We set out at dawn, 21 March, taking advantage of the south-going tide to carry *Alfred Wallace* seaward through the chain of low islands which fringe the coast. The waters were uncharted and very shallow, so we had to keep a sharp lookout for the crooked poles which local fishermen stuck in the coral to serve as channel markers. The focal point of the Marine

Enue Island

Reserve was Enue Island, the largest nesting site for sea turtles in Aru and the place where dugong had been common until the 1960s. The warden of Kobadanga, who stayed in his village, had assured us that here we would find many turtle nests. But dugongs were now rare, he said; if they did exist, we would be most likely to see them at the only anchorage at Enue, which was called Dugong Creek.

Enue, as we approached, looked like an archetypal small South Sea island. Without cliffs or hills, it rose only a few metres above sea level, and its coral core was covered with a thick mantle of small trees, mangrove and bushes. On the side facing us was its most distinctive feature, a white sand beach about one kilometre long. As we sailed along the length of the beach to reach the anchorage, Yanis was in a state of great excitement. He jumped up on the cabin roof and clung to the rigging as he

150

gazed longingly at Enue. He knew the island well, he said, because he had been fishing in this area ten years earlier when he was working aboard a Taiwanese trawler. The crew frequently landed at Enue to gather turtle eggs to eat. Now Yanis positively licked his lips as we glided past the beach, just 200 metres away. 'Eggs! Eggs! Eggs!' he exclaimed, pointing out dents and tracks which we could just see in the sand.

We sounded our way in among the coral heads cautiously, and found a spot at the mouth of Dugong Creek where we could drop anchor. Yanis could hardly wait to get the dugout dinghy unlashed from the cabin top and dropped over the side. In minutes he and Bobby were paddling hard for the shore, hopefully carrying a plastic bag to bring us back a feast of turtle eggs. It was impossible to restrain him, and ominous. Yanis, the roving fisherman from Kei, knew all about Enue as a turtle nesting site and regarded it as a happy hunting ground. There was not a hint that he or anyone he had sailed with knew or respected the fact that it was a protected site at the heart of a Marine Reserve, and that it was against the law to rob turtle nests there. It might have been argued that local natives traditionally gathered eggs there and the practice continued. But Yanis was not a local man, nor were the Taiwanese fishermen. Enue turtle eggs were clearly a free-for-all.

We waited a long time for Yanis to come back. Not until mid-afternoon did he and Bobby return in the dugout, and Yanis was looking stunned.

He climbed over the gunnel and said, 'Nothing. Not one egg. All taken.' He simply could not believe it, and shook his head in bewilderment. He and Bobby had gone ashore, left the dugout on the sand, and set off confident that they would find turtle eggs in the next few metres. They had come upon the first turtle nest immediately. But it had already been dug up and emptied of its eggs. The next nest, only a few metres away, was the same, and the next, and the next and the next. They had searched everywhere, going the entire length of the beach, until they located 60 or 70 nests. Every single nest had been plundered.

Yanis had never expected such a situation. As far as he was concerned, gathering turtle eggs on Enue was almost as easy as going into a shop and picking tins off a shelf. Yet now there was not a turtle egg to be found along the entire length of the long beach.

Yanis paddled me ashore in the dugout, and when I stepped on the sand the first sight was the desiccated skull and broken shell of a dead turtle, lying on the sand where it had died. Once the animal must have been beautiful. The shell was some 4 feet long and 3 feet across, and the rim near the tail was still decorated with a patch of elegantly mottled skin. Bobby peeled off this shred of skin and showed it to me. 'You can sell this in the market,' he said, so whoever had killed the turtle had not even bothered to harvest the valuable parts. Beyond the corpse was the first of the turtle tracks, leading from the water's edge, up the dry sand slope, and arriving at the fringe of low bushes which marked the upper limit of the beach. Here, among the roots of the bushes, the female turtles came to dig their nests in the loose sand and deposit their egg clutches. The most inexpert visitor could have located their nests. The massive animals had used their fore and aft flippers to haul themselves laboriously up the slope to reach the nest line, and with each step their flippers had scooped neat marks in the sand. Between the flipper marks ran the broad groove where the base of the heavy carapace had been dragged forward. The turtle tracks were as distinct as tyre marks left on a sand beach by a medium-sized car. Anyone could follow them to where the animal had finally stopped and dug her nest.

Most of the nests were at the final lip of the beach just before the line of bushes; in other places the nest had been dug on the flat land among the bushes themselves. But wherever the nest, the scene was now the same. A nest should have been a relatively flat area where the turtle,

after laying her eggs, scraped back the sand and loose gravel to cover it from natural predators. But this ruse had never been designed to fool the human robbers, who had dug down, found the eggs and taken them away. Instead of a flat area, every nest was a hole in the sand, surrounded by the ring of the spoil heap. There were dozens of these craters, dotted here and there along the entire beach. The empty desolate landscape looked like a casualty of war. It was as if Enue Beach had been pounded by artillery.

All of us were completely dispirited as we returned to the *Alfred Wallace* that evening. We had walked the full length of the beach, and we had never expected to witness such utter rape. Not only was every nest robbed of its contents, but under two bushes we had found the stinking corpses of turtles wantonly killed. Someone had flipped them over on their backs and left them to broil to death in the heat. One animal had been hacked across the back of the neck with a parang. We were profoundly depressed. It was obvious that no one protected this beach, and that it was pillaged regularly by raiders who either ate the eggs themselves or sold them in Dobbo for local consumption or export to gourmet shops in Jakarta and Singapore. It seemed that Enue Island was doomed as a turtle nesting ground. Unless there were other nesting beaches nearby unknown to the robbers, which seemed extremely unlikely, the population of turtles in the South-East Aru Marine Reserve was headed for extinction.

That evening we were in a very sombre mood

as we settled down to sleep, and *Alfred Wallace* lay anchored in the mouth of Dugong Creek under a sad, blood-red sky which seemed to echo our feelings. Of dugong, of course, we had not seen a single sign.

I was awakened just before midnight by Yanis tugging at my arm. He was hissing 'Penyu, penyu. Turtle, turtle,' and beckoning urgently. I struggled awake and followed him into the dugout. Budi, he told me, was already waiting on the beach. It seemed that Yanis and Budi had taken it in turns to stay on watch. In the light of the moon about half an hour earlier they had seen the lumbering black shapes of four turtles emerge from the sea and begin crawling up the beach, driven by the age-old urge to lay their eggs on Enue. Yanis and Budi watched quietly as two of the turtles failed to find suitable nesting sites. The first could not negotiate the final slope of the beach, turned, and crawled back into the water; in the morning we would see the disappointed u-shaped course of its tracks. The second turtle had failed to find quite the right spot to dig a nest — perhaps the ground was too hard, or did not have exactly the right temperature and humidity which the mother turtles demand for their eggs. She too had abandoned the attempt and gone back into the sea. Of the two remaining turtles one had reached the nesting line, stayed a short while and already gone back; Budi was not sure whether it had laid its eggs or not. But the fourth turtle was definitely in place. It was somewhere along the beach, and if we approached it quietly we would be able to witness it laying its eggs.

By now the other members of the crew were arriving, and Budi warned us to go quietly and without showing torches. He explained that the hen-turtle had a programmed laying pattern. For about half an hour she looked for her nest site and, when she found the right place, began to dig. At that time the animal was still very nervous. If disturbed, the turtle would abandoned the dig, turn round and crawl back into the sea. After half an hour, and when the hole was dug to the proper depth, the turtle lay across the hole and began to drop her eggs into it. At that stage, Budi said, the creature was locked into the laying cycle. Nothing could disturb her and for about 30 minutes she would stay over the hole, dropping her eggs. Even if you shone lights, made loud noises or touched the animal, she would not move. It was the urge to reproduce the species at its most demanding.

We walked softly along the beach in the moonlight until Budi held up his hand. Over the murmur of the sea we could clearly hear the sound of sand and gravel being flung about. It was exactly the noise of someone throwing loose soil with a small shovel in a series of rapid, short throws. Every so often the sounds would stop, and there would be a pause while the turtle rested.

Budi looked at his watch, and gestured for us to sit down and wait. The sounds continued for half an hour, then gradually subsided.

Now Budi switched on his torch and we saw

the mother turtle tucked under the branches of a large bush. It was a green turtle, and she was lying with her head towards the land. The rear of her body lay tilted at a slight angle into the one-metre-deep hole she had excavated. The sound we had heard earlier had been the sand and gravel rattling off the leaves of the bush as she dug. Now she lay there, extruding her eggs. Yanis reached forward, and the turtle completely ignored him as he scraped back the sand so that we could see sideways into the nesting hollow. The cavity was shaped like a light-bulb and into the bottom of it was falling a stream of glistening round white eggs, the shape and size of ping-pong balls. They came singly or in sudden groups of two or three at a time, and they went on and on, piling up until there were at least 60 or 70 of them. There was an inexorable continuity, as if nothing could stop the dropping of the egg cluster, and it was amazing that the animal could retain so many eggs in her abdomen. On and on they continued to fall, so that there must have been close to 100 eggs by the time the stream finally stopped. Then, slowly and tentatively, the back flippers of the turtle emerged from the shell. Elephant grey, and shaped remarkably like hands, they reached out and gently began to pull in the loose sand towards the nest, dragging the sand on to the eggs and carefully filling in the hole.

Budi clicked off the light, and we retreated for a few yards while the ritual continued. 'She will dig a false hole now,' Budi said quietly. Again the thrashing and rattling began, and was followed by some lumbering bumps and slithering sounds as the turtle repositioned herself and began to dig a shallow decoy hole to delude predators into searching in the wrong place. From time to time Budi switched on his torch, and we could see how the turtle used her back and front flippers for different tasks. The back flippers were shaped for digging and gouging downwards; the flatter fore flippers were better for skimming up the sand and throwing it in a flat arc to cover the top surface of the hole. The animal was perfectly designed for the nesting operation.

Finally, the thrashing noises stopped, and in the darkness we heard a succession of deep sighs. They were uncannily human, a poignant heavy sound as if someone was completely exhausted. It was time for the turtle to return to the sea.

We continued to wait. There was a sudden, urgent surge of activity, a burst of movement and the sound of breaking branches. Then a pause and, after a minute or so, the sound was repeated. Again Budi switched on his torch, and in its beam we could see that the turtle had managed to get herself trapped in the tough roots of the bush while digging the mimic nest. She was hopelessly entangled. A thick, strong root lay right across her shell, and there was no way that she could turn round and head back towards the water. It was also obvious that the effort to lay eggs and then extricate herself had left her completely exhausted. If she stayed where she lay, she would die.

Yanis began to break away the branches over

the animal, and then prised aside the restraining root. But the turtle was too cumbersome and exhausted to turn herself. Yanis took hold of a fore flipper, and heaved to try to pivot her around so that her head was turned towards the sea. Yanis was extremely strong, but it required all his strength to move the creature. The turtle was massive, and must have weighed at least 200 kilos. Time and again Yanis tugged, gradually slewing the huge animal around, while Budi pushed and shoved at the upper shell until the turtle lay facing the water. The two men stepped back and, after a few moments' rest, the turtle began to lever herself down the shore very ponderously. By now the tide had turned and it was a 30-metre haul down to the water.

Three times the turtle had to stop and rest, and for a while it seemed she did not have the strength to cover the entire distance. Every time she halted to rest, she issued again those deep, gasping, utterly human sighs, and it seemed that a trace of a tear glistened in the huge eyes, probably the fluid which the animal needed to lubricate the eye when out of the water. Once, when she was confused, she lost direction and began to turn back inland, until Yanis again seized a flipper and set her in the right direction. Finally she had crawled close enough to the sea for him to be able to splash her with water from his cupped hands. Then the turtle made a last effort and struggled into a few inches of the tide, and a small wave lifted her briefly. It was like a ship coming off the sand after being laid up. The land-bound mass bumped slightly, and almost as a reflex the animal gave a couple of strokes with her fore flippers. Then she was gently floating and moving out of the pool of light from our torch beams. Two more flipper strokes and the turtle was transformed, gliding majestically forward, the round hump of her shell submerging smoothly beneath the waves as she vanished into the darkness of the sea.

It was possible that the two turtles which had failed to lay that night would return the next evening or later in the week, to dig nests and lay their eggs. The urge to lay eggs was unstoppable. Nothing would deter the sea turtles from trying to continue the species. It was both the greatest danger and the greatest chance for the survival of the breeding turtles on Enue. Female green turtles lay as many as five or seven clutches of eggs in a single year at intervals of about two weeks. But they only nest every two or four years, and the eggs require about two months to hatch. During those two months the eggs are totally vulnerable to human predators and, because the mothers always seem to return to the same beach, the nests are ready-made targets.

Yet it was quite clear that there was no effective protection for Enue Island. There was no surface water so the island was uninhabited by humans, and there was no sign of a warden's hut for even a temporary stay. The nesting beach was left wide open to anyone who cared to come ashore and rob the nests. It took just ten minutes to excavate and plunder a nest. What was worse: the nest robbers had been coming methodically and staying to strip every single nest along the beach, not just to dig up a single nest as passing fishermen might do. If such wholesale pillage continued for three or four years, there would not be a single nesting turtle left on Enue.

Next morning Budi asked Yanis to return to the site of the successful nest. He was to sweep away all traces of the turtle tracks leading to the spot. One clutch of turtle eggs, at least, should remain disguised and undisturbed. It seemed a very small gesture to help animals who had survived on earth since the time of the dinosaurs.

★ ★ ★

Extricating *Alfred Wallace* from her anchorage was tricky. The tide ran so strongly that we were swept over the fringing reef, and found ourselves floating alarmingly over the coral with its beautiful but lethally jagged edges reaching up to tear the bottom of our light wooden vessel. It was then that we really appreciated the shallow draught of our Kei prahu kalulis. *Alfred Wallace* had no depth of keel; she floated in just 40 centimetres of water, so we were able to grab bamboo poles and punt the hull around the highest spots in the coral. The two heavy steering oars, which normally projected down one metre into the water where they could get a good grip, were hoisted up and laid on deck until we were clear of the danger. By brute strength we pushed our boat out to sea, while Joe in the bows pointed the best path to follow between the dark patches of the coral heads.

Until now we had relied for much of our progress on a little 9-horsepower outboard engine which we perched on a wooden bar stuck over the side of the vessel when we needed it. The engine was not powerful enough to push us up against a strong wind, but it gave us good headway when there was a calm and, just as important, charged a pair of car batteries. These supplied the power for a laptop computer and a briefcase-sized radio, so I could type up daily reports and send them through a satellite link to the University of Limerick in western Ireland. The university's education department then distributed the information on the Internet to the schools. Using the same computer I could also freeze frames from our little video camera, and send pictures to illustrate the reports. In their turn, the schoolchildren could send back questions. The whole system was unorthodox as it relied on a satellite network which was chiefly intended for navigation — so we had no voice communication and could not talk to the children — but it was to work flawlessly throughout the voyage. The chief problem was to keep the sensitive electronic equipment safe and dry inside the thatched cabin of our small boat even when *Alfred Wallace* was drenched by tropical downpours or, more rarely, waves or sea spray were landing on deck. A more domestic threat was when Yanis, in one of his frequent bursts of vigorous house-keeping, decided to wash the deck with buckets of sea-water. The hot sun always shrank the deck boards and opened the seams, so a cascade of water would come pouring into the cabin. It was a golden rule that all electronic equipment lived securely in tightly closed plastic boxes.

We sent our first satellite report, describing Kei Besar and Aru, to the distant schoolchildren just after we had floated free of the coral reefs off Enue Island. Shortly afterwards we set course for our home base at Warbal Island and a fine breeze set in from the south-east. So we made sail.

★ ★ ★

Sailing *Alfred Wallace* took special care. The boat had two, rather unusual sails, each stretched between an upper and a lower spar made of bamboo. Each sail and its two bamboos was rectangular in shape and hoisted on its own mast. But instead of being hung square, as on a square-rigged ship, *Alfred Wallace*'s sails were suspended at an angle so that they stood on one corner. Technically they were called tilted rectangular, or in Indonesian *layar tanja*. This rig had been the traditional arrangement on Kei prahus until the 1960s and 1970s. It was almost certainly the sail system that Wallace himself would have seen in the middle of the nineteenth century. But recently the *layar tanja* had been replaced on larger boats by triangular sails, and only continued to be used on very small dugouts as a single small sail. The reason for the change was that *layar tanja* were extremely powerful and drove the island boats very fast, but they are difficult to handle and require a large, more skilled crew. They can also be dangerous in bad weather.

When we first set out from Warbal, only Yanis had any real experience of using these odd-looking *layar tanja*, and though he was a brave and active deckhand, it soon became apparent that he did not have any finesse in setting or handling them. Bobby, his assistant, did not seem to know any more than the rest of us.

Our 250-kilometre passage from Enue Island to Warbal gave us a lesson we would not forget. It all started out very well. The breeze was perfect, blowing softly from the stern quarter, so we hoisted the two *layar tanja* and adjusted them to fill nicely. They were as powerful as their reputation claimed. Under their thrust, *Alfred Wallace* picked up speed immediately. In a few metres she was travelling along at five or six knots, a very satisfactory pace for such a slight breeze. The sea was calm, and our boat swayed comfortably over the gentle swells. We settled down into a relaxed onboard routine, each person taking a turn at the twin steering oars for two hours. Johnny and his building team on Warbal had done an excellent job of design, and our prahu kalulis was very well balanced on the helm. She steered beautifully with the quartering wind, running as if in a groove on the blue surface of the Arafura Sea. The helmsman rarely needed to move the wooden handles controlling the steering oars to maintain the proper course. If he did, an adjustment of just two centimetres or so was enough.

But we were aboard a native boat whose shape and construction had evolved from the Stone Age and for special conditions. The prahu kalulis of Kei were meant for sailing short distances between islands in the hands of agile experts. The helmsman's position, for example, was hair-raising. He was placed at the very rear of the boat, at the point where the sides of the deck curved in to meet the stern post. In fact there was not room there for a man to stand on deck, so a little wooden platform had been built extending over the water. This platform was about 75 centimetres square, and on it the helmsman either sat or stood, right over the sea. His little platform had no guard rail, not even a low coaming; if he missed his balance or slipped, he would drop straight into the water. To make his situation even more precarious, the big waves rolling up from astern caused the light, narrow hull to pitch heavily when *Alfred Wallace* was sailing in a following sea. Then the helmsman's little platform regularly dipped underwater, so that he had wet feet or a wet bottom and had to hang on or be washed overboard. This exposed situation meant, of course, that the helmsman tended to concentrate and not fall asleep.[1]

---

[1] In some Bugis boats this is said to have been a deliberate design feature to keep the helmsman awake. The tiller was placed so far outboard that if the helmsman nodded off, he fell into the sea.

The insecurity of our sleek little vessel was not only at the helmsman's position. *Alfred Wallace* was an extremely narrow boat for her length. The aft deck where we had placed the wooden cookbox was reasonably broad, but the passage around the cabin was a mere ledge on which to shuffle forward. It was actually safer to move up and down the boat by climbing over the top of the cabin thatch. The foredeck was also narrow, totally exposed, and had a heavy projecting post for the anchor rope, ideally placed for tripping up anyone working there. Nowhere on the boat was there a guard line around the edge of the narrow deck, nor any place to rig one. Instead we rigged a safety line down the centre line of the vessel, and I made it a rule that at night no one could be on deck unless he was clipped on with a safety harness. It would have been all too easy to take a small step, slip overboard and be lost in the darkness.

The second penalty for having such an authentically trim and fast boat was that its strange sails were awkward and potentially lethal. Whenever you needed to move the sails from one side of the masts to the other because the wind had changed direction or you wanted to alter course, the crew had to be very acrobatic. First, each sail had to be rolled up around its lower bamboo spar like a roller blind. This meant that someone had to unfasten the forward end of the spar from the deck, seize hold of a short handle which projected through the bamboo, and begin twisting the bamboo round and round so that the sail was wrapped around it. This was simple enough in light winds, but in a strong wind required great strength and agility, particularly when standing on the bouncing, unprotected foredeck and trying to roll up the big mainsail. If the sailor lost his grip on the handle at that moment, the sail promptly unwound and the furling handle spun round and round like a whirling scythe. Once the sail was securely rolled up, two cloth bands were tied around it to keep it secure, and it was safe to go to the next stage of the manoeuvre. This was to stand the sail and its two bamboos vertically on end, and twist the whole bundle over the top of the mast so that it fell on the opposite side. Then the restraining bands could be removed and the sail unrolled, again being careful not to be struck by the whirling handle. As can be imagined, the manoeuvre required a lot of muscle power and excellent teamwork, and it was easy to see why the islanders had abandoned such a fraught system for a less hazardous rig.

But the most serious drawback to *layar tanja* was that it was impossible to reduce the size of the sails in a strong wind by reefing. You had the sails either up or down; there was no practicable mid position. *Alfred Wallace*, like all prahu kalulis, had no proper keel under the boat to keep her upright if suddenly hit by a strong gust of wind, so there was a very good chance that the vessel would be capsized if you did not release the sails quickly enough and let them flap free. The greatest time of danger, of course, was at night time when a sudden squall might strike the boat out of the darkness and spin her upside down.

We were very conscious of these risks as we sailed from Aru towards Kei under a glorious sunset. Our boat continued to behave impeccably. Every time she rolled on the swells, the heavy bamboo of the mainsail swung back and tapped the mainmast with a reassuring light thump. The bow rose and fell rhythmically against the line of the horizon and Budi — who had gone forward on the foredeck with his prayer mat — was in dramatic silhouette as he knelt and offered his evening prayers towards Mecca. Wearing his white skull cap, he looked exactly as his forebears the Bugis sailors must have done over the centuries as they steered westward for

Reefing handle

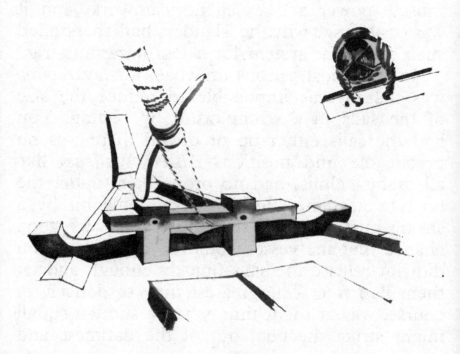

home after a trading mission in the Arus.

Our confidence in the vessel increased during the night. The wind eased, then died away entirely. We lowered the sails and made them fast to stop the cloth rubbing uselessly against the masts. An hour later the wind rose again, but from a different direction so we hoisted the sails, rolled them over the tops of the masts and set them correctly. All this was done in the dark, and we made a few fumbles and mistakes but corrected them until our boat was moving sweetly again. None of us was getting much sleep because we were not yet expert enough for the watch-keepers to handle the sails on their own, and it required all hands to make the adjustments. Barely had we got the *layar tanja* set correctly than the wind again changed direction, and we were called upon to go through the same manoeuvre once more. This second time we did the job more smoothly, even though it was by torch light. We returned to our sleep, feeling quite pleased with ourselves.

The dawn was dreary. Gone was the bright sunshine of the day before; now we had a grey sky and a muddy, lumpy sea. All around us dark cloud belts were dragging curtains of rain across sullen-looking water. The wind was now out of the north-east and soon it doubled in strength, quickly rising to force five or six and bringing driving rain. The sea began to lift into a line of angry waves rushing down on us. For a normal vessel the conditions would have been uncomfortable but not dangerous. *Alfred Wallace*, however, was not a normal vessel, and it was not safe to keep up our unwieldy sails. Getting the sails down in a strong wind was chaotic, with the mainsail requiring the most care. Yanis rushed forward to the bow, unfastened the forward end of the lower bamboo, seized the turning handle and began to twist, trying to roll up the sail.

By now the boat was pitching and bobbing in all directions. Yanis, bow-legged and barefoot, staggered back and forth on the wet, pitching deck, trying to keep his balance and still turning the handle. Joe and Beil attempted to assist him by easing out on the ropes which controlled the upper ends of the bamboo spars, and prevented the whole sail from swaying from side to side. Ropes thrashed in all directions. One loop of rope came flying aft, neatly lassoed our largest cookpot and flung it high into the air, and it was lost overboard into the sea. Waves slopped on to the deck and made it dangerously slippery. There were shouts and cries in bahasa Kei, the local dialect, between Yanis and Bobby. Yanis lost his footing and fell, but he hung on to the bamboo spar so he was swung back and forth like a pendulum. When he came upright again, he continued turning the bamboo handle frantically, winding up the sail until it was finally wrapped up. Then he, Joe and Beil lowered it to the deck. Now it was the turn of the smaller mizzen sail, and again we had the same drama. But this time Budi, the novice sailor, was handling a rope near the narrow stern. He was standing too close to the edge of the deck, looking upward at the sail, when his left foot slipped backwards a few centimetres on the wet deck and he dropped overboard. It all happened in an instant. One moment Budi was there; the next instant he was up to his neck in the sea. Two things were in his favour: first, *Alfred Wallace* was nearly at a standstill as both sails were rolled up and not driving the boat forward. Second, Budi managed to grab on to a rope as he went overboard, and he hung on. He was also very fit, and with almost no drag on him he was able to pull himself back to the edge of the boat, reach up for a handhold, and with a frantic wriggle and heave he scrambled back aboard, sodden wet and looking very shaken.

Later on our journey, I would see Budi shin ten metres up a straight tree-trunk in the jungle. It was a skill that came in handy that day on a rough sea, and got him safely back on board. But everyone aboard had taken note: you moved with the greatest care aboard *Alfred Wallace* in bad weather. Trying to keep your footing when the deck was wet was like standing on a bar of slippery soap, while our lightweight vessel heaved, tilted and pitched in the waves. The worst times were when our little boat lay parallel to the waves. Then she rolled so deeply that her gunnels dipped underwater with each passing wave. From the time when Budi went over the side, everyone saw the sense in putting on a safety harness when the wind grew strong; even Yanis, who had never seen such a safety harness before in all his days as an island sailor.

The strong wind and rough sea continued into

the early afternoon. Defensively we hoisted two small storm sails. They were not *layar tanja* but of a type known as dipping lugsails, a design used in the islands but also found widely in northern waters. Under these little sails, *Alfred Wallace* edged forward gently while her crew, tired from too little sleep, waited for the weather to improve.

By evening the wind had eased and the sea was much more calm. Until midnight we sailed again, using the *layar tanja*, and when the wind failed completely we started up the outboard engine and puttered through the night towards Kai. We arrived there in time to set Bill ashore to catch the noonday bus to Tual. His month-long stay with us had been completed, and he was on the way home with some idea of what it was to sail a prahu kalulis. The rest of us were satisfied to know that our boat could cope with sea passages of up to 300 kilometres, and that the most easterly sector of our travels had been completed on schedule. We had gone to the boundary of the Moluccas, and tracked Wallace in Kai Besar and Aru. It had been a very good start to the voyage and, with careful navigation, our prahu should be capable of carrying us the remainder of our planned zig-zag route through the Spice Islands in search of Wallace.

The experiences of Kei and Aru had also given us something to think about. It appeared that official Nature Reserves were not the only places where we could find the natural world that Wallace had marvelled at, or where rare species would survive the dangers of human interference he had foreseen. Kei Besar had shown that some sort of equilibrium was possible where the local native population seemed to coexist with rare birds, insects and plants. By contrast, we had been left with an uneasy feeling about the Baun Nature Reserve and whether it would survive official neglect. Enue with its dead turtles was, of course, a disaster. It remained to be seen whether the rest of our landfalls would support this contrary impression. Wallace's success in Aru had stimulated him to stay another five years in the Spice Islands. Much later, when writing his account of his Indonesian journey, he was to judge that his stay in Aru was 'still the portion of my travels to which I look back with the most complete satisfaction'. The next thousand miles of sailing the *Alfred Wallace* would show whether we agreed with him.

Foredeck and bilgepump

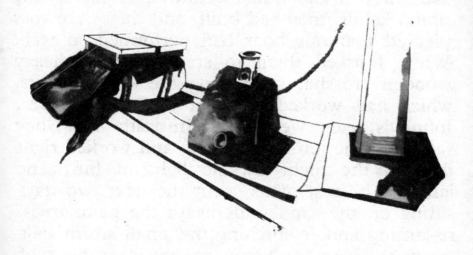

6

Jewels of the Moluccas

IN Warbal, Johnny and the building team were eager to know how we had got on. *Alfred Wallace* had ventured as far as any prahu kalulis they had built, and they were very pleased that our boat had performed so well. When I asked them to strengthen the heavy wooden crossbar supporting the steering oars, which had worked loose in the rough waves, Johnny's team were so enthusiastic that they set about the job immediately and worked right through the night by the light of hurricane lamps. The rest of us spent the next two days sitting on the sand underneath the palm trees, re-cutting and re-stitching the small storm sails to make them set better in our next bout of heavy weather. Now we had a different status on Warbal. The islanders knew that we were capable of taking a prahu to Aru and back, and we were regarded as sailors, where before we had been seen as slightly eccentric foreigners who might not know what they were doing. I suspected also that the Warbal people were relieved by our return, having feared that we might go off and drown ourselves, and then the Warbal community would get into trouble with the local authorities.

Many seafarers had come to Warbal over the years, ordered boats, and stayed while their vessel was completed. When they sailed away with their purchase, the islanders probably never saw them again. We had taken delivery of our boat and, as far as the local people were concerned, as soon as Johnny's team had made the final adjustments we would now go about our business. So it was with no ceremony at all that on the morning of 27 March we left Warbal for the last time. *Alfred Wallace* had been moored in her usual spot in the lagoon behind the village, and soon after dawn we poled our vessel out through the shallows and into the channel which curved past the headland. Here, where the village straggled down to the water's edge, we hoisted sail; Yanis looked across to the nearest houses, gave a shout and waved to a friend. The man waved back briefly, and then returned to his work. No one else took the slightest notice of us. As far as they were concerned, another Warbal-built boat was gone.

Our life on board had taken shape. The trip to Kei Besar and Aru had taught us where and how things were best stowed on our prahu. With six of us on board — Yanis, Bobby, Joe, Leonard, Budi and myself — we needed to be as tidy as possible. The entrance to the cabin was from the stern where a low doorway, not much bigger than for a large dog kennel, let in light and air. A similar doorway at the forward end of the cabin allowed a through draught; but this forward door was half blocked by the foot of the mainmast, so you had to be very agile to wriggle in or out through the gap. The bamboo floor of the cabin was heaped with twenty or more waterproof kitbags which contained our clothes and sleeping-bags as well as professional gear like Leonard's painting and drawing materials, Budi's bird-identification books and so forth. A space was left down the middle between the kitbags for people to move up and down, and there was just enough height under the cabin ridgeline for a six-foot man to stand with a slight stoop. Three home-made canvas stretchers hung by cords from the rafters and made sleeping places in the corners of the cabin. The fourth corner was left clear, for this was where we strung up our wet-weather clothing and life-harnesses. Next to it was a small open space where I could sit on the cabin floor with the computer on my lap, and type out the reports for the schools programme.

At each end of the cabin we had built rough shelves. There we kept our collection of rusty tools, the saws, drills and chisels for looking after our boat, and an essential item — the small hand-pump through which we filtered every drop of water we used for cooking or drinking. The hand-pump removed impurities and sterilised the water, a vital precaution as we had to collect our drinking water wherever we could find it: from wells, from village taps, from streams in the forest. There was no chart table. Instead, the spare charts were kept on my cot berth under a straw mat. And beside my forward berth was the emergency radio beacon, ready for use if our small and insubstantial vessel was hopelessly stuck on an isolated reef, run down by a larger ship, or capsized.

Our small, dim cabin was cramped for

Interior of cabin

Westerners, but an Indonesian crew would have found ample room for seven or eight people. We managed quite well by having three people sleeping in the hanging bunks and one person lying on the floor, while Joe and Budi preferred to sleep on the foredeck under a light awning. Only when it rained heavily was there a real crush; then all six of us were crammed below decks, the forward entry was closed with wooden boards to keep out the wet and the cabin became very dark and stuffy.

Normally, however, the 'house' — as Johnny and his team had called it — was remarkably cosy. The slightly springy bamboo floor was a comfortable place to stretch out, and the yellow and brown patterns of the roof of bamboo and leaves had a pleasing geometry. Lying in your cot berth, you looked up and saw a line of nine wooden rafters as if in the attic of a house, then beyond them a neat lattice of split bamboos, and finally row upon row of the palm leaves of the thatch. Glancing sideways, you could see the crests of waves less than a metre away where the lower edge of the roof did not actually come down to the deck, but stopped short by a few centimetres. From time to time, somewhere in the cabin there was a flicker of movement, so quick that it seemed not to have happened, and you had to wait and concentrate. Then, if you were lucky, you saw the gecko. He must have come aboard when the boat was being built, because the little lizard was with us from the very day we launched our boat, and he never left us. To the end of the voyage we would catch brief glimpses of him scuttling along the timbers, hunting for insects. Once or twice, during a calm night in the middle of the sea, he would startle us by suddenly letting loose a string of throaty cries, 'chik chik chak chak chak'.

We used the space under the foredeck to stow the anchors and mooring lines and the more robust items such as a reserve of tinned food, spare pieces of timber in case we needed to make repairs, and extra rope. Under the aft deck was our food. Cabbages, yams, potatoes, onions and carrots, whatever we could find in the markets, were stowed in nets tied to the underside of the deck beams. Containers of flour and sugar, bags of dried prawns or dried fish, were wedged into makeshift shelves, and somewhere was always a large sack of rice, our staple diet. Beyond the food stowage, right in the stern, was the area where Yanis kept our reserves of water and fuel, stowed in plastic containers. This was his domain, and whenever anything was needed he would prise up the stern hatch, drop down the hole and disappear from view as he crawled into the dark confines of the aft hold.

Yanis was thriving. He usually wore a faded yellow tee-shirt and loose blue shorts, and of course always went barefoot. He loved caps, preferably brightly coloured and with long peaks, and he cadged a succession of hats and caps from us. But his 'wire wool' hair was a poor foundation for the headgear, and the caps and hats were always being blown overboard by a gust of wind or knocked off by a flapping rope. He tried to keep them on by attaching a safety string to the hat, and then looping the end of the string around his ear, but that did not work. When the hat departed, Yanis would clap his hand to his head and give a great broad grin. On average, we left one of Yanis' caps bobbing in our wake every six days.

Yanis awake was always on the lookout for jobs to do. He would scrub the cooking pots until the metal bottoms nearly wore out of them, sweep the deck with a disintegrating brush that left as many bristles as the debris he collected, empty the bilges of the last few drops of water using an old tin as a scoop. As soon as we reached an anchorage, he would disappear up the beach with two or three empty 10-gallon plastic watercans, and reappear soon afterwards staggering under the burden of full cans. When he needed to rest, he could curl up in the smallest, most uncomfortable corner and go sound asleep. He could make his bed in the bilges, inside an old post bag or underneath the dugout canoe which was lashed upside down on the cabin roof. And wherever he slept, he snored ferociously.

Neat, ever-helpful and diffident, Bobby was trying his best to keep up with Yanis. He trailed along in the rear, still looking doubtful and hesitating about what he should do next. At first he had done some of the cooking on board, but that chore was soon taken over by Joe and Leonard who preferred not to have their rice completely soggy in the usual island way of cooking. So Bobby fell back on washing the dishes, whenever he could intercept Yanis

Left: Alfred Russel Wallace after his return from south-east Asia. *(Oil painting over photograph taken by Wallace's brother-in-law and given by his family to the National Portrait Gallery.)*

Above: Yanis.

Below: Smoothing the hull with adzes, Warbal island

Above: Dead turtle on the protected nesting beach, Enue Island.

Opposite: Alfred Wallace.

Right: Yanis guides an exhausted turtle back to the water, after egg laying. He will then sweep away the tell-tale tracks leading to her nest.

ainforest,
ian Jaya.

aboei village,
Vaigeo.

Above: Tree rats for sale, Langowen country market.

Below: Street seller of traditional medicines, including bones from dugong flippers like huge human hands, Manado.

Above: Sea turtle on offer in Langowen country market, where protected species are sold as food every Saturday.

Above: Canoe man, Kaboei.

Right: Headman and
villagers of Kaboei
recognise drawings
of the Red Bird
of Paradise.

Left: Bird catchers spreading gum on branch, Halmahera.

Left: Applying betel juice make-up.

ht: Expedition artist n Sheil drawing the d Bird of Paradise in e field.

Evening off Halmahera

Approaching Banda

from doing the same job, and trying to make himself useful about the deck. But here he was soon outpaced by Budi. Our novice sailor had not been discouraged by his mishap when he fell overboard on the way from Aru to Kei, and he was proving to be a natural-born sailor. As a forester he could already work timber and tie knots safely. Now he was learning to handle the complicated *layar tanja*, and showing himself to be the best needle-worker on the crew, as he stitched neat repairs to the sails where they had rubbed holes, or made up canvas covers for our equipment. When he was at the tiller, Budi was relaxed, alert and competent. With his cap shading his brown Malay face, he looked as if he had been a seafarer all his life.

Our route from Warbal was north-west, towards the Banda Islands. The trip took a little more than two days, and we saw only two vessels en route, both Taiwanese trawlers which ignored us. The high point was when we received a message over our radio to say that our picture of the turtle we had rescued on Aru had been successfully transmitted over the satellite link and seen by the schoolchildren in Ireland.

At dawn on the second day the Bandas were appearing faintly on the horizon as a single peak with a plume of cloud, and by early afternoon as we drew closer, we began to see why the little cluster of islands are described as the jewels of the Moluccas.

They are dominated by the splendid profile of an active 600-metre volcano, thrusting up from the depths of the Banda Sea. Silver and white clouds streamed downwind from the peak as we approached. The clouds were the turbulence where the tip of the volcano disturbed the wind flow, but from a distance they looked exactly like gushing smoke and steam as if the volcano was building up pressure and about to explode. Before us was a small, low outlying island, Hatta Island. Across the eight-kilometre-wide channel, steep land thickly covered with coconut plantation and forest climbed away to a crest. Beyond that lush green ridge, but set well back so that there was a sense of perspective, was the cone of the volcano, dark and dramatic. Flights of gannets glided past us, and in the Hatta channel a school of 20 or 30 dolphins was lazing on the surface. They bobbed and rolled and blew small spouts, and their dark skins glistened in the sun. The entire spectacle would have been a fit backdrop to a story by Jules

Verne, and it seemed highly appropriate that the local people called their volcano Gunung Api, or Fire Mountain.

The smouldering volcano had led Alfred Wallace, who visited the islands on three different occasions, to reflect how differently from most Europeans the local people must view the ground on which they stood. People in Europe, he said, regarded the earth as solid and firm, but in Banda and the other volcanic areas of Indonesia the inhabitants were always aware that the land might suddenly shake in earthquakes or erupt in showers of hot ash and terrifying lava flows. 'Almost every year there is an earthquake here, and at intervals of a few years very severe ones, which throw down houses and carry ships out of the harbour bodily into the streets.' He saw an area of forest where the trees were all dead, but still standing, where the sea had broken in during an earthquake and flooded their roots, killing them with salt water.

There was not much for him to collect by way of animals or insects, because Banda was highly cultivated. His three visits were made largely because Banda was a regular port of call for the Dutch colonial steamers on which Wallace travelled throughout the more developed parts of Indonesia. The only interesting animal he found was a species of 'fine and very handsome fruit pigeon'. This bird flourished because it lived off a small round fruit, about the size and shape of a peach, which had once made Banda phenomenally wealthy.

When the fruit was ripe, it split open and

revealed a brilliant crimson net of lace wrapped around a large, shiny, dark brown seed. This seed was the nutmeg, and the crimson net was mace. The two spices, nutmeg and mace, had been so valuable in the early seventeenth century that Holland resorted to 'ethnic cleansing' to gain control of their production. At that time the native Bandanese were the greatest trading fraternity in the southern Spice Islands. They alone had vessels large enough to sail direct to the Asian mainland, and their society was ruled by the *orang kaya*, literally the 'rich men', who had trading links as far as China and Malaya. The Dutch resolved to put an end to all this, to create a monopoly of the spice trade for themselves and make Banda their sole nutmeg garden. They provoked the *orang kaya* and their followers into armed resistance, and then brutally eliminated them. Small flotillas of refugees escaped to Kei Besar and other islands at a safe distance, but the great majority of the inhabitants were shot down or rounded up to be hung. Some were ceremonially decapitated by hired Japanese mercenaries. Fewer than 600 native Bandanese survived out of an earlier population of 15,000 people. The Dutch then imported a docile population to work the nutmeg plantations; they shipped in slaves, indentured labourers, even convicts, from as far away as Burma, India, China and Mozambique as well as from the other Indonesian islands.

The conditions of soil and climate on Banda were so perfect for nutmeg trees that most of the trees were planted naturally by the same species of 'fine and very handsome fruit pigeons' which Wallace observed. These birds had such a wide-opening beak that they could swallow an entire nutmeg fruit and pass the round seed undamaged through the gut, so that it grew where it fell. The labourers had to keep the saplings free of weeds, tend the tall kenari trees which provided essential shade for the nutmeg trees, and pick the fruit. Obligingly, in that warm equatorial climate, the nutmegs gave their crop all year long. It is calculated that, in nearly two centuries of colonial rule, Holland produced a billion guilders' worth of these spices from their tiny Banda holdings. The income from the Banda spice monopoly so dominated Dutch foreign policy that Holland offered the island of Manhattan to the British if they would drop their claim to the minuscule islet of Run in the Bandas — barely three

Nutmeg

Banda waterfront

kilometres long and one and a half kilometres wide. Even more remarkably, Run itself grew no nutmeg trees. The Dutch ripped them up in order to concentrate virtually the entire world production of nutmeg and mace on the other Bandas.

Slavery in the Dutch Indies was not abolished until 1862, so there must have been slaves on Banda when Wallace visited there in the late 1850s. Yet he says nothing about them and — astonishingly for an Owenite socialist — he voiced his strong approval of the Dutch system of monopoly plantation though he knew this opinion would raise hackles in Victorian England. State monopolies, he argued, were the only way for a colony to be viable. The mother country had to find some way of paying the huge cost of its colonial efforts, bringing education, peace and a 'civilising influence' to unruly native peoples, and if the state controlled a lucrative monopoly, that cost could be met. It was far better, Wallace argued, for the state to reap the profits than to allow the local economy to pass into the hands of private businesses, who would exploit the natives and give nothing in return. The only condition which Wallace put forward was that the monopoly should be of a product not essential to the natives, who must be able to live without it. In this respect, of course, nutmeg was ideal; it was a luxury, not a subsistence food.

In truth, by Wallace's time the state's monopoly in nutmeg was in tatters. Nutmegs were being grown illegally elsewhere in the Moluccas, and the French had established nutmeg plantations in Mauritius, using seeds smuggled in from the Spice Islands. Corruption had been so widespread among the superintending officials in Banda and Amsterdam that tight control of the nutmeg trade was a sham. The Dutch authorities abandoned the system within a decade of Wallace's visit, and handed over ownership of Banda's nutmeg gardens to the *perkiniers*, the planters who had previously held them on licence. They in their turn would go under, unable to survive in world competition. The nutmeg plantations fell into neglect and Banda began a long, slow slide into obscurity while, ironically, the impoverished planters came to be replaced by a new generation of Bandanese *orang kaya* who re-established the age-old trade links. Twenty years after Wallace's visit, the wealthiest man on the islands was a Javanese Arab trader, Bin Saleh Baadilla, who traded in pearls and bird products. His warehouse contained skins of Birds of Paradise prepared by the natives of Kai, Aru and New Guinea, as well as the feathers of other exotic and coloured species from the rainforest. Where his predecessors had sent the bird-skins to decorate the fans and turbans of a few Indian and Malay potentates, Bin Saleh now had a larger and more voracious market. He shipped his bird-skins to the milliners of Europe, who at the peak of the fashion craze were said to be importing 50,000 bird-skins a year to provide decorations for ladies' hats.

At 4.30 on the afternoon of 29 March, *Alfred Wallace* skirted the low yellow cliffs of Lontar Island and turned into the north entrance of Banda's superb landlocked harbour. Ahead of us opened the roadstead where broad-beamed, triple-masted Dutch East-Indiamen had anchored while they loaded their cargoes of spice. Neatly packaged in boxes made of palm leaf, sun-dried mace was reputed to be amongst the easiest, cleanest and most profitable cargoes in the history of trade. To our right were the grey battlements of Fort Belgica, one of several forts the Dutch had built to protect the anchorage. Down by the water's edge gleamed the white frontages of two or three mansions which had once been the residences for the Dutch governor and wealthy *perkiniers*. Beyond were the little red roofs of the ordinary dwellings of the town, set in the greenery of their small gardens. There were no factory chimneys, modern docks or electricity pylons — not even the government office blocks which had so disfigured Dobbo. Banda seemed to have been left out of the twentieth century. Towering over the harbour was the inescapable presence of Fire Mountain, backlit by the setting sun. The evening shadow of the mountain fell across the town as people were lighting their cooking fires. The smoke from their hearths oozed over the roof-tops and hung in a thin blue-grey haze. It looked as if the whole settlement was smouldering at the foot of its volcano.

A walk through the little town of some 7,000 inhabitants reinforced the impression of timelessness. We saw only three cars and one small pick-up truck in the narrow, well-swept streets of Bandaneira town. Most Bandanese walked or bicycled. If they were burdened with shopping from the small market near the harbour, they hired a bicycle rickshaw. There was no traffic noise. Many of the small neat wooden houses which lined the roads had pleasant verandahs. Occasionally a much larger house survived from the nutmeg days, with tall colonnades and high, cool rooms. None of the local people seemed to be in a hurry. Everyone we met had a pleasant and welcoming smile. Banda was still as Wallace had described it, 'a lovely little spot'.

How had it managed to survive like this? Where were the dilapidated shacks, broken gutters and open drains, drooping electricity cables and ugly hoardings of towns like Dobbo and Tual? Banda's small size and a modicum of natural wealth provided some of the answer.

Banda harbour

It was not large enough to attract the overload of bureaucracy we had seen elsewhere, for the entire island group could be administered by nothing bigger than a town council. Nor was there any need for a large, ugly modern bazaar when there were not enough people in the islands to make it worthwhile. The seas around Banda were rich in fish, and the gardens supplied fruit and vegetables, so there was plenty of locally produced food. If people wanted special purchases, they boarded a ferry and travelled overnight to the shops in Ambon, the regional capital. For ready cash, Banda still sold about 200 tons of nutmeg every year, and nowadays the nuts of the kenari shade-trees, the tropical almond, were also a valuable side crop. It was little wonder that the Bandanese seemed more content and relaxed than their neighbours in other islands.

They were also aware that Banda had a resource which should prove as lucrative as the nutmeg trade. Everyone, from the owner of the smallest street kiosk to a coconut farmer on the outer islands, knew that Banda might well become a major tourist centre. Visitors would be drawn there by the spectacular scenery, the beaches, the underwater reefs and the historic charm. In Indonesia, as so often in developing countries, tourism was seen as the quickest way of getting rich. It was just a question of how and when the islands would be developed for tourism, and much depended on an *orang kaya* whose great-grandfather had met Wallace.

Des Alwi was the island's most famous citizen,

its most influential landlord and also an elected leader of adat or traditional custom. Now in his sixties, he was typically Bandanese in his mixed descent; he had Javanese and Arab grandparents, and could also trace his line back to Chinese workers imported to Banda in the seventeenth century. Des Alwi's grandfather on the maternal side was Said Baadilla, 'The Pearl King', and

Bandaneira town and Gunung Api volcano

his father's family had served as courtiers and religious advisers to the Sultan of Ternate. Born and raised in Banda, Des Alwi's life had been interwoven with the rise of the Indonesian republic. As a small boy he had met two leaders of Indonesia's national revolution, Mohammad Hatta and Sutan Sjahrir, who would become Vice-President and Prime Minister respectively. The Dutch had exiled them to Bandaneira, where Sutan Sjahrir became Des Alwi's adopted father. At 14, during the Japanese War, Des Alwi left the island and joined the Indonesian resistance movement. Then he fought and was wounded in the struggle to evict the European colonial powers. With powerful friends from his revolutionary days he had gone into national politics, worked as his country's Press Attaché in several foreign capitals and eventually become a man of influence in Jakarta. Returning to the islands in 1968, after 24 years' absence, he had been appalled to find that the historic houses had been stripped of their furniture and fittings and the fine trees lining the streets cut down for firewood, while the harbour was run down and decayed. Worse, the Bandanese felt neglected and demoralised.

Using his influence with the government, Des Alwi plunged into promoting and developing the islands. He obtained government money for public services, for the building of a small airstrip, for the preservation and restoration of old colonial houses which were turned into schools or used to house local government offices instead of building office blocks. He

Banda colonial house

organised the restoration of Fort Belgica and set up a cultural foundation. His vision for the future of the Bandas was that they would become a high-quality tourist resort; he built two hotels, and converted his family's old mansion into a guest house for the overspill. It was little wonder that he was referred to, half seriously and half mockingly, as 'the King of Banda'.

Of course there were people on Banda who objected to his autocratic style and entrepreneurial approach. They resented the control he exercised on the pace of tourist development, his ownership of prime land sites, the special treatment he arranged for guests at his hotels and the monopoly of key tourist facilities. Yet it was due to Des Alwi, more than any other individual, that the island had stayed unspoiled relative to other places in the Moluccas. He had played the leading role in creating a public awareness of the commercial value of Banda's charm. He had succeeded not just because he had influence in Jakarta, but also because he was descended from the orlima, the five-man council which traditionally ruled Banda. This gave him local respect, and placed him in a position to mould events. Des Alwi's status on Banda recalled the authority which had allowed the Rajah of Maur Ohoiwut to encourage traditional ways of fishing, harvesting and protecting the forest resources on Kai Besar. On Banda a new-style *orang kaya* had similarly held the line against destructive exploitation, though with a view to harvesting the island's tourist potential rather than maintaining a rural quality of life.

To see what might have happened without the restraining influence of a Des Alwi, we needed to look no farther than the city of Ambon, less than a day's sail away. Though many times larger than Banda, Ambon had merited a very similar enthusiastic description from Wallace in the 1860s when he found the town to be neat, well-run and charming. Ambon had been chosen by the Dutch as their capital for the south Moluccas, and the place was organised with a certain prim orderliness. The centre of town was laid out in a grid pattern, and on the outskirts the hedges of flowering shrubs enclosed small huts surrounded by fruit and palm trees. 'There are few places more enjoyable for a morning or evening stroll than these sandy roads and shady lanes in the suburbs of the ancient city of Ambon,' observed Wallace. His greatest praise was for Ambon's huge natural harbour:

The clearness of the water afforded me one of the most astonishing and beautiful sights I have ever beheld. The bottom was absolutely hidden by a continuous series of corals, sponges, actiniae, and other marine productions of magnificent dimensions, varied forms and brilliant colours. The depth varied from twenty to fifty feet and the bottom was very uneven, rocks and chasms and little hills and valleys, offering a variety of stations for the growth of these forest animals. In and out among them moved numbers of blue and red

197

and yellow fishes, spotted and banded and striped in the most striking manner, while great orange or rosy transparent Medusae floated along near the surface. It was a sight to gaze at for hours, and no description can do justice to its surpassing beauty and interest. For once, the reality exceeded the most glowing accounts I had ever read of the wonders of a coral sea. There is perhaps no spot in the world richer in marine productions, corals, shells and fishes than the harbour of Amboyna.

Yet when we took *Alfred Wallace* to Ambon, after our stay in Banda, we had barely entered the great bay and were still ten kilometres from the modern city when we encountered a slimy yellow slick of plastic bags, old bottles and raw sewage floating out on the tide. One look at what was bobbing in the water was enough to discourage us from going closer to the city. In line ahead we counted a dead cat, followed closely by what looked like a small raft of goat's intestines, and then the corpse of a rat, so bloated with putrefaction that it was lying on its back as if wearing an inflated lifejacket, four paws pointing to the sky. We edged over to the shore and found a shallow patch where the anchor would take hold. Here Budi volunteered to go overboard to work on a stern fitting which needed attention. He was in the water for twenty minutes, standing up to his chest; by the time he scrambled back aboard, a light skin rash was already appearing all over his body.

The pollution of Ambon's harbour was explained when we took a bus into the city centre and saw that three or four small creeks cut through the town and emptied into the harbour. All of them were serving as main sewers. Private householders simply threw their refuse into them, and the municipal rubbish trucks which collected town garbage dumped their contents into piles beside the streams. A crust of rubbish, thick enough to walk on, floated on each surface. Every day there were thunderstorms and heavy rains, and the floodwater washed all the detritus into the bay in a great, putrid mass. There it floated up and down with the tide, and was joined by oil and filth directly discharged into the water by the ships, some of which looked fit to be scrapped. The Korean trawlers were so rusty and dangerous that they were manned, so it was said, by convicts. The superb corals which Wallace had described were long vanished. Those close to the town had been dynamited and dredged up to provide material to rebuild Ambon after the Second World War, and all the others were choked to death in the opaque brown water. The change in Ambon since Wallace's day was common to all the expanding cities of Indonesia. What had once been a pleasant local capital had been overwhelmed by the arrival of poor migrants from the villages and outer islands. They were looking for work and opportunity, and Ambon simply could not cope with the influx. The city sprawled out sideways into makeshift suburbs, and the services in the centre collapsed under the strain.

Wallace's lyric description of Ambon's harbour, even allowing for the hyperbole, might still apply to Banda's harbour where we stayed for a week. Here the water was still so clear that we could see ten metres down to the coral beds, watch the bright kingfisher-blue specks of tiny fish drift among the corals, and see shoals of purple- and yellow-banded angelfish nibble algae and sponges. One morning a lionfish wandered by, its long poisonous spines waving gently as it seemed to ride on the slightest current. Here Julia was finally able to join us after the completion of her contract working on a Forestry Conservation project in Borneo, so the team had a very welcome interpreter. But sadly, Julia's first task was to explain to Bobby that he would have to go home. Since the start of the trip we had noticed how Bobby suffered bouts of listlessness. He would complain of aches in his bones and a sore back, and found it difficult to concentrate. The pattern had become so frequent by the time we reached Banda that I asked Joe, our doctor, to give Bobby a thorough medical examination. There, on the deck of *Alfred Wallace*, Joe had no hesitation in diagnosing that Bobby was suffering from recurrent malaria, and Julia explained to him that once we had got him to Ambon, he would have to give up the trip and return to Kei to get proper treatment. Poor Bobby was crestfallen.

This was the other, darker side to the apparent tropical paradise of palm trees, green forests and sandy beaches through which we were sailing, and where Wallace had soldiered on for six years

200

of field work. During the Spice Islands Voyage all of us suffered at one time or another from chills and low-grade fevers, even though we had modern medicines and, in Joe, we had our own doctor on board. In Banda a small insect bite on my leg turned septic in six hours and puffed up as if I had been bitten by a venomous insect. I felt giddy and unwell as if I had severe flu, and was dosed with antibiotics. Leonard developed blotches on his face, and Joe was tormented by rashes all over his body. Even Yanis with his iron constitution and india-rubber physique could sometimes be seen curled up miserably underneath a scrap of sailcloth, shivering and with his eyes dull with fever. Julia was by far the most vulnerable. In the twelve months during

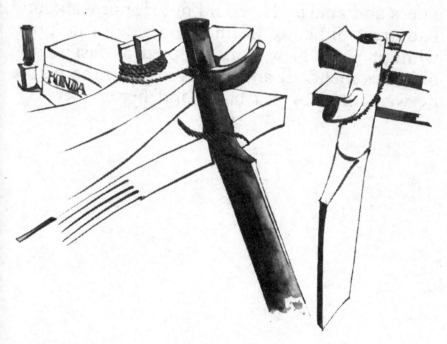

Steering oar and outboard

which she assisted the project, she contracted one bout of typhoid and had dengue fever twice.

This was nothing compared with Wallace's experience, however. In Dobbo he had been badly afflicted by mosquitoes; they bit him on his legs and feet, and the bites turned into such painful ulcers that eventually he could not even stand or walk, but had to crawl down to the river to bathe. Three years later much the same thing happened to him in the island of Seram, when he was bitten by the hordes of harvest bugs for which the Seram forest was notorious, and had to beat a retreat to Ambon where he rented a house to convalesce. By then he had come out in a rash of severe boils. He had them on his eye, cheek, armpits, elbows, back, thighs, knees and ankles. He could not sit nor walk, and had great difficulty in finding a side to lie upon without pain. New boils erupted as fast as the old ones mended, and it was a long time before he was cured by sea baths and better diet.

7

The Sago Zone

WALLACE found that Ambon and
its region was — like Banda — a
disappointment for the insect and bird
collector, and for the same reason: the area
around Ambon was too cultivated to shelter
much wildlife. So it was all the more of a surprise
to encounter a large python when visiting the
north side of the bay for some beetle-hunting.
He had heard some rustling in the thatch roof
of the small house where he was staying, but
thought no more about it and went to bed as
usual. The next afternoon, feeling tired, he lay
down on his couch to relax with a book. Looking
up into the rafters, he noticed a strange shape
which at first he thought was a tortoiseshell put

up in the roof for safe keeping. But as he looked harder, he saw that it was a massive python with black and yellow markings, tightly curled into a knot and watching him, and he realised he must have slept the previous night with the snake not more than a yard above his head. He summoned his Malay assistants for help, but they were too frightened to come close. Eventually a man from the island of Bouru, where there were many snakes, appeared and took control. He contrived a strong noose of rattan, and poked the snake into movement with a pole, at which stage he slipped the noose over the reptile's head and dragged it down from the rafters. There was a great thrashing and confusion with chairs and furniture being overturned, as the python flailed about. Eventually the Bouru man managed to seize the big snake by the tail and rushed out of the hut, dragging it behind him. He tried to knock the snake's head against a tree but missed, and the animal escaped under a fallen log. 'It was again poked out,' wrote Wallace, 'and again the Bouru man caught hold of its tail, and running away quickly dashed its head with a swing against a tree, and it was then easily killed with a hatchet. It was about twelve feet long, and very thick, capable of doing much mischief, and swallowing a dog or a child.'

We had followed Wallace from Banda to Ambon at the end of the first week of April, and I was in a hardware shop in the city, buying rope for *Alfred Wallace*, when I stumbled upon the continuing trade in Birds of Paradise, a trade supposedly banned by law. The shop had formerly been a ship chandlery. Old-fashioned paraffin navigation lamps hung from the roof beams, along with wooden steering-wheels and brass foghorns. But they were all very dusty, and most of the business now was in selling modern tools and general ironmongery. At the back of the shop I came across a treasure — several coils of first-quality natural manila rope. This was unusual in a country where the fishermen normally use pale blue polypropylene rope, so I ordered 50 fathoms of manila and was waiting while the shop assistants carefully measured out my purchase by pulling lengths of rope between marks carved into battered wooden floorboards. As I waited, the son of the Chinese shop-owner strolled over and wanted to know where I was from, what I was doing and why I should want traditional rope. When he heard that I had sailed from the Aru Islands in a prahu and was bound for Irian Jaya, to look at the wildlife, he asked if I wanted to see the skin of a cendrawasi, a Bird of Paradise. He had three cendrawasi skins at home, he said; they had been purchased from an islander who had come into his shop the previous year and offered them for sale.

Where had the bird skins come from? I asked. From the Aru Islands, he replied. Everyone knew that you obtained this particular species of the Bird of Paradise from the Aru Islands. If you wanted other species like the Red Bird of Paradise, then you bought them from traders who came down from Irian Jaya where that bird was hunted. That evening at his home he showed me one of the bird-skins. It was a Great Bird of Paradise in all its splendour, from the green sheen of the throat to the golden cascade of the tail, and it must have been poached from Aru. The young Chinaman was keeping it as a curiosity, and was not much interested in it. But he said that he knew of at least one living Bird of Paradise in Ambon which was kept as a pet.

The incident recalled the rumours I had been hearing. Someone had talked about hitch-hiking a ride on a military aircraft out of Dobbo, and climbing on board to find that the rear of the plane was filled with cage after cage of living Birds of Paradise being smuggled out for illegal sale. In the homes of senior civil servants, the same people who were supposed to be enforcing the protection of the species, I had seen the ornamental glass cases inside which a stuffed chandrawasi was mounted, spreading its display feathers. The stuffed birds looked comparatively fresh. Whatever the law said, a Bird of Paradise — alive or dead — was still a prestige symbol in Indonesia for whoever owned it. Streets were named after it, the greatest bay in northern Irian Jaya was called Chandrawasi Bay, the bird appeared on a national bank note, and the local regiment in Ambon wore the Bird of Paradise on their shoulder flashes.

A breeding pair of Birds of Paradise were among the most expensive, the rarest and the most illegal of the birds in commerce. But many other species of wild birds were being bought and sold, and again the rule applied that the more spectacular and rare, then the more valuable they were. Birds trapped in the outer islands found their way to the holding cages of professional bird dealers in cities like Ambon for the south Moluccas, Sorong in Irian Jaya, and Ternate in the north Moluccas. From there they were taken by ship to the markets in Surabaya and Jakarta. Most of the trade was in common species such as the small bright parrots, and it was perfectly legal. Many Indonesians liked to keep parrots and lories as pets. But mixed in with the tide of legal birds were the protected species such as the black cockatoos and violet-necked lories. To carry them — so we were told — some of the large ferry-boats had special hidden compartments built into the accommodation decks. So many birds died in transit that the wholesale dealers usually paid only if the birds were still alive 30 days after delivery. So, despite the extra cost, more and more captive birds were being sent to market as air freight, accompanied by false documentation.

Budi and Julia had arranged a meeting with the Department of Education in Ambon. One theme of our expedition was to offer teaching material and talks on environmental awareness to the local schools around our route, particularly for the village schools in the more remote islands. For this programme Julia had prepared an educational booklet based on Alfred Wallace's own story, and Budi had drawn the illustrations. For the next two weeks they would visit a number of schools in Ambon and the nearby island of Seram, while the rest of the team sailed

Ejecting an intruder
(*taken from* The Malay Archipelago)

west in the prahu to visit the Gorong archipelago where Wallace had himself purchased a native boat. Later we would reassemble on the north coast of Seram, and sail together to Irian Jaya and the home of the Red Birds of Paradise.

When Wallace went to the Gorong Islands from Ambon, he proceeded along the Seram coast as fast as possible, paddled by relays of local tribesmen whose incessant singing and tom-tom beating, he said, gave him a headache. A swift passage along the Seram coast suited us well enough too. Although Seram is very spectacular and wild, the island is so close to Ambon that it has been visited by many scientific expeditions over the years. Moreover Wallace had very little to say about it, and so we had no comparison to make with the conditions he observed.

It took *Alfred Wallace* a full two days to sail the length of Seram's long southern coast, staying prudently offshore until we were level with the distinctive mountain which marks its eastern tip. Half cone, half tabletop, the mountain stands behind the domes of a dozen or so mosques. Each is the site of a small village, where in Wallace's day the passing native vessels touched to trade because this part of the Spice Islands was a natural crossroads for the prahus. Wallace particularly noted one islet so covered with houses on stilts that it reminded him of an eastern Venice. Today we found that same islet was virtually deserted, with just a few coconut groves and a little hamlet of huts. Clearly eastern Seram and the small islands beyond it had lapsed into obscurity.

The wind began to pick up strength as the three islands of the Gorong archipelago came in sight. Made cautious by our rough passage between Aru and Banda, I started to look for shelter for our lightweight boat. But there was no harbour marked on the map, and the islands were no more than 7 or 8 kilometres in length and seemed to offer little chance of refuge. Soon the wind made the decision for me, changing direction and growing even stronger, forcing us to aim for a gap between the first two islands to reach shelter behind the third. *Alfred Wallace* put her lee rail to the water and began speeding along. As we came closer to the gap between the islands, we could see how the coral extended from each side in pale turquoise ledges, beautiful but deadly. A dark blue patch of water, quite narrow, marked the only gap through the reef, and was indicated by a crooked branch stuck in the coral. With *Alfred Wallace* racing through the water, we steered for the spot while Yanis clung anxiously to the mainmast, trying to point the track. But the channel was indistinct, and he would indicate one direction, then point in another. Then he would hesitate and his arm would droop, and he would tip back his hat and scratch his head.

After six weeks of steering amongst coral, I felt it was worth the risk of pressing on towards the most likely mark, even if Yanis was baffled. So I committed our boat fully to the run. Within a kilometre there was no way we could turn back or even come to a stop, because the wind would drive us sideways on to the coral ledges. We were right in the jaws of the channel when the tide changed. The effect on the waters ahead of us was very dramatic. Where there had been a ruffle of modest waves it quickly changed into lines of steep white breakers appearing to march towards us, but in fact heaving up and down, nearly stationary. The waves were tumbling in confusion as the tide pushed against the wind. Our prahu shot pell-mell through the gap in the reef, without touching rock, and ran straight into these overfalls. Short steep waves tossed and broke on all sides. The hull hammered into the waves, and the boat lurched from side to side like a train going over a series of points on the track. The jolting was sharp enough to make the dugout dinghy, lashed to the cabin top, jerk and rock in its lashings. Joe and Leonard fastened down the heavy canoe with extra ropes.

In a splendid demonstration of the power and speed of a Kei Island prahu, *Alfred Wallace* literally bounced and powered her way through the upheaval of water. There were various bangs and crashes from down below in the cabin as unseen objects came adrift and were thrown about, but the vessel herself put her shoulder to the water and charged onward. Once I had realised that *Alfred Wallace* could cope with the rough water, it was so exhilarating that I almost forgot to halt our vessel before we hit land. We came pounding through the overfalls and then closed with the next island at such speed that we were in danger of running on to the fringing reef if Leonard had not suggested quietly, 'Shouldn't we drop at least one sail?' Startled, I gave the order, and Leonard and Joe scrambled to roll up the sails in double-quick time. If *Alfred Wallace* had been a car, it would have been fair to say that she came screeching to a halt with a smell of burning rubber as Yanis then threw overboard our main anchor and we came to a brisk stop, watched by the villagers who were highly appreciative of such a dashing arrival by a strange boat.

There is a moment, when you come to safe anchorage after a strong wind and a breakneck ride, when the wild motion of the boat and the clatter of the sails have ceased and a calm descends, that you wonder what all the fuss was

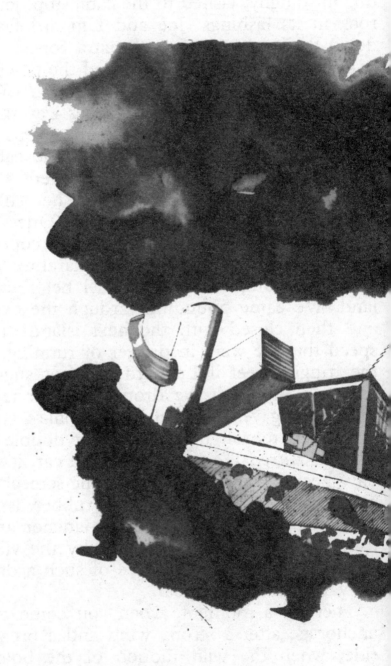

The Alfred Wallace *in overfalls*

about. The wind in the anchorage often seems much less than when you were out in the open sea. Safely moored off the little unnamed village on Pulau Gorong, this was no exception. Within half an hour the weather conditions had eased to the point that a swarm of dugout canoes were putting off from the beach and paddling out to see us. The dugouts were tiny. Some of them were no more than just over a metre long. But they were beautifully made, and their hulls were so light and thin that one man could carry them. Most of the paddlers were children, and soon we were surrounded by our little flotilla of naked invaders, yelling and shouting and waving and clowning as they skittered about the sea in their little wooden peapods. Or they would come alongside with a slight bump, so that at any one time half a dozen dripping-wet youngsters would have wriggled up on deck and be squatting, gazing at the strangers preparing their evening meal over the stove on the stern deck before we finally turned in to get some sleep.

We were wakened at 2 a.m. by the alarming sound of the twin rudder blades scraping on coral. The tide was dropping, and *Alfred Wallace* was about to be impaled on the rock. We tumbled out on deck and punted the prahu with bamboo poles until we could find safer depth according to our home-made depth finder — a large hammer-head bought in Ambon market and tied to the end of a long cord. After the rest of the crew had returned to their sleep, I stayed on deck for another hour to check that the anchor was holding. It was a warm starlit night and the adjacent village — unusually — must have had electricity, because its small mosque was outlined garishly in green striplights. Around our boat the plankton was on the move, glowing in strange patterns. Sometimes it rippled in whorls or broke into random pools of luminescence; often it appeared in individual yellow and green ribbons, roughly two metres long, which undulated through the water so that I would have sworn we were surrounded by banded yellow sea snakes. The illusion was so convincing that several times I switched on a powerful torch and shone the beam at one of these wriggling shapes, but could see nothing alive on the surface. The beam of torch-light would penetrate down through the clear water and illuminate the coral heads below, throwing them into light and shadow and making a strange optical effect as if the coral was swelling up and down with a great pulsating heartbeat.

Daylight revealed that we had shifted our anchorage over a magnificent coral garden. Below the hull spread every imaginable type and shape of coral. There were broad umbrella corals extending 1.5 metres across, antler corals, brain corals, tracery corals as delicate as lace, corals that looked like massive doughnuts, others that grew like sprays of lavender. The main colours were pale yellow and grey, but there was also mauve and purple. Some corals were the blooms of flowers, dark indigo tipped with yellow and white. The impression of plants growing under water was strengthened by one species of coral which appeared to be unfolding crumpled leaves.

Another resembled a delicate brown fern, and many others were exactly the shape of field mushrooms, brown in the centre and with a white fringe. Among these underwater growths glided the reef fish, yellow and purple or silver with a yellow stripe. Lying below them on the bottom were the outlines of dark mauve starfish, and large shells with the shape of cowries and the same brown and yellow patterns but much more substantial.

The unnamed village beside us had begun its daily routine in the unvarying rhythm of the equatorial year. The day began with the cries of lories and parakeets fluttering and screaming in the half-light of dawn among the clumps of tall trees behind the village. At about 7.30 the birds began to take off in flights, 20 – 30 birds at a time. They called and shrieked to one another as they climbed high over the village, gaining altitude before setting their course across the straits to their feeding grounds on the neighbouring island which Wallace called Manowolko. The village itself was a line of weatherbeaten huts fronting the beach, mostly roofed with palm thatch though a few had rusty corrugated-iron roofs. At the centre was the mosque, and towards one end on a small bluff stood the newer corrugated-iron roof of the schoolhouse. It was a Saturday morning and we could see the schoolchildren in their white shirts and red shorts and skirts assembling beside the flagpole. Their fathers, uncles and grandfathers had put to sea an hour earlier while the sea was still calm before the onshore breeze. Each man went by himself in one of the small dugout canoes and paddled out about half a kilometre to his favourite spot, where the coral platform suddenly dropped away vertically in a submarine cliff to plunge three hundred metres into the black depths. This drop-off zone was the fishing ground, and the man would sit there in his tiny canoe, drifting with wind and current, almost lost among the slightest waves, as he jigged up and down his single handline baited with five or six hooks. If he was lucky, he came paddling home after three or four hours with a dozen fish, each barely 15 centimetres long.

Eight kilometres up the coast we came to Kataloko, the stopping place for the local inter-island ferry. It was a hangdog little town, whose rickety ferry pier gave a clue to its character. The massive wooden pilings leaned in every direction like loose teeth, and the heavy planks of the dock

Corals and fish

rattled and shifted. Each step threatened to send you dropping five metres into the foreshore mud. At the foot of the pier was an empty warehouse which, according to the signboard, doubled as the harbour master's office. When I walked in, the harbour master was sitting at a bare table in a side room, and he looked pleased. It seemed that strange boats hardly ever called at Kotaloka and it was nice to have someone drop in for a chat. When I asked if he wanted to check the ship's papers, he waved the question aside graciously. This was something of a relief because *Alfred Wallace* had never been formally registered, not even at Warbal, and I had no papers to show.

When Wallace came to the Gorong archipelago in April 1860, he was in the final phase of his explorations in the Spice Islands after more than three years' travels in the Moluccas. He was hoping to pay a second, more leisurely visit to the Kei Islands, and Gorong was a stepping stone on the way there. A village chief provided him with a small boat, very low in the water and manned by an unwilling crew. Soon after setting out towards Kei, they were swept here and there at the mercy of the powerful currents, and Wallace became extremely seasick. Wisely he decided to turn back, before he and the men finished up on the coast of New Guinea where they risked being murdered by the natives. Abandoning his scheme to get to Kei, Wallace came up with the idea of buying a second-hand prahu in Gorong, fitting it out as his own exploring boat and then manning it with his own hired crew. That way, or so he thought, he would be more in control of his own travel arrangements.

He found the prahu he was looking for on the island of Manowolko, bought it for £9, and had it delivered across the strait to Gorong where there were some itinerant boatbuilders from Kei to help him with the conversion. A Kei island shipwright did the major overhaul, putting in new ribs, but Wallace found that it was easier to do the inside work by himself. His hard times as a youth helping out the carpenters in a London builder's yard now paid off. The islanders were amazed to see a white craftsman working with his hands. 'Luckily I had a few tools of my own, including a small saw and some chisels,' wrote Wallace, 'and these were now severely tried, cutting and fitting heavy ironwood planks for the flooring and the posts that support the triangular mast. Being of the best London make they stood the work well, and without them it would have been impossible for me to have finished my boat with half the neatness or in double the time . . . My gimlets were, however, too small; and having no augurs, we were obliged to bore all the holes with hot irons.' This was Wallace at his very best: practical, skilled and energetic, prepared to roll up his sleeves with no concern for what the local people thought of him, keen only to get a job done properly and quickly.

The five Gorong islanders whom Wallace hired to do general work on the boat and then sail as his crew took the attitude that if the white man was crazy enough to work at such a pace, then it meant they could do less. They avoided showing up for work, and invented every excuse: 'The uncle of one had commenced a war, or sort of faction fight, and wanted his assistance; another's wife was ill and would not let him come; a third had fever and ague, and pains in his head and back; and a fourth had an inexorable creditor who would not let him go out of his sight. They had all received a month's wages in advance; and though the amount was not large, it was necessary to make them pay it back, or I would get no men at all. I therefore sent the village constable after two, and kept them in custody a day, when they returned about three-fourths of what they owed me. The sick man also paid, and the steersman found a substitute who was willing to take his debt, and receive the balance of his wages.'

Wallace was now in an area of the Spice Islands which might have been called 'the sago zone'. It was a region where the main diet came from the sago palm which grew particularly well in the low swampy areas of eastern Seram and the nearby islands. As a believer in Robert Owen's ideas, Wallace believed that the environment had a profound effect on the way people developed. The sago-eating peoples, he concluded, achieved little in life because they had no real need to work. The sago palm provided enough food to keep them and their families alive with the barest minimum of effort, and he set about to prove it. By simple arithmetic he showed that a single good-sized sago palm produced enough sago to make 30 blocks or tomans of sago flour, each weighing 30 lbs, and that each toman could be baked into 60 sago cakes. Five of these cakes were enough food for one man for one day, and the raw sago flour kept very well so that once it was prepared it could be stored for many months in reserve. Wallace described how the sago palm was felled, its trunk chopped up and turned into flour, and he reckoned that in just ten days' work a man could supply himself with enough cheap food for a year. 'The effect of this cheapness of food is decidedly prejudicial,' he concluded, 'for the inhabitants of the sago country are never so well off as those where rice is cultivated. Many of the people here have neither vegetables nor

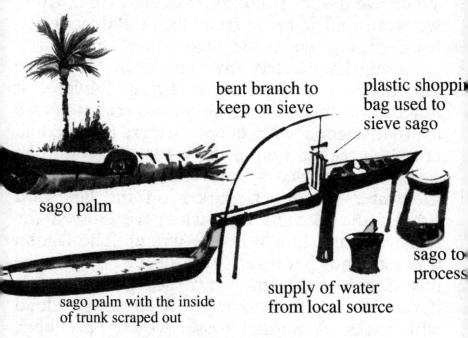

bent branch to keep on sieve

plastic shoppi▸ bag used to sieve sago

sago palm

sago to process

sago palm with the inside of trunk scraped out

supply of water from local source

Sago-making utensuils

fruit but live exclusively on sago and a little fish. Having few occupations at home, they wander about on petty trading or fishing expeditions to the neighbouring islands; and as far as the comforts of life are concerned are much inferior to the wild Hill Dyaks of Borneo or to many of the more barbarous tribes of the Archipelago.'

More than a century after Wallace's visit, the people of Gorong were still habitual sago-eaters. Toman upon toman of sago flour was stacked up in the little shops of Kataloko. The tomans were the shape of small solid drums wrapped in green palm leaves, or you could buy the sago flour already baked into biscuits and neatly tied with string into bundles often. Then they looked exactly like small, hard, light brown floor-tiles. When we asked where all this sago came from, we were told it came from the island opposite, from Pasang where the sago palms still grew.

Pasang had a deceptive approach. From the direction we arrived with *Alfred Wallace*, it looked as if the usual fringing coral reef protected a broad lagoon with deeper water; if we could cross the reef and enter the lagoon we would be safe. At least, that is how it appeared, because the water was much darker on the landward side of the reef. In fact, when we crossed the reef we found that we were wrong. The lagoon was dark not because it was deep, but because it was carpeted with brown sea grass. In fact it was barely 50 centimetres deep and studded with rocks. A normal vessel would have been stuck fast, but again *Alfred Wallace* needed so little water to float that we could pole our way through the shallows for a kilometre or more until we were able to anchor off the main village of the island. From there a guide took us into the sago swamps.

The sago palms appeared to be wild, but were in fact planted as seedlings in the muck and stagnant pools of the swamp. For 12 – 15 years the palm tree grew until its trunk was approximately one metre thick. Then, quite suddenly, the tree flowered and was ready to harvest. The owner felled the tree, peeled off the skin and chopped his way into the thick white soft trunk. We found a sago harvester at work, sitting inside the tree-trunk as if in a large dugout canoe. In front of him was the unworked face of white sago pith, and he was steadily hacking at it with a long handle which had a tiny sharp metal blade set at right-angles in the end. As he struck, the blade sliced away a sliver of sago pith which fell inside the hollow trunk and on to his feet. The blade also came alarmingly close to his feet with each blow, and it seemed he risked chopping off his toes. Occasionally he wriggled his feet and toes, pushing the growing pile of the sago shavings back down the hollow tree-trunk. When he was tired of chopping, he climbed out of the tree-trunk, filled a sack with sago shavings and carried them off through the squelching mud to a trough which he had set up beside a pool of stagnant swamp water. He dumped the shavings into the upper end of the trough, poured water over them from a bucket, and squeezed the wet pith against a cloth strainer. The water ran out of the sago pith as white as milk, carrying sago flour with it, and drained away into another trough where it was allowed to settle. Within an hour, a thick deposit of pure white edible sago flour had settled in the trough and could be scooped out with the hands. It was ready to bake and eat.

The sago gatherer claimed that in just two days' work he could produce enough food to feed his family for a month. As for the sago palm, he said, once you had planted the seedling there was no more work involved. You merely had to let it grow. Apart from Joe, who rather liked the taste of sago biscuit, the rest of us wondered if it was even worth that much effort. We compared eating sago with buying a packet of breakfast cereal, throwing away the contents and eating the cardboard packet.

When, late in May 1860, Wallace was ready to leave Gorong aboard his re-fitted prahu, he laid in a supply of freshly baked sago as ship's stores. His new plan was to cross to Seram, then coast around to a Dutch coaling station at a place called Wahai. From there he would strike across the open sea towards the 'Bird's Head' region of Irian Jaya. This was where, in a region called Waigeo, he believed he would be able to collect specimens of a little known and very valuable Bird of Paradise, called the Red Bird of Paradise. His crew for the venture had been recruited in Gorong, though there were so few volunteers that he had been obliged to take on one man who was a self-confessed opium addict.

As it turned out, the voyage was to be one emergency after another, beginning at his first port of call in Seram where his crew from Gorong deserted en masse, taking with them, as he wryly put it, 'all they had brought with them, and a little more'.

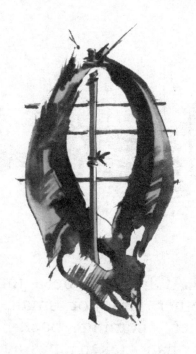

Dried fish on stick

8

Red Birds of Paradise

WALLACE could be a Jonah in boats, whether large or small. Eight years earlier, coming back from South America, he had taken passage aboard a small and unlucky brig, the *Helen*. His luggage consisted of hundreds of new species of insects and bird-skins gathered at great effort in his jungle travels, and a 20-strong menagerie of parrots and parakeets, several rare monkeys and a forest wild dog. These he planned to sell in London, with the help of his agent Samuel Stevens, and make a profit on his four years' explorations in the Amazon basin. Unfortunately the *Helen* also shipped 40 casks of a volatile natural oil, known as 'balsam-capivi', used in the making of varnish. This oil was a fire hazard, as it could ignite by spontaneous combustion. Twenty casks of the oil were properly stowed, packed in wet sand; but the remainder were packed, with almost criminal negligence, in rice chaff and placed deep in the main hold. Three weeks into the voyage the captain approached Wallace after breakfast one morning, and calmly said to him, 'I'm afraid the ship's on fire. Come and see what you think of it.' Going on deck, Wallace saw thick smoke oozing up from the forward deck. The crew began opening hatches, and throwing cargo overboard to try to get at the source of the fire. But the blaze came from the buried balsam-capivi and it was impossible to reach the source before the worsening smoke drove them back. By now the main cabin, where Wallace had his own accommodation, was also filling with smoke, and it was becoming dangerous to go below.

The captain of the *Helen* decided it would be prudent to prepare an evacuation. The sailors were ordered to get the two small boats — the long-boat and the captain's gig — over the side and ready. When they touched the water, the boats were found to be leaky, and the leaks had to be plugged with corks. Then the sailors dropped in so many of their personal belongings that the boats began to sink and had to be baled out. Meanwhile poor Wallace, unable to get to his precious collections due to the suffocating smoke, could only gather up a small shirt box in which he put his drawings of Brazilian plants and fishes, his watch and a purse with a few

227

sovereigns. This was his entire luggage as he stood on deck, awaiting captain's orders. With the boats towing astern the crew again tried fighting the fire. The balsam capivi could be heard bubbling and hissing below the cabin floor, and soon the flames broke through and came belching up through the cabin skylight.

The captain ordered everyone to abandon ship, and Wallace slid down the rope to the boat. 'Being rather weak it slipped through my hands, and took the skin off all my fingers, and finding the boat still half full of water I set to bailing, which made my hands smart very painfully.'

It had been just three hours since the fire was spotted, and for the remainder of the afternoon the crew — safe in the boats — watched the *Helen* burn spectacularly. The flames rushed up into the rigging, the sails went ablaze, and soon the masts toppled overboard. As the fire continued to eat away the ship, the ironwork became red-hot, the decks caved in and finally the bowsprit fell away. With only a slight swell on the ocean there was no immediate danger to the ship's boats, and the captain decided to keep close to the dying *Helen* in the hopes that the great pillar of smoke and flames from the burning cargo of rubber would attract passing shipping. But by the next morning no rescuers had appeared, the *Helen* had burned to the waterline and rolled over, and the two lifeboats hoisted sail and moved clear.

Wallace watched his precious collections slip beneath the waves. Fortunately he had already sent ahead from Brazil a portion of his specimens, which would raise enough to cover his field expenses. But he had counted on making a profit of £500 on the remainder to recompense his four years' toil. Far worse, though, was the destruction of his private collection which he had hoped to study in England, then to publish the results and lay the foundation of a reputation as a scientific naturalist rather than a mere commercial collector. The collection included hundreds of previously unknown species. Now they were all gone, along with his notes, sketches and even his personal journals. 'You will see,' he wrote to a friend describing the disaster, 'that I have some need of philosophic resignation to bear my fate with patience and equanimity.'

After ten desperate days in the ship's boats, scorched and blistered by the sun and living on dry biscuits, preserved pork and water, the castaways were picked up by a passing merchant vessel. To add to their trouble, their rescuer was a ship so old, decrepit and slow that it too almost went to the bottom in a gale, and eventually limped into port at Deal on the Kent coast after a record slow passage. Wallace stepped ashore with no other worldly possessions than '£5 and a thin calico suit'. He was saved from utter financial ruin by the fact that his agent Samuel Stevens had — unasked — taken out insurance on the lost cargo.

Wallace's bad luck with boats now reappeared and bedevilled his efforts to sail from Seram to Waigeo in command of his own small prahu. At Wahai he recruited four men to replace the

Gorong runaways, then he set out for the island of Mysol as his first stage on the route. His prahu was unable to sail close to the wind, so the elderly Muslim pilot he had hired in Wahai used the land breeze to work eastward along the Seram coast until they were opposite Mysol and could strike directly northward, a crossing of about 60 miles. The pilot knew these waters well and he assured Wallace that an east-going current would help them keep a good course. Unfortunately, a strong cross-wind tossed the little prahu about so badly that once again poor Wallace fell very seasick. Worse, the waves beat the prahu off course until they missed their landing on Mysol and had to head for a small island just off the coast. At 9 in the evening they had sailed within 200 yards of this island, and Wallace was looking forward to getting on dry land and having a hot coffee, a good meal and some sound sleep, when the wind failed. The crew got out the oars and began rowing, but 'a ripple of water told us we were seized by one of those treacherous currents which so frequently frustrate all the efforts of a voyager in these seas; the men threw down their oars in despair, and in a few minutes we drifted to the leeward of the island fairly out to sea again, and lost our chance of ever reaching Mysol!'

Wallace and his men now had no choice but to press on, hoping to land on the next island along their route. But the wind teased them. It blew them one way, then in the opposite direction, and finally whipped up such a short, tumbling sea that the travellers feared their undecked vessel would be swamped. They had to drop the heavy mainsail and run for safety under jib alone. In this haphazard fashion they were blown past first one island, then another and, after four days of misery since leaving Wahai, finally managed to come to anchor in the lee of two small islands and get some rest. It was a poor place to halt, with a fringing reef and the unreliable holding ground strewn with rocks. Wallace had kind words for the elderly pilot, who had never left his post at the helm except for an hour at a time to get some rest. Wallace now proposed that two men go ashore to cut some jungle vine to use as extra anchor rope, so that they could put down additional anchors to hold the prahu as the wind was blowing offshore. His crew overruled him, and assured him that they could row the prahu into a safer anchorage. But the moment they hoisted anchor and began to row, the current again began to carry them farther offshore. Once more they dropped anchor, and two of the best men swam to the beach with a hatchet to cut the extra rope. While they were away, the anchor began to slip. Hastily Wallace and the remaining crew threw their spare anchor overboard to try to hold the boat. But it was useless, and the prahu began to drag farther. Desperately Wallace fired off muskets to alert the shore party, and they could be seen running up and down the beach gesticulating wildly. The prahu continued to drift out to sea, though slowly enough for Wallace to hope that the castaways could make themselves a raft and paddle out to rejoin them.

To his astonishment, he saw them stop running up and down and proceed to light a fire to cook some shellfish they had gathered.

The prahu now drifted off towards the second island, leaving the two men marooned, perhaps to die of thirst. Conditions on the prahu were little better. The crew was so short-handed that they had barely enough strength to hoist the heavy mainsail, and there was only two days' supply of water on board. By dint of hard rowing they succeeded in bringing the prahu close enough to the second island to anchor there, though once again it was on a coral-strewn sea floor. Wallace resolved to stay at that spot as long as he could, still hoping to give his two castaways a chance to make a raft. He waited two days on the small uninhabited island, lighting signal fires to let his men know that the prahu was nearby. He and his remaining crew also searched for water, but found only a dirty stinking stagnant pool in a sago swamp which was filled with muck and rubbish. Believing it to be a spring, they emptied the pool and cleaned out the rubbish hoping it would refill. But when they returned, they found it contained only a few cups of liquid mud and was merely a rainwater catchment. They cut bamboos as digging sticks and were preparing to dig for water when, by chance, Wallace came across two rock holes which held enough rainwater to refill their canisters. By then it was obvious that they could stay no longer. Their anchor cable had already been cut through by chafe on the coral, and if it had happened in the night they would have been carried away helplessly. Besides, Wallace calculated that the castaways must also have found sago palms on their island and could survive until he sent someone to pick them up. So he set off once again, and by the following morning the coast of Waigeo was in sight.

Their misfortunes continued, for the little prahu ran on to one coral reef after another, fortunately without harm. For eight days it bumped and lurched its way along the coast seeking a path through the maze of small islands. Wallace was looking for the channel which would take them through to the settlement of Mukar, where they might find help. Eventually, after several false attempts and seeing not a soul for day after day, they came across a small native village of just seven huts, where they could get guides. The entrance to the channel, they learned, was so well hidden in the jungle that it needed local knowledge to find it. Once through the channel and arrived at Mukar, Wallace immediately hired a small boat and three men to go back and pick up the two castaways. The first rescue mission was thwarted by bad weather, but the boat eventually returned with the two men who were thin but well. For a month they had lived on shellfish, the roots of wild plants and turtle eggs. They told Wallace that they had been too frightened to cross the straits to reach the second island, though they had seen his signal fires. However, they were confident that he would eventually send help. It was a brief glimpse of how his men trusted their tall, bespectacled leader who, in his turn, 'felt much relieved that my voyage, though sufficiently unfortunate, had not involved loss of life'.

★ ★ ★

Wahai, where Wallace had recruited his unlucky crew, almost wrecked our own vessel. We had come up the coast of Seram on a fine easterly breeze; it was superb sailing, with the imposing spectacle of Seram steadily unfolding on the port side. Behind the coconut groves of the shoreline rose range upon range of jungle-covered mountains, increasing in altitude as we headed north. On both evenings of the passage a flamboyant sunset turned these ranges into every shade of purple, and set them against a pink sky with towering white thunderclouds as a backdrop. Then, after sundown each evening, the wind died away completely for about three hours, and we ran the little outboard engine until the wind would pick up soon after midnight. So by chance we approached Wahai with the engine running.

The lights of the town, only the second group of shore lights we had seen since leaving Pasang, beckoned. The rest of the Seram had been dark. Turning our boat towards the lights, I decided to get close to the town and then wait, drifting, until daylight came and we could see our path into harbour. Some sixth sense made me stop the engine sooner than normal, at least a mile offshore. In the sudden silence that followed, we heard the frightening grumble and crash of surf very close by. Joe shone a torch over the side, and the light bounced back off a coral ledge barely four feet beneath us. The surf was coming from waves breaking on a coral reef 100 metres ahead. If we had continued on, we would have smashed our boat.

Even in broad daylight it was difficult to find the dog-leg passage into Wahai, and we had to follow a big canoe loaded with fishermen to the gap through the reef. The town itself kept only one sign of its colonial past — a crumbling stone jetty where the Dutch coaling ships had tied. Here Budi and Julia joined us from the educational programme — 27 talks at different schools in Ambon and west Seram in the previous fortnight.

Leaving Wahai to go north in Wallace's wake, we diverted to investigate a ship which seemed to have run ashore some miles down the coast. It was a tall, old-fashioned freighter of about 10,000 tons, and from a distance it looked as if it had its stern on the beach. But when we came closer we saw that it was anchored in a natural basin within yards of the beach, with stern lines running to some palm trees. On the sand were piles of enormous logs, 15 metres in length and up to two metres in diameter. They had been cut from the rainforest in the interior and were being pushed into the sea, one by one, by massive bulldozers. From there they were hoisted aboard the freighter and then carried to Kalimantan to be sliced into plywood. It seemed utterly wasteful to squander

Logging camp, Seram beach

magnificent timber in this way, quite apart from the destruction of the rainforest in Seram. The timber companies had already levelled most of the forests of Kalimantan and now they were turning their attention to Seram. The great trees which supplied those enormous logs had taken at least a century to grow, and even with the best forest conservation practice they could never be replaced.

We spent the night anchored alongside the freighter, and in the darkness several of the great logs broke free. They came bobbing in the tide, nuzzling *Alfred Wallace* like enormous battering rams, and we had an active evening as temporary lumberjacks, running up and down the floating logs and poling them clear. Each of the massive runaway logs, if delivered into Europe, would have been very valuable. But in Seram no one bothered to retrieve them; they simply drifted away on the tide.

The Admiralty Pilot book cautioned that the coast of Waigeo, where we were now headed, was not fully examined, and great care should be taken in the approach. The usual telltales were not be trusted, and the mariner should not rely on the discoloration of water to indicate reefs and shoals, as these could exist without any outward sign. The warning was underlined by a bizarre incident as we crossed the Seram Sea when a large ship radioed an alert. The captain reported that his vessel had scraped her keel on the sea floor. The ship drew nine metres, but at that point in the middle of the Seram Sea the chart showed the water to be 600 metres deep. The uncharted obstacle was a complete mystery.

The first sight of Waigeo was nothing like any coastline we had previously seen. It was neither the low outline of coral islands like Kei and Aru, nor the steep volcanic cone of Banda, nor the high razor-back ridges of Seram. Instead Waigeo was a low, flattish land covered with dozens and dozens of small rounded hills, so that it appeared rumpled and bumpy as far as the eye could see. The land was also far more extensive. It lay right across our horizon as one of the least populated regions of Indonesia, a mass of dense forest and scrub, often without fresh water and hostile to settlement. There were no roads, and the few villages were scattered along the immense contorted coastline. Waigeo was so isolated and unappealing that its condition and population had hardly changed since Wallace's time.

The hummocks and bumps of the landscape, where they were submerged by the sea, became dozens of islands and coastal islets. They came in every shape and size, from small isolated rocks to substantial chunks of land steep-sided with cliffs and crowned with vegetation. They were all uninhabited except for one small atoll which had a ring of coconut palms and a small fishing village, and they bore strange names like Gag and Fam. The impression was of a wilderness, half land, half water, where the only creatures were small flocks of black-cap terns and the occasional frigate bird. As we threaded our way through this strange empty landscape where Wallace and his little prahu had spent so much of their time bumping off the coral reefs, it was easy to see how this had happened. There were no obvious channels, and the many islands were so confusing that it was impossible to tell which pieces of land were joined to the coast and which were true islands. The Waigeo coast was riddled with deep bays and inlets, and it was easy to be misled and to wander uselessly — turning into a bay, hoping that it was a channel, but then finding that it was blocked.

Wallace gave no name for the little village of seven huts where he had picked up his guides, but the clue to its whereabouts was the channel which he described. It 'resembled a small river, and was concealed by a projecting point so that no wonder we did not discover it amid the dense forest vegetation which everywhere covers these islands to the water's edge. A little way inside it becomes bounded by precipitous rocks, after winding among which for about two miles, we emerged into what seemed a lake, but was in fact a deep gulf having a narrow entrance on the south coast. This gulf was studded along its shores with numbers of rocky islets, mostly mushroom shaped, from the water having worn away the lower part of the soluble crystalline limestone, leaving them overhanging from ten to twenty feet.'

His description fits only one place on the Waigeo coast: the Kaboei Channel. This is an oddity, a natural canal made by a deep winding sea cleft which cuts right through a high jungle-covered neck of land and joins two wide bays. The Channel was marked on our chart, but even with the advantage of the modern map it was not clear just which bay hid its entrance. The sides of every inlet were so thickly clothed with virgin forest that it was impossible to tell. The coast itself appeared utterly deserted and, after we had passed the little settlement on the offshore atoll, we did not see a single hut or column of smoke for half a day as we twisted and turned our way among the islands. We wanted to locate the unnamed village where Wallace had obtained his guides, but there was no certainty that it existed any longer. Even if we did come across people, it was not sure that they would still be settled on the same spot where Wallace had found them. The small villages of the Moluccas have a habit of relocating suddenly. The villagers — usually no more than a dozen families — frequently change the location of their houses which need only a couple of days to erect on a new site. They may move to find better fishing, to a safer anchorage and — above all — to an easier source of fresh water.

It was well into the afternoon when the last of the large bays opened up. Ahead of us the afternoon thunderstorms were rolling across the forested ridges and slopes of Waigeo. Surges of grey-black cloud flowed across the tree canopy on a broad front. The wind came ahead, whipping the tops off the wavelets in the bay. Lightning flickered in the depths of the cloud, and then the curtain of grey rain blotted out everything. When the rain cleared we had a glimpse of a tiny white dot in the murk at the back of the bay. It might have been a landmark erected for navigators, but there are no such marks in Waigeo. We set course for it, and crossing the broad bay we found the spire of a tiny, white painted church. In front were a dozen or so palm-thatch houses set on stilts on the water's edge. The jungle came down the hillside to within yards of this tiny village, which looked as if it was about to be swallowed in the vegetation.

We anchored and, minutes later, there was the usual response when four canoes put out from the village to visit us. But these were canoes like nothing we had ever seen before. The central hull was a very narrow dugout log, tapering to a fine bow. From each side sprang delicate outriggers that would have done credit to a modern high technology aircraft. They curved out in a beautiful downward line so that the floats barely kissed the water. There was not a nail nor ounce of metal in the entire construction. The sweeping outriggers had been carved from naturally curved wood, and were bound in place with neat strips of jungle rattan. They were so well made and exquisitely balanced that they flexed like the wings of birds, and the entire canoe floated high and light as it skimmed forward.

The men in the canoes were pure Papuan with not a trace of Malay in their features. They had tightly curled wiry hair, broad nostrils, deep-set eyes, and very dark skins. In the lead canoe the grey-haired headman of the village was obvious from the deference paid to him by the other men. The canoes clustered around the stern of our prahu, and half a dozen men scrambled on deck. Budi and Julia made introductions and explained why we had come there. The villagers were intrigued to know about their unexpected visitors because the last time they had seen a foreigner was seven years earlier when a butterfly hunter had come to their village.

Now we explained about Wallace and how he had travelled to Waigeo in search of one particular species of Bird of Paradise, the rare Red Bird of Paradise. His long voyage, his tribulations at sea, had all been devoted to the idea of obtaining specimens of this species which, as far as he was aware, could be found nowhere else on earth.[1] As he fumbled his way along the coast, he had heard the calls of the Birds of Paradise from the nearby jungle. At the Kaboei village where he had picked up his guides for the canal he had caught a glimpse of one or two birds, but not been able to shoot them for collection. Even more tantalising, when he got to Muka the birds were very scarce and shy. It was some days before he got within shot of one of them, and then his gun missed fire and the bird was 'off in an instant among the thickest jungle'. Another day he and his hunters saw

---

[1] In this idea he was largely correct. The main population of the Red Bird of Paradise is in Waigeo, with a smaller population on the island of Batanta 50 kilometres to the south.

no fewer than eight fine males, and shot at them four times, but missed on every occasion until, 'I began to think we were not to get this magnificent species.' Finally he was successful in shooting one of the birds which came each morning to feed on a ripening fig tree close by the little house where he lodged. He shot a second bird a few days later, but after that the Red Bird of Paradise disappeared from the locality 'either owing to the fruit becoming scarce, or they were wise enough to know there was danger'.

Given that Wallace himself had the greatest difficulty finding Red Birds of Paradise in the area of Kaboei some 140 years earlier, we were not hopeful about our own chances. There were very few modern reports about these birds in Waigeo, and although the area had been declared a protected area for wildlife this was largely an administrative fiction. We never saw a warden or a forest patrol, and the area was so remote that almost anything could happen there without the central authorities knowing. Nevertheless, when the village boarding party had sat down in a circle on the aft deck of the prahu, Budi produced his bird-identification book and opened it on the page showing coloured illustrations of all the different species of Birds of Paradise. He laid the book down on the deck so that our guests could see the illustrations clearly. Had anyone ever seen any of these birds near their village, Julia asked. At least four brown hands shot out, and pointed at the picture of the Red Bird of Paradise. Were they sure? Our guests nodded in an absent-minded way. They were looking with great interest at the pictures of the other species which, it turned out, were entirely new to them. Were they absolutely certain about the Red Bird of Paradise, Julia enquired once more. Again they all nodded without hesitation. Did they see them often? 'Oh, yes,' replied the headman casually, 'there are many of them.'

This was remarkable, if it was correct. 'Ask

Red Bird of Paradise

them where we could we see the birds for ourselves,' I said to Julia. She relayed the question, and the village headman replied that the birds were nearly everywhere in the forests around the village, but the best place to see them was in the trees where they 'played' in the morning and evening. Was there just one tree? No, replied the headman, there were several trees and in different places, and different birds came to each tree. Could he show us where the trees were? The headman rose to his feet and, standing on the deck, pointed in several directions around the bay. There were dancing trees there, he said, and there, and there.

It seemed too good to be true. Far from being threatened with extinction, a large population of Red Birds of Paradise was apparently thriving near Kaboei, unrecorded. 'Do you catch the birds?' asked Julia. 'Oh no,' said the headman promptly, 'the government does not allow that. It is forbidden to hunt these birds.'

Next morning, still a little sceptical, we went ashore to check whether there were really any Red Birds of Paradise. We were led into the forest by two guides from the village, and struggled through the dense vegetation for two sweat-drenched hours without seeing a single Bird of Paradise, nor hearing one. We feared that our suspicions were being confirmed when finally Julia asked when we would reach a 'playing tree', and our guides looked puzzled. Julia explained that we had asked specifically to be shown Red Birds of Paradise, and the senior guide became embarrassed. There had been a

Kaboei hut

mix-up; he thought the village headman had asked him merely to take us on a trek through the forest.

It was now too late in the day to see the birds easily, the guide said apologetically. They would have scattered from the 'playing trees' and gone into the forests to feed. But the guide did his best to oblige. As he took us back to the village, he stopped from time to time and listened. Then he pinched his nostrils shut with one hand and, by making a sharp squawking noise in the back of his throat and expelling the air from the side of his mouth at the same time, he gave a strangled puffing cry. It was a very close imitation of the tuneless 'wawk, wawk, wawk' of the Bird of Paradise we had heard in Aru. Once or twice we thought we heard an answer and finally, right towards the end of our walk as we were nearing the village again, we saw a single Bird of Paradise fluttering high up in the branches of the tall forest. Our search had been most unsatisfactory, and a little puzzling. Where were the Red Birds of Paradise? And if the natives did not hunt them, how was it that they knew how to imitate their calls?

The misunderstanding, it turned out, was genuine. The village headman had not realised we wanted to see the birds themselves in a display tree, and that afternoon his younger brother paddled over from the opposite side of the bay in his canoe and invited us to visit the 'playing tree' near his hut. The best time, he said, would be about 7 o'clock in the morning when the birds assembled to 'play' before going off into the forest to feed.

Next morning in the dawn light we set off as passengers aboard a little flotilla of three elegant canoes, skimming forward as our hosts paddled along the shoreline. They landed us in a small inlet where a large tree lay in the water as a landing pontoon among the tangle of mangrove roots. From there we scrambled up a steep bank to the start of a well-defined path. Our leader was the headman's younger brother, a cheerful man in his mid-thirties and built like a champion wrestler. He had tremendous gusto and was always smiling and chuckling. It would have been pleasant to dawdle, but he was obviously keen to get us to the dancing tree before the Birds of Paradise arrived for their morning display. So we went along briskly, clambering over tangled and exposed roots, slipping on brown leaves lying on the dark red earth, and occasionally balancing our way along huge tree-trunks which served as footbridges over small ravines. The woodland colours and shapes could just as well have been in a gigantic, overgrown beech forest in Europe, but for the amazing bird-life we startled at that early hour. Flights of white cockatoos went shrieking and screaming overhead. Several giant ground pigeons leaped up from their feeding on the forest floor, and went flying up through the lower branches of the trees with a great, heavy slow thrashing of their massive wings as if they were wild turkeys. Smaller pigeons raced off with the more typically explosive clatter of their wings, and two pairs of hornbills stolidly flew overhead, one after another in a straight flight path, with the steady

Watching the Red Birds of Paradise

swishing of their wings reminiscent of swans in flight.

We had been walking fast for about twenty minutes, following the ridge line, when we came to a small clearing in the forest. Here several tall trees stood apart, and our genial guide gave a great grin and motioned us to sit down and wait. Sure enough, at about a quarter to seven, the Birds of Paradise flew in, assembling from different directions. The first glimpse was of a quick russet-brown flicker of quite a small bird flying with very fast wing-beats, and abruptly settling on a branch high up in a tree. You would think nothing of this creature until you used binoculars and brought into focus a bravura display of plumes. The bird had a fine yellow head, green throat, and its tail was a brilliant scarlet cascade of feathers hanging in an arching curve. Drooping from this amazing tail were two elegant feathers, more like wires, which hung in a spiral and gently swayed in the air. These were the male Red Birds of Paradise, of a most extraordinary beauty and variety of colours.

At least half a dozen of the birds settled on their individual branches at any one time, and from these superb creatures came that remarkably ugly 'wawk, wawk, wawk'. Then they would fall silent and follow up with a gurgle and chirrup, like the sound of a wet cork being drawn slowly out of a bottle. They would repeat this sound two or three times, and then return to the 'wawk, wawk, wawk'. After calling back and forth, they began to perform their dance. The display trees were very tall, about 25 metres high, and the birds stayed high up, so binoculars were needed to see the details of the dance. They would raise their wings and shuffle up and down the branch from side to side. Then they would halt and spread their superb scarlet tails and shiver the cluster of feathers by waggling their rumps. Behind them the long black tail wires swayed from side to side. All the while, as they showed off, they were shouting their coarse 'wawk wawk, wawk'. They appeared to be displaying towards one another, but they were really showing off for the benefit of the females — little drab birds which flicked back and forth across the display area, watching the males in all their glory.

Quite suddenly, after about twenty minutes, the male birds flew away, heading in different directions to the fruiting trees in the forest where they would feed. Our cheerful guide led us back to the landing place, grinning mischievously as he stopped from time to time to mimic the Birds of Paradise by waggling his bottom and going into a stuttering dance. If we cared to come back to the same spot at about 5 in the evening, he said, we would see the display all over again. And the same would be true the next morning and following evening, and the day after that, and the next day too. The Birds of Paradise never failed to appear and 'play' in the trees.

By now it was obvious to us that the villagers of Kaboei knew a great deal about the Red Birds of Paradise, and that this interest was not accidental. They also had more confidence in us now, and they answered Julia's questions rather more truthfully. The headman's denial that they hunted the birds was a lie. The villagers (or rather half a dozen of them), did hunt the birds, and they did so very professionally. One technique, our cheerful guide told us, was to shoot the birds with a bow and an arrow tipped with a hard round fruit he called the 'eyeball fruit'. Struck by such an arrow, the Bird of Paradise was killed yet his plumes were not spoiled. Or the hunter would climb into a fruit tree with a length of fishing line and set a noose as a snare. Sitting patiently until the bird landed to feed, the hunter tugged at the snare, trapping the bird by the leg, and brought it down alive.

It was almost exactly what Wallace himself had described, though in his day the bird-hunters had fixed decoy fruit as well. They took

a red reticulated fruit of which the birds are very fond. They (the hunters) fasten this fruit on a stout forked stick, and provide themselves with a fine but strong cord. They then seek out some tree in the forest on which these birds are accustomed to perch, and climbing up it fasten the stick to a branch and arrange the cord in a noose so ingeniously that when the bird comes to eat the fruit its legs are caught, and by pulling the end of the cord, which hangs down to the ground, it comes free from the branch and brings down the bird. Sometimes, when food is abundant elsewhere, the hunter sits from morning till night under his tree with the cord in his hand, and even for two or three whole days in succession, without even getting a bite; while on the other hand, if very lucky, he may get two or three birds in a day. There are only eight or ten men . . . who practise this art and it is unknown anywhere else in the island.

'Are many birds caught alive?' Julia asked. That depended on the season of the year, the market and the luck of the hunters, came the reply. Normally, the village sold two or three pairs of live Birds of Paradise every month. They were sold secretly to bird-dealers in the town of Sorong, a couple of days away by boat, and the price was usually 125,000 rupiah for a pair, male and female. The smart little church which had guided us to Kaboei had been built from the profits made from selling Red Birds of Paradise. 'How about the government officials?' Julia enquired, asking if there was not a problem with illegally trading these protected birds? The guide shrugged genially. He didn't know anything about that. The bird-dealers in Sorong paid bribes to officials as necessary, and this was the dealers' responsibility. The hunters merely delivered the birds and left such matters to the money men. The only irritation was the greed of the minor officials in the local administrative centre at Saonek. Most traffic en route to Sorong called at Saonek and, if the local officials there knew you were carrying Birds of Paradise, they demanded bribes as well. To avoid this, the hunters preferred to take the birds direct to Sorong and not call at Saonek, though this was a difficult and rather dangerous sea crossing in a small boat.

These blithe revelations of a flourishing and highly illegal trade in the Red Birds of Paradise were, at first sight, completely at odds with the fact that Kaboei boasted such a thriving population of the birds. Quite possibly, Kaboei possessed the most significant population of Red Birds of Paradise in Waigeo, or indeed anywhere. Then, as Julia continued her questions, the explanation became clear: the people of Kaboei were not ruthless in their exploitation of the bird population. They and their forebears had been cropping the Birds of Paradise for generations. Wallace had mentioned that the Sultan of Tidore demanded a small annual tribute of feathers from the Red Bird of Paradise, and these feathers had been supplied by native hunters. Over the years a system of exploitation and ownership had developed. Around Kaboei the display trees and the birds which danced in them were not public property. Each tree was owned by a Kaboei family or a group which had the right to take the birds from that tree. Naturally, if too many birds were taken from a particular tree so that the population failed, then the owners had ruined a major source of income. By the same token, the owners of the tree would make sure that no one poached or destroyed the tree and its surrounding area. At a wider level, the entire community benefited from the harvesting of the Red Bird of Paradise, for all the village shared in the revenue when it was devoted to such communal matters as church-building.

The risk, of course, was that individual tree owners would be too greedy, or the community would apply pressure for too much ready cash and so destroy the resource. But as yet that had not happened, possibly because Kaboei remained a small enough community, and very few outsiders knew that there were so many Red Birds of Paradise in the area.

We were so impressed by the 'dancing tree' we had seen that we shifted *Alfred Wallace* across the bay and anchored in the nearby inlet which we nicknamed Bird of Paradise Creek. There we stayed for three days until our food began to run low. Every morning and evening we would clamber up the hill to watch the birds 'playing' in the tops of their trees, such a magnificent spectacle that it was easy to see why the rumour had spread that they danced in the sunlight and never came down to earth. Each evening we returned to our vessel, and in that still backwater listened to the night sounds of the forest which extended its tangle of mangrove roots into the shallows. We heard the trickle of water draining off the hillside, the gurgle of the tide, the plop of fish and the calls of the night birds. There were heavy crashes and cracking sounds as branches broke away and fell to the forest floor. Much closer there was the noise of heavy bodies pushing through undergrowth and occasionally entering the water. Yanis swore they were the sounds of crocodiles, but more likely they were the noises made by herds of wild pigs foraging in the forest.

Alfred Wallace would have been delighted that Kaboei, where he had found so few birds, now had such a successful population of his treasured Red Bird of Paradise. After his poor luck at Muka, where in a month he shot only two male Birds of Paradise, he shifted his base of operations to a little coastal village called Bessir, and employed local hunters to scour the forest and gather specimens for him. When they brought him live birds, he had a large bamboo cage made, with troughs for food and water, and tried to keep the creatures alive. The captive birds were given a diet of their preferred red jungle fruit and large numbers of live grasshoppers, as well as boiled rice. On

'My house at Bessir, in Waigeo'
(*taken from* The Malay Archipelago)

the first day of captivity the birds were always vigorous and active, in constant motion hopping from one perch to the next and clinging to the sides and top of the cage, and eating greedily. The second day they were less active, but still had good appetites. Sadly, by the morning of the third day the birds would be found dead at the bottom of the cage, and for no apparent reason. Wallace tried keeping alive the immature birds as well as the mature, but the experiment always failed. Sometimes the glorious creatures would be seized with convulsions and fall dead within hours. In the end, Wallace had to give up the attempt and concentrate on preserving specimens in as good a condition as possible.

He spent six weeks at Bessir, in what he called 'a dwarf's hut'. It was just eight feet square, and raised on posts so that the floor was four and a half feet above the ground. In this lower part, open on all sides, he set up his table, crouching almost double to get to his chair and remembering not to stand up too quickly and bang his head. There he sat, making his notes, dealing with his specimens, pinning rare butterflies, totally engrossed and knowing that he was the first white man ever to stay in that place. He even took his meals in this strange little shelter, though food was so scarce that he nearly starved. There was scarcely enough to eat in Bessir to feed the usual number of inhabitants, let alone their visitors. The natives were so hungry that they would eat unripe fruit, dig up vegetables before they were ready and even consume a fleshy seaweed which Wallace, half-dead with hunger, found too bitter and salty to stomach. Instead he gathered and ate the boiled tops of ferns for greens, and in place of fowls ate cockatoos.

The poor diet sapped his health, and he suffered from fevers and what he called 'brow ague', an intense pain on a small spot near the right temple. As bad as the worst toothache, it set in directly after breakfast each morning and lasted for two hours. At one stage he became so ill with fever that he thought he was going to die. He opened the last of two tins of soup, which he had been keeping for just such an emergency, and this he believed saved his life. Yet he refused to move on, knowing that this was the only chance he would ever have to make his collections in such a remote and unvisited location.

Finally he could stay no longer, but had to catch the last of the east monsoon to bring his 'small prahu' homeward. He had collected 73 species of birds, not a great number, but 12 of them were previously unrecorded, and he had assembled the skins of 24 fine specimens of the Red Bird of Paradise. 'I did not regret my visit to the island,' he concluded, 'although it by no means answered to my expectations.'

His final day in Waigeo ended on a happy note. He had already paid his local bird-hunters in advance, giving them axes, mirrors and beads against a promise of the number of birds each hunter thought he could collect. Most of the hunters had delivered their quota when it came time for Wallace to leave. One man, who had been unable to catch a single bird, very honestly returned the axe he had been given. Another hunter had promised he would catch six birds, but had only managed to catch five. The moment he had delivered the fifth one, he turned back immediately into the forest to fulfil his contract. On the final day, as Wallace had his boat loaded and was about to shove off, this hunter came running after him, holding a sixth bird. This, wrote Wallace, 'he handed me, saying with great satisfaction "Now I owe you nothing". These were remarkable and quite unexpected instances of honesty among the savages where it would have been very easy for them to have been dishonest without fear of detection or punishment.'

9

Bacan

WE carried away from Kaboei as favourable an impression of the villagers as Wallace had formed of the people at Bessir. During our visit the people were patient and friendly when answering our questions, or whom Joe was taking his photographs and Leonard was drawing their portraits. A young man from the village, Cornelius, paddled across to see us whenever he had a good catch of fish, and when we set out to continue on our journey he volunteered to act as our pilot, showing us the hidden entrance to the Kaboei Channel. Cornelius steered us clear of the hidden patches of coral in the bay — just as the Admiralty Pilot warned, there was no telltale discoloration of the water — and when the gap in the trees which marked the mouth of the channel became obvious, he nimbly dropped back into his outrigger canoe, which had been towing astern, and paddled off — to go hunting Birds of Paradise with a length of fishing line as his snare.

The Kaboei Channel was much more impressive than Wallace's description had led us to expect. Perhaps he travelled through it at low water, or on a slack tide, because he gave little impression of the power of the stream and the grandeur of the scenery. We travelled through it on 2 May, and on Cornelius' advice tackled the channel at high tide so that there was maximum depth of water. We also went against the last of the tidal flow so that we had better steering control through the twists and turns of the cutting. At its entry, the straat — as the Kaboei people called it, using the Dutch name — was about 50 metres across with mangrove forest on each side. Then the channel quickly narrowed to little more than half that width, and the mangroves gave way to a series of coral cliffs and crags which hemmed the channel into a number of sharp corners. Here the water came rushing through against us, swirling and sucking, and creating deep eddies in the tideway. The straat cut through a high ridge, so that all we could see of the sky was a broad blue strip overhead. Across that strip of sky flew an unlikely assortment of birds. On the one hand there were the birds of the sea — gulls, fish eagles and terns. But mingling with them were the birds of the rainforest, lories, parakeets and cockatoos crossing from one forested slope to the other.

At its narrowest point the channel turned almost at a right-angle between sheer walls. Here the current was running at five or six knots, and ricocheted from one cliff face to the other. To our right was the mouth of a deep cave in the cliff. According to Kaboei tradition, this was the place from which the ancestors of their people had first emerged. Opposite, and a few metres farther on, the rock face rose sheer from the racing water. This was a sacred site; tied against the rock about a metre above the surface of the water was an eclectic, selection of offerings to the spirits — several fish spears with barbed heads, a length of net, and some plastic squeezy bottles.

It took us half an hour to twist and turn our way through the channel before we emerged through a scatter of small islands where, in Wallace's words, 'every islet was covered with strange-looking shrubs and trees, and generally crowned by lofty and elegant palms which also studded the ridges of the mountainous shores, forming one of the most singular and picturesque landscapes I have ever seen.' This was Kaboei Bay itself, and on the far shore Waigeo again spread its characteristic panorama of low, rounded hills. Turning south to the mouth of the bay we made for Saonek, a settlement of drab houses on a small island with one new concrete jetty. Saonek was the administrative centre for the vast district of western Waigeo, and offered the only secondary school in the whole territory. The pupils had

Through Kaboei channel

to live on the island during term-time because they came from so far away, and for this reason the school was not well attended; most children in the remote parts of Waigeo never progressed beyond their village primary education. Saonek's tall water tower displayed the navigation light which guided the occasional ferry across the strait from Sorong, the chief town of north-west Irian Jaya and the modern hub of all communication with the rest of Indonesia.

Wallace never got as far as Sorong, preferring to return directly from Waigeo to his base of operations at Ternate. But he did hear that Sorong was a place where you could buy rare birds from the interior of New Guinea, and he sent a scout there — a young man by the name of Charles Allen who had ambitions to become a collector — with instructions to track down new species of Birds of Paradise.

Wallace had originally recruited Charles Allen in London to help as a field assistant, mending butterfly nets, pinning insects and generally making himself useful. During the first months in Indonesia, he had tried to teach Allen the necessary practical skills, but his pupil quickly showed that he was not really cut out to be an explorer-naturalist. He was very young — only 16 — and so clumsy that he was always dropping and breaking items and leaving a mess behind him. Poor maladroit Charles Allen could not even saw a piece of wood straight, even though his father was a carpenter, and he seemed incapable of doing neat work. 'Every day,' wrote Wallace to his sister in exasperation, 'some such conversation as this ensues: "Charles. Look at these butterflies that you set out yesterday." "Yes, Sir." "Look at that one — is it set evenly?" "No, Sir." "Put it right then, and all the others that want it." In five minutes he brings me the box to look at. "Have you put them all right?" "Yes, Sir." "There's one with the wings uneven, there's another with the body on one side, then another with the pin crooked. Put them all right this time." If he puts up a bird, the head is on one side, there is a lump of cotton on one side of the neck like a wen, the feet are twisted soles uppermost, or something else. In everything it is the same, what ought to be straight is always put crooked.' In short, Charles Allen was a hopeless apprentice and, after about a year, he decided to throw up his job with Wallace and to train as a mission teacher for the Bishop of Sarawak.

Three years later, however, Charles Allen had changed his mind again. He rejoined Wallace at Ambon and Wallace, perhaps remembering his previous frustrations, preferred to employ him as a roving collector, sending him on errands to places where he himself had no time to visit. However, Allen's trip to Sorong was not a great success. The Sorong bird-dealers feared he was a competitor, and put every obstacle in his way to prevent him getting up-country to contact the tribesmen who actually trapped the birds. On his first attempt to get inland, there was an ugly scene between his escort and local villagers brandishing knives and spears, because they had been warned against him and refused to sell supplies. On a second trip he did manage to spend a month in the interior, but with very little to show for it. He was still too distant from the major bird-hunting areas, and the local people had only one new species to sell him. They told him that the tribes who prepared the skins of the rare birds were so fierce and unpredictable that they were barely known.

Sorong is still a place where Birds of Paradise can be bought and sold, as we already knew from the villagers in Kaboei. So we sailed *Alfred Wallace* from Saonek to Sorong to pick up more supplies and visit the conservation section of the Forestry Department, whose job was to monitor the bird trade. The officials proved to be more congenial and conscientious than their colleagues at Dobbo, but almost as helpless. They had heard reports about Red Birds of Paradise near Kaboei, but could not afford to go to see them for themselves. They barely had enough of a budget to travel into town by bus, let alone to take a boat and explore deep into Waigeo. So they stayed at their office in Sorong and tried to monitor the bird trade there. Their great coup had been the arrest and prosecution of a local doctor who had ordered 200 Red Birds of Paradise for export, a number so grotesque that the authorities had been forced to act. The doctor had been arrested and sentenced to six years in prison, of which he had not served two years before being released. Now, we were told, he was back in town openly practising as a doctor again, with no stigma attached to his criminal activities. The remaining bird trade in Sorong was entirely legal, the officials of the conservation department assured us. They showed us a holding cage behind their office which contained a dozen parrots of protected species which had been seized and would be released into the wild. Of Kaboei's illicit bird trade, there was no mention.

Our other reason for visiting Sorong was to pick up a second expedition artist, Trondur Patursson. He was due to arrive from his home in the Faeroe Islands by a roundabout route through Denmark, London, Jakarta and Ambon. This was a three-day journey by air, which would eventually bring him to Sorong's airport located at a former Japanese wartime runway on a small island about ten kilometres offshore from the city. The island lay on our route out of Sorong so, after we had picked up fresh food in the market, we shifted *Alfred Wallace* to the island to wait at anchor for Trondur.

The weather was a capricious mixture of sudden rainstorms and heavy squalls followed by periods of bright sunshine, and the aircraft which served Sorong often turned back because of dangerous landing conditions on the short runway. We had barely anchored off the island when a fierce squall hit. For ten minutes the wind rose to full gale force, and the rain fell so heavily that there was a complete white-out; it was impossible to see more than five metres or to stand upright on deck. Just as suddenly the squall passed on, and about half an hour later a single canoe arrived, bringing a man from the little fishing village that was the only settlement on the island. Our visitor told us that we had to move our little boat because our mast would interfere with the approaching plane. I was incredulous. We were about a kilometre away from the end of the runway, and *Alfred Wallace*'s mast was only seven metres high. Any aircraft would be at least 100 metres above us, and we were not even anchored in line with the end of the runway. No matter, said our guest cheerfully, it was risky to stay. A few months earlier an approaching aircraft had missed its approach completely; instead of landing on the end of the runway the plane had hit head-on into a nearby cliff which he pointed out for us. Forty people including the pilot had been killed, and there were only two survivors from the wreck. He knew the exact number of dead, he said happily, because he had helped loot the bodies. To make his point, he mimed tugging a wallet out of his pocket.

On this sombre note, I was relieved when Trondur showed up safely next morning. Apart from a tinge of grey in his trademark beard, he was little changed from the person who had sailed with me on several previous voyages including the Pacific raft voyage with Joe. So it was after a pleasant reunion that we set sail next morning and turned into the narrow Sagewin Strait which links the Pacific and Indian Oceans, and brought us back to Wallace's homeward track with his 'small prahu'.

Wallace's maritime mishaps had begun again even before he left Waigeo, when he discovered that rats had gnawed some twenty holes in the mainsail while he had been ashore, and ruined it. His crew had to rig a clumsy replacement sail made of matting, and this meant that his prahu would not perform nearly so well. His plan was to sail south-west to go around the long island of Halmahera, then coast up the far shore until he reached Ternate, the city where he rented a house as a base camp. In theory it should have been an easy journey, because this was the time of the favourable winds of the east monsoon. Yet it took four days just to clear Waigeo due to contrary winds and difficult currents. Fearful of running out of fresh water, they stopped at Gag to replenish and lost their first anchor in the process. While crossing to Halmahera they were overtaken by a line of strange, roaring waves in an otherwise calm sea which Wallace could only explain as being caused by an earthquake. Luckily the waves did not trouble them. However, when they arrived on the Halmahera coast they were just downwind of the southern cape, and the wind died away so that an adverse current carried them helplessly up the coast in the wrong direction. For several days he and his dispirited crew struggled to get around the cape. They tried rowing, but the current was too strong for them, and the local people mistook Wallace for a pirate and refused to supply extra oarsmen. When they tried sailing, the wind either dropped or turned against them. Finally they attempted to anchor and drift alternately, according to the direction of the tide. But this technique lost them the last of their anchors.

Wallace himself was in a poor way. Half-starved, his lips were so badly sunburned by long exposure at sea that they bled at the slightest touch, and he could only put food in his mouth by opening it very wide. For weeks afterwards he had to keep his lips smothered in ointment. On the final run-in to Ternate, he and his crew were struck by one squall which tore adrift the small dinghy they were towing, and a second bout of strong winds shredded their jib to rags. In the worst of the gale, the pilot so feared for their survival that he stood up at the helm and cried out his prayers at the top of his voice, asking Allah to preserve the boat and her crew.

It was the first week of November when Wallace's 'little prahu' finally limped into Ternate. He had owned the boat for six months, and summed up the experience resignedly. 'Looking at my whole voyage in this vessel from the time I left Goram in May, it will appear that my experiences of travel in a native prahu have not been encouraging. My first crew ran away; two men were lost for a month on a desert island; we were ten times aground on coral reefs; we lost four anchors; the sails were devoured by rats; the small boat was lost astern; we were thirty-eight days on the voyage home, which should not have taken twelve; we were many times short of food and water; we had no compass lamp owing to there not being a drop of oil in Waigeou when we left; and to crown it all, during the whole of our voyages from Goram by Seram to Waigeou, and from Waigeou to

Ternate, occupying in all seventy-eight days, or only twelve days short of three months (all in what was supposed to be a favourable season) we had *not one single day of fair wind!*' His Bugis pilot, the same old man who had steered the boat up from Wahai, had an explanation. He was convinced that their prahu was cursed, and he told Wallace that a mistake must have been made when it was first launched. The boatbuilder had failed to drill a hole in its keel and pour through some oil. If that ceremony had been done properly, their journey would have had less grief.

The good luck ceremonies on Kei for the launch of our *Alfred Wallace* must have been effective, because our own crossing to Halmahera was not nearly so gruelling as Wallace's ill-fated voyage. Our only difficulty was that, with Trondur aboard, we now had to fit seven people on our little vessel. We managed by having Joe, Budi and Yanis all sleep on the tiny foredeck, sometimes clipped on with life-harnesses for fear of tumbling overboard in their sleep. Julia, who was the tallest of the crew, slept on the cabin floor as it gave her more room to stretch out than a cot berth. Joe and Leonard did the cooking, and our midday and evening meals now alternated between noodles and rice, flavoured with one or two onions or a handful of fried peanuts. To accompany it, we would open a couple of tins of fish or a cheap brand of corned beef which we could find in the larger bazaars. We would have preferred to eat locally dried fish, but it was very difficult to find and not very enticing. The fish was offered in heaps, seething with flies, and the market choice was between chunks of dried tuna — which looked and smelled so unappetising that Joe was reluctant to cook it — and an unidentifiable pale yellow fish so bony that the only way to eat it was to fry it up and then crumble it to powder. For snacks during our night watches, we had biscuits made in China for the Indonesian market. Packed in large square tins, a design long since disappeared from most countries, the biscuits came in sickly pastel shades reminiscent of nursery food, and were flavoured with what seemed like sweet perfume. They also tended to disintegrate, so that the tin contained a sludge of multi-coloured crumbs. However, we were usually hungry enough to eat whatever handful we dredged up.

On 8 June we had rounded the southern cape of Halmahera which had given Wallace so much difficulty, and were preparing to stop at the nearby island of Bacan. Here, in October 1858, he had made one of the most exciting discoveries of his career when he located an entirely new species of the Bird of Paradise. It was a major discovery at a time when only 12 such species had yet been identified, and even then there was some dispute about their classification.

The event took place on only his second day on Bacan. He had gone for a walk to scout the area around the small house where he intended to establish himself and begin collecting. Just as he got home, he overtook his Malay assistant Ali, who had been out shooting birds and had several dead birds hanging from his belt. Ali seemed very pleased with his game bag and, holding out one of the birds, said to Wallace, 'Look here, Sir, what a curious bird!' At first glance, Wallace was completely puzzled for he had never seen any such bird before. It was about the size of a large starling, and had a mass of splendid green feathers on its breast which tapered off in two glittering tufts. But what was really odd were the two long white feathers which stuck straight out from each shoulder. Ali assured him that the bird was able to spread out these white feathers like banners, when fluttering its wings.

I now saw that I had got a great prize [wrote Wallace]. No less than a completely new form of bird of paradise, differing most remarkably from every other known bird ... The neck and breast are scaled with fine metallic green, and the feathers on the lower part are elongated one each side to form a two-pointed gorget, which can be folded beneath the wings, or partially erected and spread out in the same way as the side plumes of most of the birds of paradise. The four long white plumes which give the bird its altogether unique character spring from little tubercles close to the upper edge of the shoulder or bend of the wing; they are narrow, gently curved, and equally webbed on both sides, of a pure creamy white colour. They are about six inches long, equalling the wing, and can be raised at right angles to it, or laid along the body at the pleasure of the bird. The bill is horn colour, the legs yellow, and the iris pale olive.

Wallace eventually sent a specimen of this new bird to the British Museum for identification and classification, and his initial summary was confirmed: it was a species of Bird of Paradise, never previously seen or reported. It was duly named *Semioptera Wallacei* or 'Wallace's Standard Wing' in his honour, though this name seemed rather prosaic in comparison with other members of the genera which had been given such dashing names as the Superb Bird of Paradise, the Golden Paradise Bird and the Magnificent Bird of Paradise. In a letter to his sales agent Samuel Stevens, Wallace provided a more down-to-earth reason why he was so thrilled to find a new and spectacular species. 'I have got here a new Bird of Paradise! Of a new genus!! quite unlike anything yet known, very curious and very handsome!!! When I can get a couple of pairs I will send them overland to see what a new Bird of Paradise will really fetch. I expect £25 each!'[1]

---

[1] He managed to send Stevens a consignment of six male Standard Wings, one female and one juvenile, all for sale. He tagged a seventh male Standard Wing as 'Private', which Stevens was to put aside for him to study when he got back to England.

Wallace's Standard Wing, in fact, proved to be so rare that during the following century the bird was seen only once again, and there were fears that it had become extinct. Then reports began to filter out from Ternate that the bird had been seen not on Bacan but on Halmahera, where — unlikely though it may seem — it had been reported by a group of Boy Scouts on an adventure trek.

Was there any chance that Wallace's Standard Wing really did survive on Bacan? We thought it was worth checking with the local people as we passed along the coast of the island. So we steered directly for the first settlement we saw and put Budi and Julia ashore with the bird-identification book to try the same technique that had worked so well in Kaboei. When they returned an hour later, after showing pictures of Wallace's Standard Wing to the headman and several villagers, they had drawn a complete blank. The villagers were coastal farmers and fishermen and did not venture much into the forest. They had never seen or heard of such a bird, though they did catch small common parrots in their crop fields and sold them to traders who came down from Tidore. If we wanted up-to-date information about rare birds, they suggested, we would do far better to contact the people of a village called Gandasoli in the interior of Bacan. There we would get more accurate information because the people of Gandasoli were professional bird-catchers.

We sailed on to the next village along the coast, and made the same enquiries. Again we received the same answer. No one had ever seen such a strange-looking bird with its four fluttering shoulder feathers and the bright green extending gorget at its throat, and the only people who might know about it were the bird-catchers of Gandasoli.

That evening we anchored at the little port where the ferry came in from Ternate, and next morning Julia, Budi and I took a bus across the heavily cultivated isthmus of Bacan to Gandasoli. It was a typical rural settlement of the Spice Islands. The long street was lined with small bungalows behind gap-toothed wooden picket fences and small gardens. There were a couple of tiny shops, and a mosque. The only noteworthy feature was a number of surviving traditional houses, elegantly made of timber and raised above the ground on wooden posts. With their long, steeply pitched roofs they must have been far more comfortable and cooler to live in than the more numerous little bungalows of concrete block walls and corrugated tin roofs.

The village headman was absent, so we were invited into his house by his deputy, and over glasses of tea he told us about the bird-catchers. There were about 15 men in the village who did this work for their living. All of them were away on bird-catching expeditions at that time, and no one knew when they would return. They came back home when they had caught enough birds or their food supply had run out. Normally they operated in teams of 3 – 5 people, who would travel to an area of forest where sufficient numbers of wild birds of commercial species had been reported, mostly lories, parrots and cockatoos. There the team would make their camp, close to the birds' feeding areas. The hunters would hang ripe fruit in the trees, next to branches they had covered with gum. The birds, coming to feed, would land on the sticky branches and get caught. In a two-week period a team might reasonably expect to catch about 200 saleable birds, and would be able to sell a common white cockatoo, for example, for the rather modest sum of 17,500 rupiah.

Two hundred birds caught in two weeks by a single team was a very heavy drain on the wild bird population, so we were not surprised when our informant told us that it was increasingly difficult to catch commercial species of birds on Bacan itself. The main island had largely been stripped of birds and, to make a living, bird-catchers were now going to small offshore islands to catch birds there. In fact they did not trouble to bring the captive birds back to the village, and instead had built a holding facility on one of these islands. From there the cages filled with birds could be collected directly by the Bugis traders who sailed with their live cargoes back to Sulawesi, from where many of them were shipped on to Singapore.

Once again the frankness of our informant was unexpected. When Budi showed him the bird-identification book, he pointed to the birds that were caught and traded. Most of them were the usual commercial species such as red lories, but a few — like the black-headed parrot — were not. These species were officially banned from trade, so were more valuable. Clearly, too, the deputy headman knew that all was not strictly legitimate. The technique of assembling the bird catch on a small island and shipping the birds directly aboard the Bugis smuggling boats reduced the chances of being caught in the illegal trade, and when he talked about these details the deputy headman had a habit of twisting his watch-strap nervously.

Yet at the same time there was a very basic similarity between the activities of the bird-catchers of Gandasoli and what Wallace had been doing 140 years ago. The modern bird-catchers captured and sold for a living, just as Wallace had done. The new problem was one of numbers: the harvesting of wild birds was so severe that it was destroying the species. It was difficult to see how the bird population of Bacan or any other island would survive such a professional onslaught. Unlike Waigeo, where the villagers owned every dancing tree, the bird-catchers of Gandasoli operated freely over areas in which they had no long-term interest.

Bird-catching was no longer as lucrative as it used to be, said our informant — but then he brightened up. A new buyer who had recently opened a shop in Bali dealt in butterflies, and there was one large special butterfly for which he was prepared to pay 250,000 rupiah — much more money than any single bird — and the bird-catchers would turn to hunting that insect. Here again was an echo of Wallace. In Bacan he had caught several glimpses of a new species

Coastal scene

of butterfly, a huge Bird Wing, so gloriously coloured that he knew he had to have it. Two months passed before he managed to catch a male specimen; it was seven inches across, and velvet black and fiery orange, and he named it the Croesus Bird Wing. Knowing their rarity and monetary value, he delayed in Bacan until he had gathered no fewer than 100 specimens, of both sexes, including perhaps 20 very fine males, 'though not more than five or six were absolutely perfect'. Very likely, this was the very same species for which the mysterious butterfly dealer in Bali was prepared to pay the equivalent of almost two months' wages.

As for Wallace's Bird of Paradise, the Standard Wing, no one in Gandasoli had ever seen or heard of such a bird, and we were coming to accept that the species probably no longer existed on Bacan. However, we decided we should make one last enquiry in the north of the island, where Leonard was keen to go ashore because Wallace had mentioned in passing that the people of north Bacan made a living by collecting a tree resin called dammar. This resin burns with a bright clear flame, and was used in Wallace's day for making torches. But gum dammar had a quite different significance for our two artists, Leonard and Trondur. They mixed it with turpentine to produce a varnish which they applied as a finishing coat to their paintings. This dammar varnish gave a particular richness and depth to the final colours which could not be obtained with any other material. The problem for the artists was that dammar was very expensive in Europe, even in small quantities. Was there any chance, Leonard asked, that we could try to obtain some dammar cheaply by going to the source?

In Gandasoli we were told that dammar was rarely collected nowadays. The price was too low, and it was too much effort to collect it, as you had to go deep into the forest to find and tap the resin-bearing trees. However, there were still dammar traders at a place called Sabatang on the north-east shoulder of the island.

When we arrived off Sabatang the following evening, a Bugis trader was just packing up his display tent. He had anchored his boat close inshore and set up a marquee on the beach, where he had laid out his wares of plastic goods, pots and pans and clothing. It was obvious why he had chosen to set up his pitch at Sabatang. Though it was only modest in size, perhaps 200 families, it was a well-run place with neat well-kept wooden bungalows, swept sandy streets and a general air of prosperity. Julia, who went ashore to ask about dammar, soon brought back news that there were three or four dammar traders living in the village, and that one of them had a stock of dammar in a shed behind his house.

The house was newer and smarter than most. Behind a neatly carved front door was a spotlessly clean living room furnished with new plastic chairs and a table. There were photographs hanging on the wall, and a hi-fi set in one corner; there was even glass in the windows. It seemed that the dammar business had its rewards. Behind the house was a small shed in which the trader kept his stock of dammar, which Julia had reported looked like gravel. It was a one-metre-high heap of white, translucent, angular pebbles, which were slightly sticky and smelled of turpentine. These were lumps of resin which had been collected, as rubber is gathered, by making cuts in the trunks of the dammar trees and catching the sap that oozed out. The trader explained that the nearest dammar tree was a 7-kilometre walk into the forest, and that the trees were owned communally by the village. In a good year a single tree might produce as much as 100 kilos of resin, which was collected and stored in the village until it was picked up by the Bugis traders. They carried the raw resin to Ternate, where it was transhipped for Java and used in the manufacture of the very best quality paints and varnishes.

When the trader heard that Trondur and Leonard wanted gum dammar for their oil paintings, he was astonished. He had never heard of it being used by artists, but he had something special to show us. Three bundles wrapped in rags were brought from his bedroom, and opened. Inside each bundle was a large lump of what looked like low-grade amber or beeswax. Each lump weighed about three kilos, and had its own shape and texture: one was the shape of a round flat loaf of bread, the second a fat crescent moon, and the third resembled an old-fashioned smoothing iron. These, said the trader, were pieces of the natural dammar which was usually found buried in the ground and discovered by chance. It came not as the result of artificially cutting the tree, but as a natural excretion oozing from it. A tree might take 7 – 10 years to produce a lump of natural dammar of such size and consistency.

This natural substance was much harder, more pure and of far higher quality than the tree-cut dammar.

We invited the dammar trader to come out to *Alfred Wallace* and discuss the price of this special dammar. That afternoon he arrived, paddled by his friends in a dugout canoe, and a solemn inspection took place on the aft deck. Trondur and Leonard examined each lump in turn, turning it over, scratching it, holding it up to the light, even biting it as if it was some precious substance. The owner of the dammar looked on, bemused. He admitted that he had no idea that the quality of dammar could mean so much, and that he had kept back the lumps of natural dammar because they were rare and unusual rather than for any specific purpose. Eventually each artist decided he could afford to buy one lump. The selection was made, and a price was agreed. Then, after the negotiation of price had ended and the two selected lumps had been handed over to their happy new owners, the dammar trader leaned down and picked up the unsold piece. 'Here,' he said, offering it to Leonard, 'please accept this as my gift.'

So it was with two very contented artists on board that we headed on towards the north, for Ternate. We were passing down the long strait that divides the big island of Halmahera — studded with volcanoes and covered in forest — from a chain of offshore volcanic peaks which form a series of conical islands. It is one of the most spectacular channels in the world. On each side rise volcanic cones, some of them active, and on one of them — the island of Makian — the hole in the crater wall can be clearly seen where a tremendous explosion has literally blown the top of the cone apart. The sea around us was particularly rich in marine life. Six-metre-long minke whales surfaced and blew, three or four of them in view at once, and we were entertained by schools of dolphins which swept up the channel in their hunting pattern. Their chase was announced by the frenzy of a cloud of gulls shrieking, chasing and wheeling above the water, and diving to dart at the fish being driven to the surface by the dolphins. Below them was a constant flash and gleam of black backs and fins dipping and churning the water as the dolphins remorselessly drove the fish shoal, attacking the fringes and gradually concentrating the fish into a more vulnerable mass. Then the dolphin pack surged into the

Dolphins off Makian

final attack, dashed through the killing zone and gorged on its prey.

Here, on 17 May, we sailed across the Equator and observed the crossing by requiring Julia, as the youngest member of the crew at 26, to jump overboard with a rope tied around her waist. She was hauled under the boat and up the other side by Trondur, who looked a suitably bearded King Neptune. Yanis upheld a rather different maritime tradition by pointing out a small village as we passed along the Halmahera coast. There, he said in a matter-of-fact tone, he had a second wife and a grownup son who were the result of his previous voyages in those waters!

10

Ternate

THE volcanic island of Ternate, where Wallace first stepped ashore in January 1858, was at that time nominally ruled by an eccentric one-eyed Sultan.[1] An octogenarian, he liked to be addressed by his full title of Tadjoel Moelki Amiroedin Iskandar Kaulaini Sjah Peotra Mohamad Djin. He was the twenty-third Sultan, and traced his authority

---

[1] He had lost his right eye to a bullet during the British attack against the Dutch in Ternate in 1811. He refused to have the bullet removed, and continued to wear it in the eye socket.

back to the ruler of Ternate who had been on the throne when the English adventurer Francis Drake came there in 1579 looking for the fabled Spice Islands. Drake had found what he was seeking, because Ternate and the small islands to the south were then the main source for cloves, a spice which cost more than its weight in gold when brought to Europe. The Sultan of Ternate — with his equally autocratic neighbour the Sultan of Tidore, who ruled another little volcano island a mile away — controlled virtually the entire world's supply of the spice, and a good proportion of the nutmeg and mace as well, because these spices happened to grow in domains which paid them tribute. In fact the suzerainty of Ternate and Tidore extended, in theory at least, as far as Waigeo, where nearly three centuries later Wallace found the natives still obliged to send a tribute of feathers from Birds of Paradise to decorate the turbans of the Sultans and their clusters of courtiers.

In Drake's day the Sultan of Ternate had been a splendidly barbaric figure, wearing a cloth-of-gold skirt, thick gold rings braided into his hair, a heavy gold chain around his neck, and his fingers adorned with a glittering array of diamonds, rubies and emeralds. By the time Wallace arrived, the effective power of the Sultan had been eroded by more than two centuries of bullying by larger nations who coveted the spice trade. In the mid-nineteenth century Sultan Mohamad Djin was frail and very forgetful, living on a Dutch pension as a doddering semi-recluse who spent his days in his shabby and dusty palace surrounded by his wives, a brood of 125 children and grandchildren, the princes of the blood and their families, courtiers, servants and slaves. Most of them were poverty-stricken. A memory of the glamour remained, however. The Sultan himself would emerge from his palace, the kedaton, for state occasions or to call on the Dutch authorities in the town. These appearances were like mannequins come to life from a museum, and greatly enjoyed by the Sultan's citizens who continued to ascribe semi-divine powers to their overlord. The Sultan and his court would sally forth dressed in a magpie collection of costumes which had been acquired piecemeal from earlier colonial contacts, or had been copied and recopied over the intervening centuries by local tailors. They donned Portuguese doublets of velvet, Spanish silk jackets, embroidered waistcoats and blouses, parti-coloured leggings and Dutch broadcloth coats. Their exotic headgear and weapons ranged from Spanish morions and halberds to swashbuckling velvet hats with drooping plumes and antique rapiers set with jewels. The *pièce de résistance* was the state carriage, which had been given to an earlier Sultan by the Dutch and was a period piece. It was so badly in need of repair that, to climb aboard it, the elderly Sultan had to mount a portable ladder. Safely ensconced, he was then pulled forward in his rickety conveyance by 16 palace servants harnessed instead of horses, who towed him slowly along to the Dutch Residency a few hundred metres distant.

The real power in Ternate when Wallace arrived was not even the Dutch Resident but the chief merchant, Mr Duivenboden. He was of Dutch family but born in Ternate, and had been educated in England. Locally known as the 'King of Ternate', he was extremely rich, owned half the town as well as more than 100 slaves, and operated a large fleet of trading ships. His authority with the Sultan and the local rajahs was considerable, and he was very good to Wallace who, with his help, was able to rent a run-down house on the outskirts of the town and fix it up well enough to serve as his base of operations. He kept this house for three years, returning there regularly from his excursions to the outer islands. Back in his Ternate house, he would prepare and pack his specimens for shipment to Europe, write letters to his family and to friends like Bates, and begin preparations for the next sortie into the lesser-known fringes of the Moluccas.

Here, too, Wallace could recuperate from the strains and stresses of a field trip. Very often he came back to Ternate malnourished and sick with fever or tropical ulcers, and his little house was part haven, part sanatorium. It had its own well of cool water, a great luxury in that hot climate, and it was only a five-minute walk into town where he could buy the fresh provisions so badly needed to bring him back to full health. 'In this house I spent many happy days,' he wrote. 'Returning to it after a three or four months' absence in some uncivilised region, I enjoyed the unwonted luxuries of milk and fresh bread, and regular supplies of fish and eggs, meat and vegetables which were often sorely needed to restore my health and energy. I had ample space and convenience for unpacking, sorting, and arranging my treasures, and I had delightful walks in the suburbs of the town, or up the lower slopes of the mountain, when I desired a little exercise, or had time for collecting.'

The house itself was modest. A bungalow, it was just 40 feet square, with a verandah front and back, four medium-sized rooms and a hall. It was surrounded by fruit trees, and was built in the local style where the walls were made of stone up to a height of three feet and then extended upward by a screen of leaf stems made from the sago palm. The roof would have been of thatch.

But where was this house situated, and did it survive? Wallace stated that 'just below my house is the fort, built by the Portuguese below which is an open space to the beach, and beyond this the native town extends for about a mile to the north-east. About the centre of it is the palace of the Sultan, now a large, untidy, half ruinous building of stone.' The Portuguese built at least two forts whose walls are to be found within the limits of what is now Ternate town, and neither really fits the location he describes. One is too far to the north and the other, which the Portuguese never finished, is too far in the opposite direction. The best candidate is Fort Oranje which is central to the town, but that is Dutch. Today the town is far larger than the place Wallace would have known, and sprawls for several kilometres along the shore. The Sultan's kedaton is towards the northern end, and in the same general direction there are only a dozen or so houses which retain the vernacular architecture Wallace describes. However, this has not discouraged the town authorities from designating one of the few remaining old houses as 'Wallace's House'. It has almost the same floor plan, a well in the garden, and is of about the right vintage, with a picturesque tumbled-in thatch roof. But it is much too large and substantial, with outside colonnades, to have been Wallace's rather more modest home, and its stone walls extend to the ceiling. In fact it has survived because it was once an overspill residence for members of the Sultan's family.

'Wallace's House', Ternate

It seems more likely that the expansion of Ternate town has long since swallowed up the little building where Wallace, recuperating from fever, wrote his ground-breaking essay on 'Evolution by Natural Selection'.[1] To it he added his covering letter to Charles Darwin, asking if he would bring the essay to the attention of his eminent friend Sir Charles Lyell, and then entrusted the small package to the agent for the Dutch steamship lines which operated a service to Singapore. From there it would go by mail steamer to Egypt, and thence overland to the Mediterranean and onward to Southampton. Wallace could reasonably expect the letter to arrive at its destination in three months. The delivery address was Down House, Bromley, Kent.

The progress of that letter and essay, written 'on thin foreign paper' in February 1858 and posted in early March, has been reconstructed by historians of science with the meticulous care of detectives checking an alibi which will clear a suspect of a very grave accusation. The reason for their close attention is that there is just a

---

[1] Though Wallace wrote 'Ternate' at the head of his cover letter to Darwin, he may have had his 'flash of inspiration' about the theory of evolution when on a field trip in nearby Halmahera. The dates and places in his journal and his collecting notes sometimes differ, and his later recollection is imprecise.

possibility that Charles Darwin may have taken advantage of Wallace's Ternate essay in a serious act of plagiarism. It is a very slim possibility, but the more it is checked by scholars the more it lingers. In 1980 it caused something of a furore when proposed by an American journalist-writer. Four years later the suspicion received heavyweight support from an American academic, J. L. Brooks, after extensive research into the Darwin archives.

The background to the suspicion is straight-forward. After more than 20 years of labouring on the problem of the origin of species, in 1856 Charles Darwin had begun to write a monumental work provisionally called *Natural Selection*. Painfully, chapter by chapter, he was pushing forward with it. But he had amassed such a mountain of information, whether from his own research in breeding plants or domestic animals such as pigeons, or from his worldwide network of correspondents like Wallace, that he was always going back to add bits here or rewrite them there. He worked with excessive secrecy, and when he did send the occasional details of his ideas to his scientific friends, he expected them to maintain absolute confidentiality. Above all, he had never made a public announcement of an over-arching theory which would explain the process of evolution.

In the early summer of 1858, when Wallace's letter was on the way to Darwin, he was mulling over the problem of how the different species diverge, and making very slow progress. Then, on 8 June 1858, he wrote to his friend and confidant Dr Joseph Hooker that he had achieved 'the keystone' of his theory, which was to understand the principle of species divergence. Later he was to recall 'the very spot in the road, whilst in my carriage, when to my joy the solution occurred to me'.

The suspicion that the 'keystone' may have been lifted from Wallace is based on the possibility that his Ternate essay had arrived at Darwin's house in the first week of June. Darwin himself would claim that the letter reached him on 18 June but, oddly, another letter which Wallace had written to the brother of his old friend Bates, then living back in Leicester — and presumably posted by the same mail steamer from Ternate — arrived in Leicester on 3 June. There was no reason why the letter to Bates' brother in the Midlands should have arrived at its destination two weeks earlier than the letter to Darwin in Kent. The exact date of the arrival of the letter to Darwin will never be established, because its envelope has not survived, whereas the envelope to Bates' brother, Frederick, is intact with its postal frankings showing its route via Singapore and London and Leicester, both the latter dated 3 June. Thus, in the same week or at very least the same fortnight when Darwin found the solution to the divergence of species, an essay arrived in the post from Wallace entitled 'On the Tendency of Varieties to Depart Indefinitely from the Original Type'. It was a core concept in the Theory of Evolution by Natural Selection, and the coincidence is, to say the least, rather uncomfortable.

Even if Darwin did not quarry vital information from Wallace's Ternate essay, which would have been impossible if Darwin's own timing of events is to be believed, he already risked being outpaced by Wallace's originality of thought. Two and a half years earlier, Wallace had sent from Indonesia another essay on evolution, which he had submitted to a workaday journal called *The Annals and Magazine of Natural History*. The circumstances of writing this paper were remarkably similar to his Ternate essay. This time he had written the essay in Sarawak, where he had been staying in a hill cottage loaned to him by the 'White Rajah', James Brooke. Once again Wallace was recuperating from a bout of fever, and once again he was on his own, apart from a Malay cook, because Brooke and his secretary were absent. Left to himself and unable to do field work, Wallace had free time to review his reference books and notes and to think once more about the 'Great Problem.'

He drew up a list of what he described as ten 'well known geographical and geological facts'. These ranged from the fact that similar environments, even if widely separated, produce similar species, to the fact that the geological record shows 'no group or species had come into existence twice'. Deducing from these facts, Wallace came up with what he described as 'The Law which regulated the Introduction of New Species', namely that 'every species has come into existence coincident both in time and space with a pre-existing closely allied species'. Put another way, Wallace proposed that a gradual continuous progress of evolution must have taken place through the ages in order to produce all the different species on earth. He had not yet worked out how the mechanism of that change took place — that would come in his letter from Ternate — but it was the most significant advance in evolutionary theory since the time of Lamarck and until Darwin published his own work.

Astonishingly, Darwin himself missed the significance of the Sarawak essay, when he first read it in the *Annals*, and his copy of the magazine still exists. Against one fact he noted, 'Can this be true?' And when Wallace produced the image of evolution as a tree growing and sending out branches and twigs, Darwin observed patronisingly: 'uses my simile of a tree'. Finally he went on to dismiss the essay as 'nothing very new'. Yet the Sarawak Law, as Wallace's idea came to be called, was to be another concept vital to the Theory of Evolution by Natural Selection.[1]

Between Darwin and Wallace there was now something of the relationship occasionally found between the long-established eminent university

---

[1] On the basis of Darwin' s revisions to his own book draft, the American academic J. L. Brooks believes that Darwin looked again at Wallace's Sarawak paper, and quarried the ideas for his own explanation of divergence theory.

professor and his most gifted research student. On the one hand looms a mass of scholarship, the years of research, the professional status and reputation, and the power over the future advancement of the junior. On the other hand there is the respect due to the senior, the eagerness to please, but also the originality of thought which can result from coming new to a subject or having done more recent primary research. The situation sometimes leads to the senior ignoring the genuine contribution of the junior, or — worse — taking advantage of the junior's work. Of course Darwin and Wallace were not professor and researcher; they were two private individuals separated for much of the time by huge distances and, perhaps more significantly, by a social gulf which meant that Wallace's work was unlikely to be given the same regard as Darwin's efforts.

Darwin could be patronising in other ways when it came to dealing with outsiders like Wallace and other less qualified researchers. He had invested so much time and effort in the study of evolution that he had come to regard it as his private preserve, and he took care to let outsiders know it and to warn them off. When the Sarawak Essay produced little reaction in the world of scholarship, Wallace had the temerity to write to Darwin asking if he had read it and what he thought. Darwin wrote back disarmingly, 'I can plainly see that we have thought much alike & to a certain extent have come to similar conclusions'. But then he went on to add a blatant warning:

'this summer will make the 20th year (!) since I opened my first note-book on the question how & in what way do species and varieties differ from each other . . . I am now preparing my work for publication, but find the subject so very large that . . . I do not suppose I shall go to press for two years . . . It is really impossible to explain my views in the compass of a letter . . . But I have adopted a distinct and tangible idea — whether true or false others must judge.' The response was typically Darwinian. He was telling Wallace that he, Darwin, had been working on the subject of evolution far longer than the younger man, that he knew more about the subject but was not going to tell him what it was, and that he was planning to publish his views in due course. The implication was that Wallace should wait his turn.

The shattering impact of Wallace's new submission, the Ternate essay, when it arrived in Darwin's mail can be imagined. Darwin was appalled. Here, in a few pages, was virtually the entire theory of evolution which he was gradually trying to hammer out. Darwin knew instantly that it was no longer possible to sidetrack or ignore the uneducated specimen collector. He could not imagine that Wallace had borrowed any of his own ideas, because Wallace had come up with his notions from the far side of the world, with just a dozen or so reference books. Nor could he suppress the letter from Ternate, because Wallace would soon be communicating his ideas to friends like Bates.

Darwin was a contradictory bundle of self-pity, honourable intentions and consternation. He was also sick, having suffered for years from mysterious illnesses which may or may not have been acquired on his South American travels, and members of his family were unwell too. For year after year Darwin had havered about publishing his evolution ideas for fear of upsetting his High Church friends or being caught out in small errors of research. Now he had the choice either to step back and allow Wallace to be the first person to expound the main thrust of the Theory of Evolution by Natural Selection, or he had to put aside his obsessive secrecy and doubts and go public.

To compound the problem, Darwin had nowhere near finished his 'big book' on evolution, and had virtually nothing ready to publish. He had been wrapped for so long in his cocoon of research, introspection, ill-health and comfortable living that he had failed to realise that someone else might come up with the same idea.

He sent Wallace's Ternate essay, as Wallace had requested, to his friend and confidant, Sir Charles Lyell. But he made sure that Lyell was aware that if he suggested publishing it, this would forestall Darwin's own work. The way Darwin put it was to tell Lyell that he was prepared to send the essay off to whatever publication Lyell recommended, even though this would mean that 'all my originality, whatever it may amount to, will be smashed'. Lyell took the point. Indeed he had already warned Darwin that someone, and it might be Wallace, could beat him to the pronouncement of the idea of Natural Selection. Now Lyell consulted with Hooker, and these two powerful grandees of English science decided that if Darwin was willing to put together some brief account of his ideas, then the two men would arrange for the work of Darwin and Wallace to be announced in tandem, and also to acknowledge Darwin's early lead. Darwin agreed to the stratagem but knew perfectly well that something was wrong, and that the action could be construed as taking unfair advantage of Wallace, 9,000 miles away. He consented to provide 'a sketch of my general views in about a dozen pages or so. But I cannot persuade myself that I can do so honourably . . . I would far rather burn my whole book than that he (Wallace) or any man should think that I had behaved in a paltry spirit.'

Darwin might find it dishonourable to agree to the scheme suggested by Hooker and Lyell, but he was willing to take part in it, and on 1 July the fateful meeting took place at the Linnean Society when the Darwin-Wallace Theory of Evolution by Natural Selection was first proposed.

Only 28 Members and two Guests attended the Linnean meeting. Most of them must have been taken aback to discover that the secretary of the Society had added an extra item to the scheduled programme. The addition had been slipped on to the agenda the previous day under pressure from Lyell and Hooker, and it was rather odd. Although dressed up as a joint paper, it was nothing of the kind. It was an uneasy mishmash of extracts from an essay which Darwin had written in 1854, then part of a letter he had written in 1857 to an American professor outlining his theory of evolution, and finally Wallace's complete and well argued Ternate essay.

Darwin's pieces were read out first, and not surprisingly they were not very coherent. The extract from the letter to the American professor, for example, had only been handed in the previous day, and no one except Darwin even knew it existed. Most of the audience had a right to be perplexed. Darwin's contributions were disjointed and cryptic, and he was not there to discuss them.[1] Wallace was relatively unknown, and it was puzzling to the audience that two such eminent authorities as Hooker and Lyell had obviously sponsored the announcement of his work. The meeting ended rather lamely, with scarcely any discussion and some confusion. The President of the Society, for one, had no clear concept of the importance of that meeting. Later

---

[1] Though Wallace wrote 'Ternate' at the head of his cover letter to Darwin, he may have had his 'flash of inspiration' about the theory of evolution when on a field trip in nearby Halmahera. The dates and places in his journal and his collecting notes sometimes differ, and his later recollection is imprecise.

that year he lamented that the Society had not been provided with any particularly innovative papers.

It was left to the quicker-witted members of the audience to work out what had happened: that the idea of gradual evolution by natural selection, as opposed to the unchanging nature of animal life or a divinely created Universe, had been proposed rather incoherently by the renowned Charles Darwin, sponsored by Lyell and Hooker, and summed up forcefully by a specimen-collector working in the Spice Islands. One of the sharper members present was the Vice-President, a botanist named Bentham. He was scheduled to read a paper on exactly the opposite view — that species were immutable. After he heard what had been read, and presumably appreciating the heavyweight sponsorship of Lyell and Hooker, he withdrew his contribution. The evening's programme ended after six other uncontroversial and scheduled papers had been read, and the Linnean Society meeting was declared closed.

In the strictest sense, Wallace had been given his proper due and more. As he had requested, his paper had been brought to the attention of Sir Charles Lyell, read and recommended. It might be said that Lyell had been generous in going further, by laying it before such an influential audience as the Linnean Society, and in association with such an eminent scientist as Charles Darwin. As a further bonus, the paper would be published in the *Proceedings of the Linnean Society*.

While these events were unfolding in London, Wallace was getting on with the pressing chores of making a living as a collector. After posting his essay he had gone across to Halmahera, the huge and sprawling island just 11 kilometres away from Ternate. On the previous occasion when he had sent off an essay, the Sarawak Law, he had received a chiding letter from Stevens, his sales agent, informing him that his English clients were disappointed. They were waiting to receive tropical insects and bird-skins from Wallace which they could add to their collections, not theories which merely caused dissent and arguments.

Halmahera, then known as Gilolo, was *terra incognita* for naturalists and covered with primary forest, so Wallace had high hopes for making a good collection there. But he

Portuguese fort, Ternate

was to be disappointed. He had not yet fully recovered from his fever, so was not well enough to do much active hunting. He got only 'some nice insects', and his assistant Ali shot a very colourful ground thrush with 'a breast of pure white, shoulders of azure blue, and belly of vivid crimson. It has very long and strong legs, and hops about with such activity in the dense tangled forest, bristling with rocks, as to make it very difficult to shoot.' Dissatisfied with his haul from Halmahera, Wallace returned to Ternate where he found that his friend the merchant Duivenboden had the schooner *Hester Helen* preparing to leave on a trading voyage to New Guinea.

This was too good an opportunity to be missed, and Wallace took the chance to be dropped off with a small team of hunters and bird-skinners on the north coast of New Guinea, in a region known as Dorey. For three and a half months he lived there, part of the time by himself — the only European inhabitant of that vast island — and part of the time in the company of landing parties from a Dutch warship, its attendant collier and a coastal steamer. These newcomers were more of a nuisance than a blessing. Food in Dorey was scarce, and the visitors bought up most of the surplus from the natives. Wallace was reduced to eating the corpses of parakeets he had shot for skinning. A single scrawny parakeet, he lamented, had to serve him for two meals. Worse, the coastal steamer brought the Sultan of Tidore and the Dutch Resident of Banda, and both had come to buy Birds of Paradise skins for trade. Their men swept the neighbourhood, and poor Wallace was unable to acquire a single new species. For several weeks he was kept in his hut by a badly infected foot, the result of cutting his ankle while clambering over dead trees and logs looking for new insects. The foot swelled up so badly that he could not move without a crutch and he had to sit in his hut — tantalised by the sight of gorgeous butterflies flying past the open door, yet unable to move.

All in all, his stay in New Guinea was not a happy one. The weather was atrocious, and the climate was extremely unhealthy. Wallace and his team were repeatedly going down with dysentery and fevers and one of his men, a young Butonese, died. Wallace himself suffered from a gum infection which made the inside of his mouth so sore that he could only eat liquids. His main consolation was the astonishing richness of insect life. Going out at 10 in the morning and returning at 3 in the afternoon, he could gather enough insects to keep him hard at work for another six hours, sorting and pinning them. On his best day he collected a record number of 78 distinct sorts of beetle, and over the three months of his visit collected more than 1,000 insect species in the space of a little over a square mile.

This profusion of insects, however, had its less attractive side. Dorey was infested with a particularly aggressive species of small black ant, and they plagued him. 'They immediately took possession of my home, building a large nest in the roof, and forming papery tunnels down almost every post. They swarmed on my table as I was at work setting out my insects, carrying them off from under my very nose, and even tearing them from the cards on which they were gummed if I left them for an instant. They crawled continually over my hands and face, got into my hair, and roamed at will over my whole body, not producing much inconvenience until they began to bite, which they would do on meeting with any obstruction to their passage, and with a sharpness which made me jump again and rush to turn out the offender. They visited my bed also, so that night brought no relief from their persecutions.' If ants were not enough, a plague of blowflies laid their eggs in the bird-skins Wallace had set out to dry. If the eggs were not removed within 24 hours, the skins crawled with maggots. The blowflies laid such masses of eggs that the bird-skins literally rose up half an inch from the drying boards on a bed of fly eggs, and as each egg was firmly stuck to the fibres of the feathers it took Wallace hours to clean them without damaging his specimens.

So, on 22 July when the *Hester Helen* arrived to take him off, Wallace was heartily sick of Dorey, because 'in no place which I have visited have I encountered more privations and continual annoyances'. His 'long-thought-of and much-desired voyage to New Guinea had realised none of my expectations.' Resignedly, he noted that his voyage back to Ternate on the *Hester Helen* should have taken five days with the favourable monsoon but lasted 17 days due to calms and head winds. His weather luck, as always, was atrocious.

★ ★ ★

On Halmahera, just a three-hour boat ride from Wallace's base in Ternate, is the place where a group of Boy Scouts on an outing in the mid 1980s heard and saw an unusual bird. They reported their discovery, and a visiting ornithologist confirmed soon afterwards that a sizeable population of Wallace's Standard Wings — feared to be extinct — lived in a forested area locally named Tanah Putih or 'White Land'. The conservation section of the Forestry Department in Ternate advised us to go there if we wanted to see Wallace's own Bird of Paradise; it was not far to travel and quite well known. We had only to sail across to the little ferry port, called Sidangoli, ask for directions, and someone would guide us up to the area where the birds lived.

The sea approach to Sidangoli was signposted by the chimneys of a massive timber factory. Smoke and steam poured upward into the sky; barges stacked with huge logs were anchored in the fairway, waiting for the tugs to pull them into the milling area. The factory complex was big enough to have its own worker dormitories, shops, offices, docks, and a ferry service which took personnel back and forth from Ternate. The ordinary citizens of Sidangoli had to have special permission to enter the compound. We sailed *Alfred Wallace* into the shallows beside the public ferry pier, anchored her there and, leaving Yanis on board as watchman, found a minibus which would take us to Tanah Putih. It seemed that the Bird Park was right beside the main road to the east coast of Halmahera.

It was only a 20-minute drive before we came to a sign on the roadside on which someone had painted a large and rather lurid picture of Wallace's Standard Wing. The bird looked like a heraldic griffin, with a fierce expression in its eye, huge muscular legs and large ugly claws gripping a branch, and an unlikely spray of long feathers projecting from its shoulders. The minibus dropped us off, and rattled away with much grinding and clashing of gears and

Countryside at Tanah Putih

the usual thudding boom of loudspeakers.

The countryside was a succession of uninhabited ridges and steep-sided valleys, mostly covered with forest. At a distance the forest appeared to consist of larger trees, but closer to the road the tree cover was much more sparse. Most of the vegetation was low bushes and scrub. On the right-hand side of the road where we stood, the land dropped away into a small, steep valley, almost a ravine which had been cut by a stream whose bed was strewn with large grey boulders. The red earth of the valley floor was planted as a small field of cassava, and on the far side of the stream rose a very steep hillside thickly clothed in what looked like secondary forest. The undergrowth was very dense, but here and there you could see the bones of bare rock.

We looked around, stunned. We had been expecting a secluded corner of forest where we would find the elusive Standard Wings, but by no stretch of the imagination could this spot be called tranquil. Every few minutes a truck or minibus came grinding past, changed gear several times as it negotiated a couple of bends, and then laboured up the slope with its engine roaring. To our left, away from the stream, the ground rose to a hillcrest. On the slope someone was constructing some wooden chalets. They were half-built, and it was difficult to say whether they had been abandoned before completion or were waiting to be finished. Below us in the valley were a couple more half-finished buildings without their roofs. On the crown of the hill was a large open-sided structure, rather attractive and well built with a thatch roof and a broad wooden floor. It looked like a giant bandstand.

We took another look at the painted sign. The picture was undoubtedly of a rather grotesque Wallace's Standard Wing, and the arrow underneath it pointed across the ravine to the forested hillside opposite. In the direction where the arrow pointed, someone was clearing the forest to make another field. The buildings, the noisy traffic, the ragged condition of the forest were the exact opposite of what we had expected. But there was worse: half an acre of bush and bamboo was ablaze. Flames were roaring and jumping spectacularly. A yellow-brown wall of smoke was billowing upward into a light breeze and drifting across the forest wall designated as the bird area. It looked like a scene from the *Inferno*, and to add to the turmoil the flames were licking through several clumps of bamboo. Every now and then a bamboo stem exploded. It was like a hand grenade or a very large firework going off.

Amazed, we walked up to the open-sided structure on the hilltop and found a young woman preparing a meal for a Chinese merchant. He had a cartridge belt buckled around his waist and was obviously the owner of the large, smart motorcycle that was parked nearby. He was very friendly and explained that he ran a hotel in Ternate, and it was he who was building the half-finished huts. They were for tourists whom he would send across from his hotel in Ternate to see the birds, as they were a tourist attraction.

When he finished his meal he invited us to visit his hotel, straddled his motorbike, revved the engine and roared off down the road to catch the ferry. Ten minutes later the husband of the Indonesian woman arrived; he apologised for not being there to greet us, but he had been away in the forest gathering freshwater crayfish for supper. He was a tall, thin man in his early thirties, very like Budi. In fact the two of them were very similar in manner and expertise. Demianus, the newcomer, was also a bird specialist. He had lived at Tanah Putih since the first days when the Standard Wings had been discovered, and had worked for various foreign conservation groups, conducting bird surveys and acting as a guide.

The story he told was part-farce, part-tragedy. In the mid 1980s, about the time the birds were discovered, the population of Standard Wings had been estimated at about 300. Now, he guessed, perhaps 20 birds remained, and it was not a sustainable population. The decline had been the result of unbridled exploitation and sheer carelessness. At first only a few visitors had come to see the Standard Wings but then, as word of these remarkable birds spread, the parties of visitors grew larger and larger. The largest single groups had been parties of tourists from cruise ships visiting Ternate, who had been brought to the site in buses. There had also been a steady stream of groups from Ternate, including school trips and more Boy Scouts. To accommodate them, the forestry department had built the big thatched tourist shelter. Of course, the building of the shelter had also contributed to the decline of the nearby bird population. The presence of builders, their hammering and sawing, the clearing of the hilltop — all had disturbed the birds. This was then followed, when the lodge opened, by a succession of noisy visitors who would come to see the birds, tramp across to their display trees in the adjacent forest and then stay up all night on the nearby hilltop, sitting around their camp-fires, playing loud music and generally making a noise. But this had been only one half of the tragedy. Worse still had been the opening and improvement of the road. As more and more traffic travelled past, so the noise and disturbance had increased. Yet, astonishingly, the birds continued to hang on; their numbers dwindled steadily, but they still returned to their favourite display trees. In fact the most important tree stood right beside the road, and here the birds would assemble at dawn and dusk to display even with the traffic roaring past a few yards beside them. Then came the *coup de grace*. One day, when Demianus was away, the display tree was cut down. He did not know who did it, nor why, except that it was a large tree and probably of value to loggers. There was no preservation order or official protection for the Bird Park, and so there was no redress. Once the main display tree had been cut down, most of the remaining Standard Wings disappeared. The few who continued in the area came to the remaining trees on the far slope of the hill, but they seldom displayed.

We went to visit the spot. Only a couple of Standard Wings showed up, and they were difficult to see in the thick foliage. Demianus suggested that we wait. The previous week a friend had reported coming across another display tree, where 20 or 30 Standard Wings were regularly assembling. The tree was a few kilometres away in the opposite direction, deep in the forest, and Demianus volunteered to go there to check whether the report was accurate. If so, he would take us there.

We waited for him to return from the reconnaissance. And the farce continued.

Yes, he reported next morning, the information was true. He had reached the area where the display tree had been reported, and confirmed that it had been a dancing place for Standard

Ternate scenes

Wings. Unfortunately, the very day before he got there, the logging road which took the lumberjacks into the forest had reached the same area. The loggers had taken a chainsaw to the tree, and cut it down.

Motor launch

11

Wallace's Standard Wing

DEMIANUS had another suggestion: if we were still determined to see Wallace's Standard Wings, then he could guide us to a large breeding population of the birds discovered only the previous year. But it would involve a long boat trip around the coast of Halmahera. We accepted his offer, and sailed from Sidangoli the following morning with Demianus on board.

The trip took 36 hours, and by the end of it a queasy Demianus was not at all sure that he had made a sensible offer. We had to go north around the end of Halmahera, and off the northern cape we again met the long, slow swells of the Pacific Ocean. They broke spectacularly on the outlying coral ledges, throwing tremendous curtains of pale green spray over the backs of the waves as they rumbled ashore and then burst into great welters of foam. It looked magnificent, and we kept a safe distance. But Demianus told me that, when our excursion was complete, he would prefer us to set him ashore so that he could return home on dry land.

On the morning of 21 June, he brought us to a landfall at the small village of Labi Labi on the north-west peninsula of Halmahera. From here to the breeding site of the Standard Wings was a three-hour walk. We decided to camp in the rainforest, so Demianus hired two porters from the village to carry our food and supplies. Though it was a hot and sultry tropical day, the two porters went back to their houses to collect heavy rubber gumboots.

Our path took us out of Labi Labi and through the village's coconut groves. Then the track turned inland and, after passing two or three small huts set beside their cassava fields, abruptly entered the rainforest. The last 500 metres was across newly destroyed forest. The people of Labi Labi, as elsewhere in the Moluccas, were steadily nibbling into the jungle. Trees lay toppled on the ground, and there were blackened fire marks where the undergrowth had been burned back in preparation for tilling and planting. The moment we entered the rainforest, it was clear why our porters were wearing gumboots. The track was wet and slippery, squelchy with mud, yet booby-trapped with twigs sharp enough to spike a naked foot.

Here the forest trees were more slender than those we had seen on Seram or Aru. The larger ones were perhaps 15 metres, with large buttress roots, and their crowns often joined to form a canopy with only an occasional gap through which we could see the sky. It was Trondur's first trip into the rainforest, and as an artist he had never experienced any environment like it. He commented how, coming from the Faeroes with its turf and rock, he had never imagined anywhere on earth with so many great trees or such richness of vegetation.

The colony of Standard Wings where Demianus and the village guides were taking us had been visited only by professional ornithologists and a wildlife documentary film crew. The track had been cut to allow the film crew to reach the site with their equipment, but already the forest was re-establishing itself. A log bridge thrown across a deep ravine was half rotten, and the hut camps left behind by the ornithologists and cameramen had collapsed into little more than mouldering piles of sticks and leaves. Only their cooking shelter survived, a lean-to of thatch and branches, and here we set up camp.

We had scarcely dropped our rucksacks to the ground when two men emerged shyly from the forest behind us. I had seen them in Labi Labi among the crowd of onlookers when we came ashore from our prahu. The taller of the two had been hard to miss as he was a muscular, bare-chested man in black pantaloons, with a stern expression, who looked as if he was auditioning

317

for a role as a pirate. Now he hovered at the edge of the camp-site. He had a wooden cage strapped to his back, and in one hand a hoop of bamboo with a wooden crosspiece. It was a bird perch on which two bright red Chattering Lories were swinging and chirruping as their name would suggest. His companion, hardly bigger than a 13-year-old child, had a dreamy smile and was wearing such a tattered pair of trousers and tee-shirt that he might not have been wearing any clothes at all. He too had a bird perch in one hand, this time with a Violet Necked Lory tied to it. Both men had parangs tucked into their waistbands, and the smaller man also had a small hollow gourd hanging from his belt, and a short stick of sugar cane. The two of them stopped a few metres away, and waited politely.

Once again there had been a misunderstanding. When Demianus was arranging for our porters in Labi Labi, I had asked him to check if there were any bird-catchers living in the village. Wallace had regularly employed professional bird-catchers in the rainforest, and I wanted to see how bird-catchers worked. I was told that no one in Labi Labi caught birds for a living, though a few men did make extra money that way. Now, it seemed, the two men had decided to follow us to our camp in case we still wanted a demonstration.

Demianus asked the two bird-catchers if our camp-site was a suitable place for them to go to work. They walked diffidently over to the cooking shelter and hung up their two bird perches, and the pirate removed the bamboo cage from his back and left it on the ground. Then they murmured with one another, glanced round the camp and picked out a slender, tall straight tree about 30 metres away, standing by itself. With a few slashes of his parang, the pirate

In the rainforest

319

cleared away the brushwood which surrounded it. Tucking his parang in his belt, he clamped his hands and feet around the tree-trunk and swarmed up it as casually as if he was on a ladder. As he climbed, he stopped now and again and cut off any branches, leaving the tree-trunk bare. Near the top he lopped off the final four feet of the trunk, then climbed lightly back down the tree.

Meanwhile his small companion had been searching in the nearby forest and reappeared carrying a smaller sapling, about two metres long, with four long slim branches protruding from the top. By the time the pirate had reached the ground, the smaller man had stripped the leaves off two of these branches, leaving a small crown of leaves at the end of each branch. Handing the sapling to the pirate to hold, he took a large bite out of his section of sugar cane, chewed vigorously and spat the sweetened saliva into his cupped hands. Then he dipped into his gourd bottle and produced a large ball of what looked like old chewing gum. Kneading and tugging, he pulled the gum into a long string and delicately began winding the gum around one of the stripped branches. Every so often he would stop, take another bite of sugar cane, and spit on his palms and fingers so that the sugary saliva stopped the gum sticking to his hands. When one thin branch was entirely wrapped in its spiral of gum, the small man did the same to the second bare branch. Finally, he slipped the three decoy parrots off their perches and attached them to the remaining leafy branches on the sapling.

Balancing the two-metre sapling in one hand, the pirate returned to the tree he had just scaled and began climbing it for the second time. Now he had to keep the awkward length of the sapling finely balanced so as not to disturb the lories who were chirping in alarm as they were hoisted aloft. Also, he had only one hand to climb with. Yet he still made the ascent look easy, going smoothly and carefully until he reached the top of the tree some 15 metres off the ground. There he gently turned the sapling until it was vertical and, using a strip of rattan he had been carrying between his teeth, carefully lashed the little sapling to the top of the tree as if it was a

Under the Standard Wing display trees

321

natural extension to it. Then, he climbed down quickly and rejoined his companion.

We all waited, gazing up at the bird-trap. The three lories, the decoy birds, shifted and fidgeted for a few moments, then settled down on their new high-level homes. They began to call out, the sounds carrying far over the tree canopy, and within minutes another lory — a wild one — had been attracted. The newcomer came flitting out of the forest, circled the decoy birds and settled into a nearby tree to watch them. The decoy birds continued to chatter and call; the wild bird shifted its perch, coming closer and closer to them. In a few more moments the wild bird would have flown across to join them and been stuck on the gum-covered branch. I had seen enough, and there was no need to catch a wild bird so I called a halt. Without a word the pirate swarmed up the tree and brought down the decoy birds. The whole operation had looked ridiculously simple and effective. With no more equipment than three tame lories, a ball of gum and a stick of sugarcane, the bird-catchers could have harvested the wild lories of that section of the rainforest. The only conditions that would hinder them, they said, were heavy rains when the wild birds did not like to leave the shelter of the forest canopy. Or, if there was very hot, bright sunshine the bird-catchers could not leave their decoy birds on their exposed tree-top for more than half an hour before they began to suffer from heat and thirst.

We spent two days at the forest camp. The pirate turned out to be an adept woodsman. He stalked through the shallows of the little stream which ran past the camp-site, gently turning over the large stones of the river bed. Now and then his hand would dart forward like a heron striking, and in less than an hour he gathered two kilos of freshwater crayfish for our meal. When Trondur joined him, and the two men came across a small grey-brown snake moving into the stream, the guide gestured Trondur to stand clear because the snake was venomous, and then let the snake continue on its way. On both afternoons we heard storms building up in the distance, with rumble after rumble of heavy thunder, but the tree cover prevented us from seeing the sky to judge whether the storm would come our way. We had to wait for the sound of approaching rain — a quite distinct drumming noise, coming closer and closer as though someone was spraying the forest canopy with a huge hose. Down below, we could hear the heavy rain striking the leaves high above us, but the foliage was so thick that very little water fell for several minutes. Then as the leaves shed their water, the drops began to patter down around us as the drumming sound of the rain ceased and the storm moved on. Then, for five or six hours the steady drip of water continued as the upper leaves released their collected rainwater, so that a brief thunderstorm became half a day's precipitation, and the paths stayed wet and muddy and the ground gave off a rich earthy smell.

Nightfall came early to the gloom of the forest floor. In the darkness, among the steady drips from the leaves, we heard the night sounds of the jungle. Occasionally there was the call of a night bird, but mostly there were the sounds of crickets and other insects, including one which was exactly the noise of a miniature smoke alarm going off. It was surprising how often there were loud crashes and sudden cracks. The equatorial forest was living, growing and dying. With no common seasonal rhythm for its plants, trees noisily shed old branches even as their neighbours put out new growth. It made the rainforest a remarkably rowdy place, and when we went in the half-light of dawn to visit the display trees of the Standard Wings there was little reaction from the bird-life of the forest if someone stood on a twig and suddenly snapped it, or brushed noisily through the undergrowth. With so many sudden noises already, and so few predators, our blundering passage caused little alarm.

We heard the 'wawk-wawk-wawk' of the Standard Wings and their excited chattering from 500 metres away. The birds were so intent on their display, and their rivalry was so focused that they were squabbling like a pack of house sparrows and paid as little regard to any other spectators. The display trees stood on the shoulder of a hill, and had two places where the birds congregated. Some preferred to assemble very high up, on the branches of two very tall forest giants. These birds were hardly visible as they were so far from the ground, and flitted back and forth energetically, though it seemed that one or two males were dominant and stayed longer on the main display branch. More interesting, because they were much closer to us, were a group of about 15 birds which chose to display in a clump of much smaller trees. Though no more than eight metres from the ground, they took little notice of us as they carried on their competition for the females. About the same size as large blackbirds, the males hopped about briskly in the branches, seeming to follow a regular route so that a bird would return again and again to the same preferred spot. This was a clear place on the branch where the bird could get a good grip with his large and powerful claws, spread his wings and show off, preferably facing across to another branch where a rival would receive the full frontal effect of the display. The demonstration involved raising and spreading the white shoulder feathers which Alfred Wallace had described, and rattling and shaking them furiously. To heighten the dramatic effect, from time to time the male Standard Wing also extended two pointed winglets which stood out on each side of his lower throat, so that he seemed to be wearing a short cape of emerald with flamboyant wing collars.

Between their shaking and fluttering, the male birds would suddenly launch themselves upward. Springing off their display branch, they would dive upward into the air a metre or more, do a tumbling turn in mid-air and then drop back on the same branch to look around, shout a challenge and then raise and shake their display plumes once again.

Wallace's Standard Wing

For Demianus this was the third time he had visited the Standard Wings of Labi Labi, and he was guardedly optimistic about the survival of the bird colony. There were enough birds concentrated in one area, he said, to make a sustainable population. The first crucial factor for their survival would be whether the villagers of Labi Labi had begun to see a value in the Standard Wings. If the villagers thought that the birds would bring prosperity, either by attracting visitors or because local people would be employed as wardens and forest-keepers, then they would try not to disturb the birds. The second urgent need was for the government in Jakarta to declare a sufficiently large zone around the bird colony as a protected habitat. Not a single hectare had yet been gazetted by the authorities for environmental protection — which, it turned out, was hardly surprising because there was no Nature Reserve or protected Area anywhere on Halmahera. The entire island was still at the mercy of logging companies, plantation interests and the expansion of land-hungry villagers. The Standard Wings were only one of 22 rare species of birds on Halmahera whose survival was threatened unless quick action was taken to shelter them. Whether that action was taken would probably depend on how well the environmental pressure groups pleaded their cause in Jakarta, and if enough money could be found to pay for the setting up of a major forest reserve. The cash would have to equal the commercial interests of the loggers.

We left Demianus on the east coast of Halmahera, as he requested, so that he could return home overland and did not have to endure the long haul back to Ternate by boat. He was lucky. If he had been seasick and nervous during the outward voyage, he would have been much more distressed during our return journey. To begin with, and for the first time, we ran on to a coral reef. The collision was in the late evening and we were moving very gently through the water, so no harm was done. But the time spent backing away from the reef,

Off Halmahera's cliffs

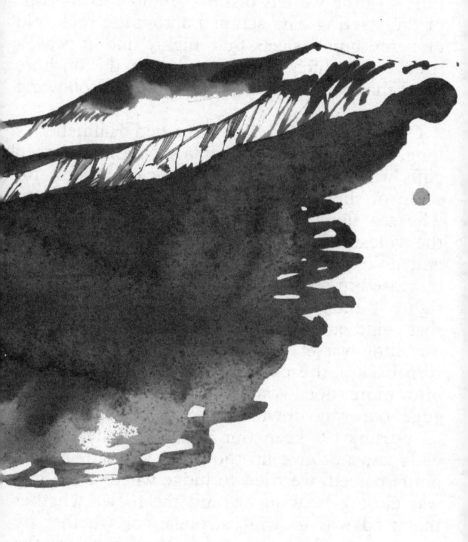

and then finding a deeper channel, meant that we found ourselves trying to get clear of the coast by starlight. All around us were the dark shapes of small islands. The coral reefs and ledges were so close under *Alfred Wallace*'s hull that from time to time we felt distinct tremors as the tips of the steering oars scraped across the rock. No one got much sleep that night, and it was a tired crew which had to deal with the onshore wind that caught us off a lee shore the following afternoon.

On our left-hand side stretched Halmahera's long, rock-bound coast with a succession of steep cliffs where there was not a single harbour nor scrap of shelter in which we could find refuge. The sea floor rose too steeply to the edge of the volcanic land to allow us to drop anchor and hold our vessel off the rocks. As the wind increased in strength, blowing onshore from our right, it built up a lumpy and hostile sea, so that wind and waves constantly tried to push our little vessel against the land. Too late to turn back and escape around the northern cape into more open water, all we could do was edge our way down the coast, trying as hard as possible to keep our course parallel to the cliffs and not give up too much ground. As the hours passed, we tried to judge whether the gap was closing between us and the rocks, whether the wind was growing stronger, or whether by any chance there was a slight change in the wind's direction which would allow us to set a safer course. This was when the shallow draught and light weight of a Kei Island prahu was a disadvantage. Our little vessel was not designed to hold up to such adverse weather. All that afternoon and well into the night, *Alfred Wallace* clawed her track parallel to cliffs and gave her crew a roller-coaster ride. At one moment the helmsman on his tiny platform at the extreme stern was thrown high in the air by the pitching of the boat. The next moment he would come swooping down, and with a shake and slap of water his steering position would be plunged beneath the waves, only to be tossed upward again. It was too unstable and dangerous for the helmsman to stand up, so he had to crouch or sit on his platform, clinging to the steering oars, and at every plunge of the stern below water level he would be half-soaked by the warm sea.

Cooking a meal on the heaving deck was difficult, even after ten weeks of living aboard our boat. Another saucepan and a kettle lid were whisked away by the wind, and Budi was overawed by sea conditions rougher than any he had experienced in his brief career as a sailor. He curled up wretchedly in the lee of the thatched cabin, while Joe and Leonard prepared a very basic meal of rice and tinned meat which we had to eat quickly before the food slithered off our plates. From time to time there was a heavier crash as a larger wave rolled out of the darkness and dumped sea water on the foredeck. This was followed immediately by the sound of water cascading through the deck seams and pouring into the forward hold. Then the deck watch had to work the bilge-pump, for it was only by keeping our boat light and the storm sails finely adjusted that we were managing to hold off the rocks of Halmahera. If we had not run our little outboard engine to keep the prahu's head closer into the wind, we would not have succeeded. In Alfred Wallace's time such a situation, with matting sails of uncertain cut and with oars for use in emergency, would have ended in disaster and a prahu broken on the rocks.

So we were numb and shaken up as we watched the grey-black peak of the Gamalama volcano take shape, dead ahead, through the poor visibility of a dull, rain-swept dawn. At the foot of 1,721-metre Gamalama, with its plume of steam and radiating gulley lines eroded in surface ash, lay Ternate's harbour, and here by 9 o'clock on the morning of 25 May we came to anchor, intent on tracing the final link in the bird-catching chain.

To find the house of the main bird-trader in Ternate, we turned off the main road leading through the southern suburbs and then walked down a maze of small laneways between tightly packed small houses which extended all the way to the beach. One confusing right-angled turn followed another until finally we came to a neat and well-appointed bungalow with a tiled entrance verandah. The house was squeezed in among its neighbours and there was no notice to announce that this was the headquarters of a trading enterprise, though Haji Muslim Kadir was well known in Ternate's central bazaar among the petty bird sellers who sold lories, parakeets and cockatoos directly to the public. Anyone could walk into the big hangar at the centre of the central market, select a bird from the dozen or so on display, pay a modest price and carry it out on a bamboo perch like the one the pirate had used in the rainforest for his decoy birds. But for real bird-trading, everyone said that we should visit Haji Kadir: he dealt wholesale.

Haji Muslim Kadir wore heavy glasses with thick lenses which made his eyes seem enormous. He also had a way of looking around nervously which gave him a rather defenceless air. A thin man in his mid-fifties, originally from Sulawesi, his business card stated unequivocally that he was a supplier of 'birds not banned for trading'. There was even a wildlife protection poster prominently displayed on the wall in his living room-cum-office. The poster had been prepared by an international wildlife protection society and showed coloured drawings of all the species of Indonesian birds which it was forbidden to buy and sell. To the sceptic, the poster might also have been a ready guide to the birds which commanded the highest price in the illegal commerce. However, Haji Kadir was adamant that he took every precaution to deal only in those birds which were legally traded under international convention. He had just returned from a lengthy trip to the government offices in Ambon, where he had spent much time in arranging to renew his official licence which allowed him to send 1,000 white cockatoos out of Ternate every three months. That figure, though Haji Kadir probably did not know it, made a mockery of all the official statistics. According to international agreement, the permitted trade in white cockatoos was a total of 1,000 birds every year from the whole of Indonesia. Yet Haji Kadir was sending that number every three months from one town, and had official permission to do so. Nor was anyone counting the number of birds sent with each consignment.

In fact, Haji Kadir was an outstanding example of good practice in the bird trade. He, at least, took the trouble to obtain certificates to buy and sell cockatoos, parrots and other species. Most of the smaller dealers and all the smugglers operated on a free-for-all basis. As one minor official in the Conservation Department at Ternate wearily put it, for every one bird captured and traded legally, 1,000 birds were traded outside the law.

Haji Kadir was also happy to show us his business premises. A door from his living room opened directly into a long shed with a cement floor; ranged along the walls and down the middle of the shed were holding cages, each about 1.2 metres high and one metre deep. There must have been 40 of them, and while most of them were empty about a dozen were crammed with birds awaiting shipment. They were red lories and cockatoos, scores upon scores of them, stuffed shoulder to shoulder in the cages. Dozens of dark shiny eyes watched from between the thin wire bars, and the noise was incessant. There was an endless shrieking, screaming, clucking and calling as several hundred captive birds shouted and squabbled. For 20 years, Haji Kadir said, he had traded in birds from the same house, and one wondered how he had managed to put up with the never-ending clamour. Compared with the bedraggled birds in the vegetable market, Haji Kadir's stock was in fine condition; they looked healthy and clean, and were being fed a special diet of soft maize from a steaming cauldron manned by three of his employees. Here, too, he was very professional. He explained that when the captive birds were brought in from Halmahera or the islands to the north, they were being fed on bananas. He took care to change their diet gradually to boiled maize, because when the birds were sold on to the Javanese dealers they would be fed nothing but maize. Later, the majority would continue on to the bird-dealers of Singapore, who would send most of the gaily coloured parrots to Pacific countries, while the majority of the cockatoos ended up in the United States.

Haji Kadir's approach was matter-of-fact. To him the bird trade was simply a business like any other; he might as well have been exporting sacks of nutmegs or tins of coconut oil. The exotic birds of the neighbouring islands were simply a crop which others harvested and brought to him to sell on. Nor had the trade much diminished during the 20 years he had been in it. Another wholesale bird-trader in Ternate had closed his business when the European market shrivelled up after protests from animal welfare groups, but the trade to North America remained steady and that to the Pacific rim countries was expanding. Haji Kadir saw no reason why his children should not take over the business, and his wife, a formidable lady in a yellow turban which matched her blouse, nodded agreement.

Haji Kadir was a modern exponent of the bird trade which had made Wallace's field work possible. Wallace had sent Moluccan bird-skins and skeletons overseas at a profit, just as Haji Kadir now shipped living birds to reach overseas markets. For every specimen that Wallace kept for scientific study, he tried to get as many specimens as possible which Samuel Stevens, his London agent, could sell to collectors in England. The better the specimen, and the more rare the bird, the higher price he obtained. To Wallace and men like Haji Kadir, the rich bird-life of the Moluccas was a resource to be exploited. What was remarkable, given the huge numbers of birds still being harvested, was that this resource had not yet been totally exhausted. If Wallace had had the means to send his bird catches back to England alive, he would very likely have done so, not just for their scientific interest as living specimens but also for the high price they would have obtained. When he finally travelled back to London in 1862 he took two living Lesser Birds of Paradise with him, purchasing them for the high price of £100 in Singapore and transporting them with the rest of his luggage. He had a large cage placed on the ship's deck, and laid in a store of bananas to feed them, but found that the birds much preferred eating insects. So he would go to the ship's storeroom each day and brush up cockroaches into a biscuit tin, in order to give them the preferred diet. This system worked well enough until the ship reached Egypt, at which point the railway officials arranging the overland sector to the Mediterranean made a great fuss about live cargo and had to be cajoled into letting the two Birds of Paradise, and some lories, travel onward with Wallace. Worse, the ship which then took him and his small aviary onward from Alexandria was too clean to have cockroaches. Wallace solved the problem by going ashore in Malta, locating a bakery and capturing a sufficient stock of cockroaches to last the rest of the trip to Southampton. The birds finished up with the Zoological Society of London, the first Birds of Paradise to have reached England alive.[1]

Indeed, one of the best pieces of news after Wallace got back, exhausted, to Ternate from his rather unsatisfactory trip to New Guinea in mid-1858, was a letter from Samuel Stevens informing him that the collection of bird-skins which he had made in Aru had sold for the

------

[1] One bird lived a year, the other for two years. Wallace suggested that, in future, live Birds of Paradise might be kept in the Palm House of Kew Gardens, where they would survive many years and provide great interest for visitors.

remarkable sum of £1,000. Aru birds including the Birds of Paradise, even dead, were so rare that they commanded an excellent premium on the London market. The other piece of astonishing news which arrived soon afterwards was that Wallace's essay explaining evolution as a result of natural selection — the same paper he had written after his bout of fever and sent to Charles Darwin — had been read out to no less an audience than the members of the Linnean Society of London. What is more, it had been presented in tandem with a similar proposition prepared by no other than Charles Darwin himself and sponsored by the great Sir Charles Lyell.

Wallace was thrilled. Writing to his mother, he reported proudly, 'I have received letters from Mr. Darwin and Dr. Hooker, two of the most eminent naturalists in England which have highly gratified me. I sent Mr. Darwin an essay on a subject upon which he is now writing a great book. He showed it to Dr. Hooker and Sir Charles Lyell, who thought so highly of it that they had it read before the Linnean Society. This insures me the acquaintance of these eminent men on my return home.' Wallace had good reason to be pleased. Nothing he had written before had appeared in such a prestigious setting. It must have seemed an extraordinary accolade to a self-taught scientist, tucked away on the far side of the world in a town where it was difficult even to buy items of a collector's basic equipment like penknives and wide-mouthed flasks. He had no way of knowing about the machinations which had led to the joint presentation at the Linnean Society, and such was his respect for Darwin that he gave no thought to the possibility that his own Ternate essay might have contributed anything to Darwin's greater knowledge. Home, indeed, was something he was beginning to think about. The grisly time in New Guinea had dampened his enthusiasm for field work, and he told his mother that 'as soon as I have finished my exploration of this region I shall be glad to return home as quickly and cheaply as possible. I will certainly be by way of the Cape, or by second class overland.'

As matters turned out, it would be another three and a half years before he saw his mother again. In the interval, in late 1859, Darwin's book — *The Origin of Species by Means of Natural Selection* — had been published, and was already enthroned as the dominant text on the whole question of evolution. In its Introduction Darwin referred favourably to 'Mr. Wallace's excellent memoir' which had been sent to him from the Malay archipelago, and he acknowledged that its author had 'arrived at almost exactly the same general conclusions that I have on the origin of species'. But once again Darwin left the reader in no doubt as to who had the idea first, pointedly mentioning his own pioneer work of 1844, fifteen years earlier, and saying that he had first started thinking about the 'Great Problem' when he was a young naturalist sailing aboard HMS *Beagle*. The reason for publishing his 'Extract', as he

12

Maleos and Bats

WHILE Darwin was checking the proofs for his book, Wallace had already moved on in both his thinking and his travels. He was in Sulawesi, where he was encountering animals so strange that he was able to extend his theory of evolution to explain why different species were found in different parts of the world.

Celebes, as Sulawesi was then known, was an anomaly for naturalists. Its bizarre wildlife seemed to reflect the island's weirdly contorted shape which has been compared with a sprawling spider, an amoeba, or the constellation Sagittarius. This fauna included a creature called the babirusa which seemed half-pig and half-deer; a deer-like forest creature which some naturalists considered an ox but others classified as an antelope; a bird resembling an oversized chicken wearing a badly fitting blue helmet which buried its eggs in hot sand and then abandoned them; and several species of black monkeys at that time thought to be apes.

Sulawesi's north-east peninsula, where Wallace landed in June 1859, was also the setting for the most rapidly successful Dutch colonial plantation in the entire Indies. In the space of two generations its native tribes had changed from being aggressive headhunters who dressed in bark and lived in stilt houses, to an orderly agricultural people settled in neat villages with rosebush hedges who tended their coffee plantations. Wallace found himself staying one night with a village chief whose father used human heads as house decorations. His own host, however, dressed in a neat black suit with patent leather shoes, and lived in a smart new house furnished in European style and lit by chandeliers. Waiters in white uniforms offered Madeira and bitters before dinner, and the food was eaten off fine china, with finger glasses and napkins. The only exotic touch was in the regional menu. Washed down with claret and beer, the main courses were chicken, wild pig and a fricassee of bat.

Again Wallace found a wealthy merchant to help him with his research. This time it was an Englishman, a Mr Tower who was a long-established general merchant in the capital of Manado. He introduced him to another Mr Duivenboden who turned out to be a son of Wallace's earlier benefactor, the 'King of Ternate'. With their assistance Wallace set about tracking down specimens of the more exotic creatures he wanted to examine, particularly the egg-burying bird known locally as a 'maleo'.

The best place to find maleos, he was told, was at the very tip of the peninsula. Here, on a beach of hot sand, the birds came in the nesting season to inter their eggs. The place was awkward to reach, but a government salt works was being built about 20 miles away, and its superintendent offered to make up a hunting party to take Wallace to the beach and drop him off there so that he could do his studies. While Wallace camped on the beach and collected his feathered specimens, the superintendent would go hunting in the forest with the local 'major' or village chief, a dozen natives and a pack of 20 dogs, and see if they could bag him a pig-deer and an anoa, the deer-ox.

The trip turned out to be only a qualified success. Its high point was supposed to be a driven hunt, involving Wallace as well as his host's team. He and his companions sat for five hours in the tree-tops, clutching their guns and waiting for the pig-deer and deer-ox to rush past in large numbers, as the local people had forecast. But nothing appeared and they did not get off a single shot. Wallace had to be content with the corpses of two anoas which had been caught earlier, but they had been so chewed by the native dogs that it was only possible to preserve their heads. Of the babirusa or pig-deer he saw no living example, though he was able to sketch the dried-out skull of one of them, showing the animal's extraordinary upper tusks. Instead of growing downwards from the jaw in the usual way, they grew upwards and then curled back into a splendid curve almost ten inches long in front of the animal's eyes. Wallace could offer no explanation for this odd excrescence except that perhaps the curved tusks protected the animal's eyes while it was rootling through thick bushes.

His quest for the maleos, by contrast, was highly rewarding. During his stay at the beach he was able to observe their unusual nesting habit at close range. The male and female birds were difficult to tell apart because both had the same black and white plumage, the white tinged with

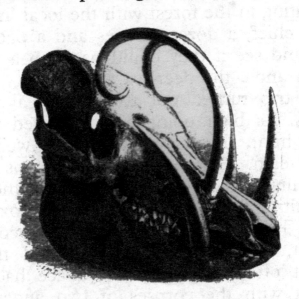

Skull of Babirusa
(*taken from* The Malay Archipelago)

salmon pink. They also shared the distinctive feature of a bright blue casque or helmet on the crown of the head which probably served to protect them from sunstroke. If startled, they would either run off into the bush, or flap up heavily into the nearest tree and strut up and down the branch looking very like domestic chickens. Both male and female worked on their subterranean hatchery, taking it in turns to scratch out a pit about three feet deep in the black volcanic gravel of the beach. In the bottom of this hole the female then deposited a single large egg, before covering it up with a foot of sand or gravel. After that chore was done, the two birds would then disappear into the bush, perhaps to reappear a few days later and deposit another egg. Meanwhile other maleos might bury eggs in the same hole, or dig their own holes nearby until the nesting area was soon pitted with a great number of holes so that it looked like a large badger sett.

Wallace was fascinated to note that, once the parent birds had completed their egg-laying, they seemed to take no further interest in their young. The male and female went off to the bush, leaving the eggs to hatch by themselves, and the fledglings struggled to the surface in the manner of young turtles emerging. As soon as they broke into the open air, the young maleos simply scuttled off and, according to Duivenboden senior, were able to fly within a day of being hatched. The 'King of Ternate' had taken a couple of maleo eggs aboard his schooner, and the eggs had hatched during the night. The very next day the young maleos had been able to fly the width of the cabin.

By this stage Wallace was constantly on the look-out for evidence to support his ideas on evolution, and the maleos provided him with a very good example of specialised adaptation. He pointed out that the maleo's sharp claws and powerful feet were specially suited for scratching and digging downwards, so that they could excavate their laying pits. The contrast, he said, was with their relatives, the brush turkeys. They also buried their eggs, but in great heaps of sticks and rubbish, so their feet had evolved to be much more like shovels so that they could scoop and throw a cascade of the necessary quantities of twigs and vegetable matter.

But it was Sulawesi's odd congregation of animals and insects which gave Wallace most to puzzle about. The island seemed to be a contradiction of everything he might expect. It was very large and lay at the centre of the Indonesian archipelago, with a number of smaller islands extending in each direction to serve as stepping-stones to link it with its neighbours. So the expectation was that Sulawesi would contain a great number and variety of species of animals which had arrived as immigrants from both directions, from Asia and from Australia. 'As so often happens in nature,' Wallace observed, 'the fact turns out to be just the reverse of what we should have expected.' In reality Sulawesi had remarkably few animals, and not very many species, but many of the species which did live there were found nowhere else in the world. Wallace counted 108 species of characteristic land birds, which was not a very large number compared with, say, Sumatra. But of these he found only 19 species extended into the islands eastward, and only 9 species occurred on islands to the west. By his calculation, no fewer than 80 species of birds were unique to Sulawesi, 'a degree of individuality which considering the situation of the island is hardly to be equalled in any other part of the world'.

What was the reason for this curious situation? Wallace pointed to a clue found among the butterflies of Sulawesi, which differed from their neighbours on the other islands. Members of similar species of butterflies in Java and Singapore, for instance, resembled one another very closely. Yet these species, or their near cousins, were very different when captured on Sulawesi. Their wing shapes were so distinct that Wallace was able to tell at a glance whether a specimen had been collected on Sulawesi or not. He offered the explanation that Sulawesi must have formed part of an earlier continental system, and had then been isolated for longer than its neighbours so that its own species had developed. He proposed that Sulawesi should in fact be regarded as its own distinct geographical zone for animals, and that the study of the present-day distribution of animals was an insight into geological history. Today that idea is a commonplace and, although Wallace's field data on Sulawesi has been expanded and modified, he is acknowledged as the founder of modern zoo-geography, the study of the distribution of animals.

★ ★ ★

On 31 May we arrived off the beach of Tangkoko to look at the place where Wallace collected his maleos. The beach was as he had described: a long, ragged sweep of loose black volcanic sand, which he had found very tiring to walk across. Some 30 metres wide at high tide, the beach was not much broader at low water because the underwater slope dropped off steeply, creating an almost constant surf. The local fishermen had to be quick about extracting their outrigger canoes from the waves. With two men aboard, the canoe would be paddled straight towards the beach until it was just short of the breaker line. At that moment the bow man would jump overboard and swim through the surf until he could stand in the shallows. His colleague would then bring the canoe forward until he, too, leaped overboard as the first rollers threatened to swamp the vessel. If he had timed his approach carefully, there was just enough of a gap between the waves for the two men to pick up the lightweight canoe, hoist it up on their shoulders by the outrigger bars, and stagger up the beach before the undertow pulled them back.

Wallace made no mention of anyone living near the beach, so the place was probably deserted in his time. Today the village of Batu Putih has expanded along a section of flat

348

Maleos

land just behind the beach, with a tarmac road leading inland towards the volcanic mountain peaks which overlook the coast. Just to the south of the village the slope of these mountains comes almost to the beach. Here the forest begins at the edge of the sand, and by happy coincidence Wallace's 'Maleo Beach' is included within a small Nature Reserve. Its wildlife includes several troops of black-crested macaque monkeys, two species of cuscus, and numbers of the tiny tree-dwelling primates called tarsiers. The Reserve is only four hours' drive away from the capital at Manado, so it is a favoured location for tropical zoologists and botanists doing research, and it receives a steady trickle of tourist visitors. 'Tangkoko Nature Reserve' is announced on a carved wooden board at the outskirts of Batu Putih, and a few metres farther on a painted sign reads 'Tangkoko Rangers' over a drawing of a round-eyed tarsier. An arrow

Off Tangkoko Beach

directs the visitor to turn aside into the front yard of a large bungalow where an outbuilding serves as a dormitory for tourists. Compared with the remote, underpopulated and rarely visited nature reserves we had seen on Waigeo and Aru, there could have been no greater contrast. The former had been reserves only in embryo, while Tangkoko was well established.

So it was interesting to find that the Tangkoko Rangers were a non-governmental organisation, independent of the Directorate General of Forestry Protection and Nature Conservation which officially controlled the Nature Reserve. There were about half a dozen Rangers on site, all local men and mostly under 30 years old. They financed their work by selling tee-shirts and other souvenirs, running the tourist accommodation and working as guides to the park. In good years they also received funding from foreign environmental groups. The Rangers described themselves as volunteers who had banded together to protect the forest and its creatures, and as it turned out they were doing a remarkably good job. They patrolled the forest for poachers and had even built watchtowers to look out for forest fires.

A visit to Tangkoko Park under their wing followed a well-rehearsed pattern. At dawn the Rangers sent an advance scout into the forest to locate a foraging group of black monkeys and report back so that visitors could be led directly to them along well-marked paths. In the evening they would bring their clients to precisely the right hollow trees where the tarsiers lived. The little furry creatures, no larger than a child's hand, would creep out of their sleeping places at nightfall and begin hunting the thickets, leaping from branch to branch as they searched for their diet of grasshoppers and the occasional gecko. For the benefit of the tourists the Tangkoko guides would illuminate the tarsiers with torches, but only briefly for fear of damaging their huge eyes adapted for low light vision.

To find maleos was far more difficult, the Rangers told us. Not since the early 1980s had maleos dug their nests on the black sand beach of Tangkoko where Wallace had found them. The birds had been driven away by the expansion of Batu Putih village, and their nest pits had been regularly plundered. Saskar, one of the senior guides, believed that a small group of maleo might still be found deep inside the park, though to reach them would involve a 7-kilometre trek through the forest and there was no certainty that the birds would appear. Their former egg-laying grounds had been overgrown by shrubs, and, because maleo eggs and maleo flesh were considered delicacies by the local people, the birds had been hunted almost to extinction.

Indeed, the immediate threat to the unique wildlife of north-east Sulawesi, according to the Rangers, was neither the destruction of the habitat nor the risk of pollution. It was that the local people liked to eat the endangered species. A regional joke was that the people of the province, Minahasa, would eat everything on legs except for a table and chairs.

To make their point, Saskar and another ranger, Simsun, took us to a country market which specialised in selling the flesh of protected wildlife for food. The market was held every Saturday at the small town of Langowen, a three-hour drive from Tangkoko, and it was supplied by poachers and illegal hunters who operated all over north Sulawesi and the outlying islands. If someone wanted python to serve at a wedding feast, plump maleo to roast, or any other protected species to eat, Langowen was the most likely place to find it for sale or to place an order with the poachers for the following Saturday. Swarms of shoppers came from miles around to take advantage of the extraordinary selection of animals on offer. Nor was the Langowen market unique. There was at least one other smaller country market where protected species were sold, and a poachers' market in the suburbs of Manado itself.

Langowen was on the interior plateau where Wallace had so admired the transformation from savagery to well-ordered plantation life, and the scenery could hardly have changed since his day. On a Saturday morning the approach roads to Langowen were choked with horse-drawn carriages piled with sacks of rice, peppers, carrots, cabbages, leeks, lettuces, fruit and cut flowers which the farmers were bringing in for sale. The rich dark red soil was extraordinarily fertile, and the Minahasans were cultivating it assiduously to produce magnificent crops.

The market was at the centre of a sprawling complex of lanes where small shops and stalls offered every sort of cheap manufactured goods, from plastic sandals to spare parts for paraffin lamps. These, of course, could be bought in any good market in Indonesia, and what made Langowen so special was the large open-sided shed at the centre of the market where the prominent colour was the red of bloody flesh. It was packed with shoppers shuffling their way down the narrow aisles as they checked the large slabs arranged with carcasses. There was fresh meat everywhere. It was laid out on the slabs, hung from the roof beams of the shed, looped around the vertical support posts and dangled from the wooden crossbars of market stalls. Nor was all the meat yet dead. To one side of the large shed were several wire mesh cages packed with live dogs like tall beagles. These were being examined by a passing trade of shoppers — mostly women, though there were some men — who would point out their selection and the animal would then be hauled out of the cage and quickly despatched. Moments later a contented shopper might be seen walking off with a heavy plastic bag, from the top of which protruded four lifeless and clearly canine paws.

Opposite the live dog stall, a green turtle was being butchered. It was a huge animal weighing at least 200 kilos, and to have transported it all the way up from the coast to Langowen would have required considerable effort. Eating turtle meat was supposed to increase a man's virility according to Indonesian tradition, and Langowen was obviously a good place to sell off the animal's flesh. The great reptile was lying

354

on its back and being dismembered by two men. The turtle was so large that it was too big to fit on the stall's counter, so the men crouched over the carcass on the blood-soaked ground as they worked. They glistened with blood and slime up to their elbows as they hacked with parangs to open up the thinner undershell, and then carve the flesh from the shell. As each lump of turtle meat came free, it was tossed up on the counter where, to make sure the customers knew it was genuine, the reptilian head of the turtle gazed out. Killing green turtle was only illegal in the marine reserves, explained Simsun sadly, though the turtle population off north-east Sulawesi was declining very rapidly.

The real disregard for the conservation laws was inside the main shed. Here, to an astonishing degree, the bodies of protected and endangered species were for sale. We arrived too late to count

The Minahasa plateau

the number of dead cuscuses, the sleepy-looking furry marsupials which were pathetically easy to catch because they climbed so slowly through the tree-tops. They were a favourite delicacy for local gourmets, and had all been snapped up by the shoppers. The last cuscus was being put into a paper wrapping even as we shouldered our way up to the stall. All that was left from that particular vendor were clusters of tree rat priced at 2,000 rupiah a time. The rats looked remarkably like barbecue sticks, as they had been roasted and neatly skewered along their length.

Tree rats did not make a very tempting gastronomic display, and it took an even stronger stomach to encounter the hanging racks of baked dogs which had received similar treatment. This was dog-on-a-stick, with the giant skewer emerging from the animal's gaping teeth, the paws curled forward over the chest, and the stomach a gaping hole filled with what looked like green stuffing. The skin itself was coal black because the fur had been singed off with a blowtorch.

There was worse. The display slabs at the centre of the meat market were cement platforms, about one metre by three metres, and they extended the full length of the shed. From end to end they were covered with great gobbets of pig meat and pig's heads. But very few were ordinary domestic pigs; the majority were wild boar from the forest. There must have been a couple of tons of meat from wild pigs, their flanks, chines and enormous thighs. Some cuts had been skilfully prepared, others looked as if they had simply been chopped up with an axe. The butchers and their assistants entreated the shoppers to buy, holding up morsels dripping with blood, encouraging the public to prod or sniff the flesh to check that it was fresh. One vendor had his son, a boy about ten years old, standing on the display slab, his feet invisible among the pig meat so that he could scan the crowd and pick out the most likely shoppers. Here and there, artistically arranged or simply tossed in casual piles, were the boar's heads, another delicacy. And among them lay the heads of babirusa, the pig-deer which Wallace had tried in vain to hunt. It was impossible to mistake their backward-curling upper tusks. Babirusa are a rare species unique to Sulawesi and the neighbouring islands, and strictly protected by law. Yet at Langowen market on a single Saturday we counted at least a dozen babirusa heads, still for sale four hours after the market opened. How many had been sold already it was impossible to tell, nor was there much secrecy about where they had been obtained. Most, we were told, came from the forests of Dumoga Bone 200 kilometres to the west. Dumoga Bone just happened to be another National Park and Wildlife Reserve. Zoologists, tourists and wildlife film crews were finding it difficult to track down babirusa, but it seemed that the poachers who supplied Langowen knew exactly where to go.

Simsun bought a kilo of babirusa meat as evidence of the illegal trade. The skin of the babirusa, he demonstrated to us, was quite distinct from the skin of wild pig, and laboratory tests would confirm the origin of the meat. But it was largely a gesture. He and his colleagues had no power to enforce the animal protection laws, and although one of the sellers of babirusa took the trouble to bury the more obvious curly-tusked heads in the pile as we approached, his colleagues were very forthright about quoting us the price for fresh babirusa. Minahasans, it seemed, preferred the flesh of babirusa to the flesh of wild boar, and paid a premium of 70 per cent to buy joints of babirusa meat, knowing that the animal was surely a wild one.

Simsun and Saskar both shrank back from taking too close an interest in the most blatant marketing of a protected species — black-crested macaque monkey — because the animals might well have come from their own Tangkoko Park. The disembowelled corpses of two black macaque monkeys dangled by their long arms from meat hooks, among the stuffed dogs. The monkeys looked appallingly human; one had its head turned upward, and its mouth was wide open in a horrible grimace. Here the salesman was noticeably more wary. He flipped a small cloth over the dead monkey's head as we came closer, but then his salesmanship got the better of him as a potential customer showed an interest in buying the monkey for the pot. The vanity cover came off, and the haggling began. Simsun later explained that the black monkeys had almost certainly been killed by poachers operating inside the Nature Reserves, as only a few bands of black monkeys existed outside the protected areas. The tragedy was that his own Reserve at Tangkoko was the most tempting target. There the black macaques had been so intensively studied by scientists working with them over long periods that the monkeys had become accustomed to being approached very closely by humans, and were equally used to tourists. So the macaques were very tame and trusting. They allowed humans to approach to within touching distance, and the poachers took advantage of this trust to get close enough to the monkeys to kill them silently.

In the starkest possible way, the meat market at Langowen illustrated how man was having a direct impact on the more exotic species which Wallace had described. Yet here, also, Wallace himself had behaved in similar fashion, just as he had been a very active bird-trader. When he was collecting maleo birds on the beach of Tangkoko, he relished their meat and eggs. The flesh, he said, provided him and his companions with an abundance of good food, and the eggs were a great delicacy. Four inches long, they were much bigger than hens' eggs, and 'when quite fresh are indeed delicious. They are richer than hen's eggs, and of a finer flavour, and each one completely fills an ordinary tea-cup, and forms, with bread or rice, a very good meal.' Wallace and his assistants killed 26 maleo, and presumably their skins and skeletons fetched a good price on the London market. The number of maleo eggs they ate is not recorded.

Wallace had also eaten fricassee of bat in Minahasa. Today bat is still a popular local dish,

359

and the President of Indonesia himself is said to enjoy a meal of bat. At our request Saskar took us to the street market in Manado city where, on most mornings, a bat-seller arrived with his box of bats for sale. He brought them in a closely slatted wooden box, with a little trap-door in the top. Inside the box the bright pinpoints of bat eyes stared out of the gloom, and it was just possible to distinguish the sharp, foxy faces of the creatures themselves. From time to time a black claw worked its way through a gap in the box slats to grasp and scrabble in the daylight. The shoppers strolled up and down checking the street market's vegetables and other foodstuffs, and a housewife stopped to ask the bat-seller if she could see his wares. He flung open the trap-door on his box, reached inside and pulled out a furiously scrabbling bat. The creature tried to grab the sides of the box with the desperation of a kitten being pulled from a bag. The bat-seller then displayed the animal and spread it out, a wing in each hand, to show off the chubby body. The shopper, after poking and prodding the bat, liked the purchase, and the seller swung the bat through the air and brought the animal's head down on the pavement with a sharp smack. Then he tossed the still fluttering corpse to his assistant for the fur to be frizzled off with a blowtorch.

I asked Saskar if he knew how the bats were caught and where they came from. Most of the bats sold in Manado, he said, came from Dumoga Bone, the same region as the babirusa. There was also a village of bat-catchers near the Tangkoko Park, and he could arrange a demonstration of bat-catching if we wanted. However, when he approached the villagers they refused to show us how they worked. It seemed that although bat-catching was legal, and most species of bats were not protected, the villagers were aware that their activities might not be approved generally, and the Rangers suspected them of being black monkey poachers as well. After some searching, the Rangers did find a farmer in Batu Putih who would oblige, and the following evening we were escorted through the jungle to the edge of the Tangkoko Reserve. Here a special bat-hunting stage of bamboo scaffolding had been erected for our benefit, strategically placed at a saddle gap in the ridge line through which the bats would fly during their evening feeding.

The bat-catcher himself appeared about an hour before dusk. He was a lean, cheerful man in his late middle age, with sunken cheeks and wearing an old army forage cap. He was carrying two very long thin bamboo poles which he was careful not to get snagged in the thick undergrowth. Looped over his shoulder was a length of fine mesh net. He had brought with him a young man as an assistant, and the two of them carefully tied the net between the ends of the long poles. He then showed the young man how to scrape a short length of bamboo up and down the metal blade of a parang, making a series of screeching sounds like chalk dragged across an old-fashioned blackboard, which presumably were meant to lure the bats to the net or to confuse their echo-sensing calls as they flew. The young man could not master the exact pitch of the scratching sound, so he gave up the attempt, and the older man scrambled up on the scaffolding and was handed the two poles. Seating himself comfortably on the top bar of the platform, the bat-catcher spread the poles apart in a vee with the mist net hanging between them like fine tennis net in the sky, and waited patiently.

For almost an hour nothing happened. The daylight faded, and stars began to appear. A crescent moon lit up a few high clouds, and there was barely a stir of wind. The forest was very quiet as we waited at the foot of the scaffolding, watching the occasional brighter flare as the bat-catcher drew on his cigarette.

Suddenly, in the stillness, he clapped the poles together. It was a very abrupt movement, and I had seen nothing, but already he was lowering the poles, hand over hand so that he could grasp the net. Someone switched on a torch and shone the beam on the bat-catcher's hands as he peeled back the mesh to reach a small struggling shape. It was a bat, a very small one, little more than a baby.

It took several moments for the bat-catcher to free his victim, and in that time the frantic squeaks of the bat could be heard clearly. It twittered and chittered in alarm. In a moment another bat, a much larger one, came swooping and fluttering out of the darkness and through the beam of the torch. It seemed that the second bat was attracted by the cries of the captive.

Bat catching

The newcomer hovered and then swept back
and forth over the scaffolding for two or three
passes before vanishing into the darkness.

The bat-catcher untangled the baby bat and,
after showing it to us, let the little creature go
free, then settled back once more to wait, the
twin poles pointing up into the sky like long
antennae and the net hanging limp in between.
Now we knew what to look for, and a few
minutes later we saw another bat flying into
range, silhouetted against the moon. It swooped
back and forth, jinking and turning, and abruptly
reversing its flight like a house martin coming

under the eaves of a house. Two or three times it approached the net and then backed off, sensing the mesh. Then it came too close. There was the clatter of the two bamboo poles clapped together, and the bat was taken. It was painstakingly extracted from the net, taking care not to damage the mesh, and shown to us. It had a piebald face and was baring its teeth in alarm and rage. The bat-catcher held it carefully, so he was not bitten, then tossed it into the air to release it.

We stayed for another hour until a gentle breeze began to sway the mist net and the bat-catcher could no longer control the aerial trap. By then three more bats had been caught — a very poor total, we were told. On a good night a bat-catcher might take as many as 30 or 40 bats in an ideal location, and sell each one the following day in the market for 4,000 rupiahs. In a single night he would earn as much as a factory worker could earn in two weeks.

Bat-catching was the final episode of our stay at Tangkoko. After four days at anchor off the black sand beach, we sailed *Alfred Wallace* around the coast to Manado. In 1859 Wallace had described it as a 'little town . . . one of the prettiest in the East. It has the appearance of a large garden, containing rows of rustic villas, with broad paths between, forming streets generally at right angles with each other. Good roads branch off in several directions towards the interior, with a succession of pretty cottages, neat gardens and thriving plantations, interspersed with wildernesses of fruit trees.' Now Manado was a substantial city and, though not as spoiled as Ambon, was nevertheless bursting at the seams. The harbour was particularly overcrowded. Overlooked on the landward side by fine but stained old buildings, it was only three small, stone-faced basins crammed with boats, their warps criss-crossing in every direction. We had to creep our way into shelter, pushing aside ropes covered with putrid matter and filth so that our prahu could slide over the obstacles. *Alfred Wallace*'s draught allowed us to find space right in the back of the basin, in stinking water too shallow for most other craft. When I called on the harbour master to ask his permission to stay in that spot for a few days, he was surprised. We could moor where we liked, he said, but warned that we should watch out for the rats. His harbour, he claimed, had more rats, and larger ones, than any port in Sulawesi.

Wallace had completed his research in Manado by September 1859 — just as Darwin, on the other side of the world, was delivering to Murray, his publisher, the final proofs for his *Origin of Species*. Darwin had sent earlier drafts to his friends Lyell and Hooker for their comments and suggestions, and the book itself was ready for sale in late November — 17 months after Darwin had received the apocalyptic 'Letter from Ternate' but 22 years since he had first begun to work on the subject. A complimentary copy of *Origin* was posted off to Wallace, and his reaction was characteristically and totally generous. Wallace sang Darwin's praises, instead of resenting that their shared ideas on evolution had been presented to the public in his co-discoverer's name. To his old friend and travelling companion Bates, who by now had returned to England, Wallace wrote:

I do not know how or to whom to express fully my admiration of Darwin's book. To him it would seem flattery, to others self-praise; but I do honestly believe that with however much patience I had worked up and experimented on the subject, I could never have *approached* the completeness of his book — its vast accumulation of evidence, its overwhelming argument, and its admirable tone and spirit. I really feel thankful that it has not been left to me to give the theory to the public. Mr. Darwin had created a new science and a new philosophy.

13

Gadfly and Guru

DARWIN'S book had been a best-seller[1] for more than two years by the time Alfred Wallace arrived back in London in April 1862, bringing his two live Birds of Paradise with him. He had been away in the East for eight years, and his photo-portrait taken on his way through Singapore shows a tall, spare man posing rather stiffly in front of the lens,

---

[1] The entire first print of 1,250 copies was taken up by booksellers on the first day it was available to them, and by 1862 *Origins* was in its third edition.

367

self-conscious but with a hint of confidence in his bearing. Wallace knew that, waiting for him in London, were dozens of boxes and crates marked 'Private'. He had been sending them back with the more commercial shipments to Samuel Stevens, with instructions that these special boxes were to be put on one side, unopened. They contained thousands of bird-skins, butterflies, beetles and landshells, many of them previously unknown, whose description would cause a great stir among naturalists in England.

Public interest in scientific travel, preferably with overtones of danger, had soared to new heights while Wallace had been in the rainforest with butterfly net and birdshot. David Livingstone had discovered the Victoria Falls of the Zambesi, and Speke, after mapping the Great Lakes region with Richard Burton, was on the verge of locating the long-sought-for source of the Nile. In the north of Canada, expedition after expedition had been searching for the remains of Sir John Franklin's expedition, mysteriously missing since it set out to find the North-West Passage to the Pacific Ocean. The world seemed to be a smaller, more immediate place to an audience interested in foreign countries and cultures. The compound expansion engine had been fitted to ocean-going ships, making them less weather dependent, and the first iron-built Cunarder had crossed the Atlantic in nine and a half days. The leviathan SS *Great Eastern*, at 27,000 tons' displacement the largest ship of her time, had shown what could be done with shipbuilding on the grand scale; and a Frenchman, De Lesseps, had recently begun a very ambitious scheme to dig a canal through the Suez isthmus which, if successful, would make commonplace the journey to the places Wallace had explored.

Like many self-exiles who spend long years away, Wallace had been mentally planning every detail of what he would do on his return. From Sourabaya in Java he had written to his widowed mother: 'I am, as you will see, now commencing my retreat westwards, and have left the wild and savage Moluccas and New Guinea for Java.' His sister Fanny, who had returned from the United States in 1847 and was now married to a professional photographer named Thomas Sims, 'wrote me last month to know about how I should live on my return. Of course my dear mother, I should not think of living anywhere but with you after such a long absence.' His only worry was that there might not be enough room in his mother's cottage for all the materials he had been accumulating in Indonesia. He would need 'a small bedroom, one large room or a small one if there is, besides, a kind of lumber room where I could keep my cases and do rough and dirty work'. If her cottage was not big enough, then he would help her and Fanny acquire a new, larger residence. His own choice was for somewhere suburban near London — 'I should prefer being a little way out of town in a quiet neighbourhood and with a garden, but near an omnibus route.'

On an even more personal matter he was

corresponding with George Silk, a friend from his days in Leicester. Wallace was now 39, and he hoped to find a wife. 'I believe a good wife,' he informed Silk earnestly, 'to be the greatest blessing a man can enjoy and the only road to happiness.' He had once held the opinion that an essential qualification in a wife was the ability to provide 'intellectual companionship', but further reflection and the loneliness of eight years abroad had changed his mind. Now 'should my good stars ever send me an affectionate, good-tempered and domestic wife, I shall care not one iota for accomplishments or even for education.'

Wife-hunting proved to be more bruising than butterfly-chasing. Soon after his return to England, Wallace moved into a house in west London shared with his photographer brother-in-law, his sister and his mother whose cottage must have proved too small for the reunited family. He also joined a chess club at the instigation of George Silk. At the club — perhaps as Silk had planned — he made the acquaintance of a widower, a Mr L (Wallace never revealed the full name) who had two unmarried daughters. Soon Wallace was paying court to the elder girl, regularly visiting the family to take tea or supper with them, and beginning to hope that 'she would become my wife'. About this time his brother-in-law took another portrait of him, and the photograph offers a contrast to his more self-confident pose in Singapore. Wallace seems to have slipped back into his more diffident manner. He has lost his austere gauntness and the air of confidence. He stands very awkwardly, with a weak smile, almost as if embarrassed by the camera and finding London society rather overwhelming.

His timid handling of the courtship reflected this change. It took Wallace a year before he plucked up enough courage to propose to Miss L, and even then he did so by letter, not in person, because he was so shy. She wrote back, putting him off politely but not definitively. It was another year before Wallace tried again, this time writing to the girl's father to ask if he would see him privately. At their meeting Wallace was told that, provided the financial arrangements between the couple were satisfactory, the match could go ahead. So the engagement became official. The courtship continued at this formal, slow pace. Wallace brought Miss L home to meet his family; he called on her at her house two or three times a week; the wedding day was fixed, and all the arrangements made.

Then, totally unexpected, came the blow. Wallace called round to his fiancée's house as usual, only to be told by a servant that she had gone away and would write to him. Astonished, he waited for the letter. It came from Miss L's father and informed him that the young woman wanted to break off the engagement. Wallace was devastated and very deeply hurt. Eventually Miss L did write. She had heard gossip that Wallace had formed a friendship with another woman, the widow of an Indian Army officer, and Wallace had concealed the relationship from her. Poor Wallace had been the victim of his own reticence. He was acquainted with the Army widow, whom he thought was a very pleasant and good-natured woman, but he had no intention whatever of marrying her. He had not mentioned her to Miss L simply because he hated to talk about himself. He explained all this in a letter to her, 'but I received no reply, and from that day I never saw, or heard of, any of the family'.

Wallace's dismay at being jilted so brusquely reveals just how vulnerable he was emotionally. Forty years later he could write that, 'I have never in my life experienced such intensely painful emotion.' His many years abroad had left him feeling out of step with normal metropolitan society. He found it difficult to engage in trivial conversation, and he realised that to strangers he appeared gloomy 'when merely I was bored'.

He was also daunted to discover the sheer quantity of scientific material awaiting him. His boxes from Indonesia filled almost the entire upper room of the Sims' house, and he had not seen the contents of some of them for five or six years. Everything now had to be opened, laid out, described and then placed in a general scheme of classification, preferably with some reference either to the theory of evolution or to Wallace's notions on the geographical distribution of animals. Even the physical task of opening the careful packaging, 'the rough and dirty work', and teasing out the closely packed specimens from their wrappings was a major undertaking. It did not help that after his return Wallace suffered from a severe attack of painful boils as his body readjusted from years of living on poor food in a sultry climate. For a long time afterwards he was also prone to fevers and chills whenever the English weather changed.

His happiest discovery was to learn that he was sufficiently solvent to get on with the work, thanks to his agent. Samuel Stevens had not been sending the full proceeds of his sales out to Wallace in the field. There was surplus cash which he had invested on Wallace's behalf, mostly in Indian Railway stock. Wallace found that he had come back to an income of £300 a year, enough for him to live frugally while tackling the preliminary classification of his collections.

He concentrated on the birds, frequently going off to the bird room at the British Museum to consult with the resident expert there, a Mr Gray, who had already seen some of the more exotic specimens and had named the Standard Wing in Wallace's honour. But there was also time to study some of the huge collection of beetles, and to write learned papers on physical and zoological geography, as well as butterflies. These papers were submitted to the Zoological, Entomological and Linnean Societies, and Wallace gave an occasional lecture though, from shyness, he disliked standing up in front of an audience and knew that he was a clumsy speaker. He expressed himself best in writing, and he kept up a long correspondence with Darwin about various aspects of evolutionary theory. By now

Darwin knew that he had no reason to fear Wallace's resentment of the Linnean Society's 'delicate arrangement' about the announcement of Natural Selection, and the two men were on cordial terms. Wallace went down to stay overnight at Down House soon after he got back to London and, when the state of Darwin's health allowed, he would visit London and the two men occasionally met for lunch. For the benefit of the naturalists, Wallace arranged a display of the best of his exotic bird and butterfly collection in his brother-in-law's photographic gallery. It made a powerful impression as 'the entire series of my parrots, pigeons and paradise birds when laid out on long tables covered with white paper, formed a display of brilliant colours, strange forms, and exquisite textures that could hardly be surpassed.'

A sum of £300 per annum was by no means a lavish income for someone living in London, and Wallace was able to supplement it by selling off yet more duplicates from his collection until that source dried up. There was the worry that Indian Railways or any other investment might suffer from the boom-and-bust cycle of the Victorian economy, and so Wallace kept a lookout for a regular job. One such post came up, as Secretary to the Royal Geographical Society. Ironically Wallace found himself applying for it in competition with Henry Bates, his friend and former travelling companion in Brazil. Each man, hearing of the other's interest in the post, offered to withdraw. In the end Bates was selected, possibly because he had taught himself

German which was regarded, with French, as being the language of new science. Wallace was characteristically upbeat about the choice because 'it brought Bates to London' and he could see more of his friend.

Fortunately the South American connection also brought a more positive addition to Wallace's life. On the Amazon and the Rio Negro he and Bates had travelled with Dr. Richard Spruce, a botanist who had gone to Brazil to collect plants and to try to cure himself of lung and heart disease. Not surprisingly, the health cure had not been a success. When Spruce came back he was in worse health, having added severe rheumatism to his other illnesses while working in the Andes. He brought back a mass of South American plants which, like Wallace's collections, needed classification. Not expecting to live very long, Spruce enlisted the help of the leading English authority on mosses, Mr Walter Mitten, and moved to Hurstpierpoint in Sussex to be near his collaborator. Wallace travelled down to Sussex regularly in the summer and autumn of 1864 to see his sick friend,[1]

---

[1] Spruce was to survive, though in very poor health, for another 29 years. By the time of his death from influenza, aged 76, he had only completed six chapters of his book about his South American journeys. The remainder were edited for publication by Wallace, who retained a lifelong affection for the botanist.

was introduced to the Mitten family and met their 18-year-old daughter Annie. In a complete reversal of the ponderous courtship of Miss L, which had only recently collapsed, Wallace wooed and won Annie Mitten in a year. In spring 1865 they were married. It was to be a partnership which lasted with great contentment on both sides for the rest of their lives, despite a difference of fourteen years in their ages. Annie was exactly that quiet, homely and affectionate companion that Wallace had been dreaming about.

Wallace had already met the Mittens when he wrote to Darwin saying, perhaps half-joking, that he could not face tackling the heavy chore of writing a book about his Indonesian travels 'unless I should be fortunate enough to get a wife who would incite me thereto, and assist me therein — which is not likely'. Marriage to Annie does seem to have provided the necessary impetus, because two years later he was composing the final chapters of his travel narrative which had not turned out to be such a burden after all.

The reason was his remarkable tenacity and fluency as a writer in the field. During all his time in Indonesia he had been keeping a journal, writing up the day's or week's events in small notebooks with mottled purple covers. His self-discipline must have been enormous, to sit down at the end of an exhausting day and find the energy to write out several hundred words. Then there followed the problem of keeping the notebooks safe and dry for years in a wet

'Orang utang attacked by Dyaks'
(taken from The Malay Archipelago)

monsoon climate, under conditions which we had found required sealing everything carefully in plastic bags against the rain and humidity.

What is even more remarkable is how well Wallace wrote while he was in the field. His journals, now held in safe keeping by the Linnean Society, were written in ink in a clear copperplate hand, and they have very few crossings-out or corrections. Reading them, there is surprisingly little difference between the prose he wrote in the rainforest or the palm-thatched hut, and the finished paragraphs he published when back in London. He could order his thoughts and find the right phrases even when he was in the most difficult physical conditions. In short, he was a born writer.

The opposite was true of his skill as an artist, however. He was so inept that the sketches of butterflies in his field notes look as if they were drawn by a schoolchild, and for *The Malay Archipelago* he selected professional illustrators, one of them being Thomas Baines — an artist who had travelled with David Livingstone in Africa. They worked from Wallace's verbal descriptions, photographs he had obtained in Java and dried specimens of his own and other Indonesian collections. By early 1869 *The Malay Archipelago* was ready to be published; it was offered in two volumes, price £1.4s. It did not have quite the runaway success of Darwin's *Origins*, though the 1,500 copies of the first print sold quickly enough for the publishers, Macmillan, to print another 750 copies six months later. However, the book was to continue in steady demand over the next 20 years, reappearing in new guises every three or four years as the text became a standard work on the East Indies, helped by its publisher's enticing sub-title: 'The Land of the Orang-utang, and the Bird of Paradise'.

Darwin was sent an early copy and, like most reviewers, was very complimentary, but then the book had been dedicated to him. 'I have finished your book', he wrote to Wallace enthusiastically. 'It seems to me most excellent, and at the same time most pleasant to read. That you have returned alive is wonderful after all your risk from illness and sea voyages, especially that most interesting one to Waigiou and back. Of all the impressions which I have received from your book, the strongest is that your perseverance in the cause of science was heroic. Your descriptions of catching the splendid butterflies have made me quite envious, and at the same time have made me feel almost young again . . . Certainly collecting is the best sport in the world.' Darwin was sure that the book would be a great success, and that Wallace's observations on the geographical distribution of animals 'will be new to most of your readers'. The most valuable data, in Darwin's opinion, came from Wallace's information about Sulawesi.

At first glance, Wallace had written a standard Victorian travelogue. The frontispiece, for example, is a dramatic picture of five Dyak natives of Borneo entangled with a huge, enraged orang-utan. The orang-utan has sunk its teeth into the arm of one spear-carrying native, and the Dyak is falling back from the onslaught. The picture immediately recalls similar illustrations of a gorilla in the Congo jungle scowling menacingly over the broken gun of a vanquished explorer, or David Livingstone sprawling under the attack of a lion which is mangling his upper arm. But the caption to Wallace's picture is unexpected; it reads 'Orang utang attacked by Dyaks', not 'Orang utang attacks Dyaks'. Wallace was making it clear that man was the aggressor, not the animal.

Nor was his book a treatise on natural selection or animal distribution. It was a 'sketch of my eight years' wanderings among the largest and the most luxuriant islands which adorn our earth's surface'. He told his readers about the scenery, vegetation, animals and peoples of Indonesia, and he introduced evidence of natural selection only when it fitted into the flow of his tale. He had seen how the black cockatoos on Aru had learned to break into a particularly tough and slippery kind of nut by wrapping the nut in a leaf so that it could be held firmly while being cracked open. The more numerous white cockatoos, Wallace stated, did not know this technique. So 'the black cockatoos have maintained themselves in competition with their more numerous and active white allies, by the power of existing on a kind of food which no other bird is able to extract from its stony shell.'

In Wallace's eyes, the peoples of the archipelago were at least as interesting as the wildlife. Across the islands he described the extraordinary tapestry of different characters, clothing, houses and customs, often with a neat turn of phrase. At the temporary trading station on the sandspit of Dobbo in Aru, the Chinese traders 'stroll about or chat at each other's doors, in blue trousers, white jacket and a queue into which red ribbon is plaited until it reaches almost to their heels'. The senior Bugis shipman, a haji who has made the pilgrimage to Mecca, walks by 'in all the dignity of flowing green silk robe and gay turban', followed by two small boys carrying his boxes containing the leaf and lime for betel-chewing. Even when local habits are unpleasant, Wallace's description could add a light touch. In a village in interior Aru he found the people drunk, dispirited and dirty. Their main income was from selling baskets of sugar cane, for which they had an insatiable appetite, so that whenever Wallace entered a house he found 'three or four people with a yard of cane in one hand, a knife in the other, and a basket between their legs, hacking, paring, chewing, and basket-filling with a persevering assiduity which reminds one of a hungry cow grazing, or a caterpillar eating up a leaf'.

Observing the local people, he was reminded of his own visit some years earlier to a London exhibition where Zulus and Aztecs were on display to a curious public. Now, he said, the roles were reversed and he was stared at and questioned by the local people, who naturally wanted to know why he was putting dead birds and beetles in boxes. The most sophisticated theory was that he would later use the animals to make medicines. Another explanation was that he could make them come alive again when he got home. To anyone who did not know a naturalist's habits, his behaviour must have seemed very odd. On the island of Lombok, he would walk quietly along the country roads, then suddenly stop and stand stock-still for half an hour, giving out a series of quiet whistles in imitation of a ground thrush, hoping to lure the bird from the undergrowth. In Timor he waited incautiously under a tree, gazing up at a man who had climbed into the branches to collect wild honeycombs. He was wondering how the man could possibly manage to withstand the stings of the irate bee swarm when a few stray bees turned their attention on Wallace. He had to go running off, with bees crawling in his hair as he swatted at them with his butterfly net; then he halted long enough to scoop up a few bees as specimens. In remote villages he had spent hours fiddling about with dead beetles, round paper labels and mounting pins among people who had never seen a pin before. They thought it was a faulty needle, without an eye in it, and that he was quite mad.

Wallace much preferred this curiosity and questioning to being regarded fearfully as some sort of foreign devil. His unhappiest experience was in Sulawesi, in a small village where hardly anyone had seen a European before, and he was unable to explain what he was doing because no one could speak Malay. 'One most disagreeable result of this was that I excited terror alike in man and beast. Wherever I went, dogs barked, children screamed, women ran away, and men stared as though I was some strange and terrible cannibal monster.' The packhorses took fright at the sight of him, and went rushing off into the jungle. Even buffaloes, normally placid, would stick out their necks and stare at him; if he came any closer they would turn and bolt, breaking their tethers and trampling down anyone in their way. Poor Wallace had to keep out of sight, hiding whenever he saw someone coming, or skulking furtively down the back alleys of the village. If he unexpectedly stumbled on people at the village well or children bathing in a stream, they would scream and run in terror. This happened day after day, and it was 'very unpleasant to a person who does not like to be disliked'.

In practice Wallace was very adept at winning the confidence of strangers. He allowed villagers to try on his pebble glasses and in Bacan, when some onlookers were intrigued by his pocket magnifying glass, he set the device in a piece of wood to fix the focal length and handed it to them with a beetle to test. 'The excitement was immense. Some declared it (the beetle) was a yard long; others were frightened and instantly dropped it.' Nor did Wallace mind being the butt of local wit. He paid far too much to an Aru islander for two sea slugs which he wanted to eat to see what they tasted like. The man took the payment in tobacco and, seeing he had been overpaid, made no attempt to conceal his glee. He showed the large handful of tobacco to his companions, and 'grinned and twisted and gave silent chuckles in a most expressive pantomime'. Wallace took no offence. Instead he used the episode as another example of the difference between the more expressive 'Papuans' of the Spice Islands and the quieter, more reticent Malays.

This anthropological difference reinforced his notion of dividing lines running north-south through the archipelago, between the biological influences of Asia and Australia. For the human inhabitants he placed a line running between Flores and Sumbawa in the south, through the Moluccas and to the east of the Philippines. On the one hand were the Malays who had arrived from Asia; on the other hand there were the Papuans from the east. They were utterly different, Wallace claimed, in physique and culture. He proposed a similar watershed, a little farther west, to mark the boundary between land animals, birds and insects, whether they had spread from the Asian mainland or from Australia. Of course there was a great deal of overlap where the fauna from one direction mingled with species from the other side, and he was particularly puzzled about where to place Sulawesi. Did the strange-shaped island belong within the zone of Asian influence, or was it more Australian in its zoology? Wallace never tried to be precise, and he rather thought Sulawesi should be seen as a half-way house between two zones of influence. His concept was soon given a precision he never intended, as well as a name: it became 'The Wallace Line', and a favourite with generations of biologists as they drew and redrew the theoretical division, shifting first in one direction and then another as new data was acquired. After falling out of favour in the early twentieth century, the 'Wallace Line' concept was revived when the new study of plate tectonics in the 1950s showed that the Line roughly matched the main geological boundary between two sections of the earth's crust. Today, the Wallace Line is still employed as a very handy concept in studying the distribution of animals, though modified to take in the realisation that the geology and zoology of Sulawesi and the neighbouring islands are far more complex than first thought, and have close links with the Philippines. Until that puzzle is resolved, most scientists prefer to think of this central area as an intermediate zone and, in deference to the great pioneer, call it Wallacea.

* * *

When he left England, Wallace had not been a practising Christian, and he was no different when he came back. In a private note to his photographer brother-in-law, he reminded Sims that in his early days he had spent a year and a half in the household of a clergyman and 'heard almost every Tuesday the very best, most earnest and most impressive preacher it has ever been my fortune to meet with, but it produced no effect whatever on my mind. I have since wandered among men of many races and many religions. I have studied man, and

385

nature in all its aspects, and I have sought after truth. In my solitude I have pondered much on the incomprehensible subjects of space, eternity, life and death. I think I have fairly heard and fairly weighed the evidence on both sides, and I remain an *utter disbeliever* in almost all that you consider the most sacred truths.' He was thankful, he said, that 'I can see much to admire in all religions.'

It is odd, therefore, that in his description of Indonesia he barely mentioned the animist beliefs of many Indonesians whose ideas, in some respects, resembled his own. Most natives in the outer islands believed in spirits and practised ancestor worship. The Albuferro aborigines of Seram, for instance, were renowned as powerful magicians and spirit people. In nearby Ambon, it was believed that they could fly through the air and speak with dead ancestors. By the time he came to write his book, Wallace had also begun to believe that it was possible to communicate with the dead: he had become a fervent spiritualist.

Spiritualism was then very much in vogue. In the 1860s and 1870s, several mediums and clairvoyants in London were household names who held well-publicised séances and arranged manifestations. Wallace attended sessions where tables moved mysteriously, people passed through walls, or hovered in the air. There were rappings and messages from the dead. Wallace himself hosted seances at the Sims house, and naïvely sent out invitations to his scientific colleagues asking them to attend, if only to probe their actual basis. But the very idea of spiritualism ran counter to the stringently scientific ideas of the people Wallace was dealing with, the empirical naturalists. He was laughed at, and his credibility as a serious scientist was greatly harmed. Refusing to be overawed, he published an appeal on 'The Scientific Aspects of the Supernatural: indicating the desirableness of an experimental enquiry by men of science into the alleged powers of clairvoyants and mediums.' A situation arose where Wallace was called as a defence witness in the trial of a charlatan medium, and Charles Darwin was contributing anonymously to the costs for the prosecution.

As always, Wallace was entirely sincere. He had come to spiritualism as a result of attending a lecture on hypnotism — or mesmerism as it was then called — in 1844 when he was a young schoolteacher in Leicester and had gone to the lecture with some of the boys from the school. The lecturer had called up volunteers from the audience, placed them in trances and explained the difference between genuine and fake hypnotic states. He also suggested that members of the audience might like to make similar experiments for themselves. Naturally the schoolboys did so when they got back to school, and some of them succeeded. This persuaded Wallace also to try his hand; to his surprise, he found he had a talent for hypnotism and could make a few of his subjects go into deep mesmeric trances. From there it was easy to proceed to the belief that someone in a trance, like a village shaman or spirit doctor, might be able to communicate with another world.

Spiritualism in a scientist was considered an embarrassment, but this was less true of phrenology, the belief that the shape of the human skull can be read as an index of the person's abilities. Wallace linked the two together. Toying with hypnotism, he found he could produce specific responses from his hypnotised subjects by touching certain parts of their heads. He also had his own skull 'read' while he was working as a surveyor in Wales. The results seemed to him to be uncannily accurate, and he was confirmed in his view that there were certain psychic phenomena which were real but unexplained. Eventually this was to lead him to differ from Darwin's view of evolution. Wallace came to believe that evolution by natural selection explained much of the present state of the living world, but there was an unexplained spiritual dimension in the case of the human race.

From phrenology it was a small step to an even more respectable science — cranioscopy, the study of skull shapes. When Wallace sailed for Indonesia, respectable anthropologists were measuring the length, breadth and shapes of hundreds of human skulls. Their aim was to build up immense collections of such data which would form a basis for the classification of man. So in Indonesia Wallace dutifully measured the skulls of natives from various regions, trying to calculate whether the different skull shapes meant anything. His results were inconclusive, and when he returned to London he found that his work had been superseded. Cranioscopy as a science had been consigned to the dustbin.

So too, literally, were some of Wallace's precious notes. During his travels he had collected the basic vocabularies for no fewer than 57 languages, most of which he considered to be previously unknown. Again he was trying to help the anthropologists; they believed, correctly, that the study of local languages was a key to understanding where the people came from. Wallace wrote down the word lists in field notebooks, and on his return to England he lent them to John Crawford, the author of a Malay grammar book and dictionary.

Unfortunately, Crawford moved house a few months later, and the notebooks containing the main material for 25 of the vocabularies were mislaid and never recovered. A lesser man might have been enraged, but Wallace was philosophical. 'Being merely old and much-battered copybooks, they probably found their way to the dust heap along with other waste paper.' Undeterred, he published short word lists of what survived.

The year after *The Malay Archipelago* was published, Wallace became embroiled in a bizarre sideshow with a dangerous crank. Mr John Hampden believed that the earth was flat, and he challenged anyone to persuade him otherwise. Specifically, he offered a £500 bet to any scientist who could prove to him that any body of water could have a curve on its surface. Wallace, drawing on his experience as a surveyor, constructed what he thought would be a simple and elegant demonstration of the curvature of the earth's surface. On the brick parapet of the Old Bedford Bridge over the Bedford Canal, he fixed a sheet of white calico with a thick black line painted across it. This black line was exactly 13 feet 3 inches above the surface of the water. Moving six miles along the canal to the iron Welney Bridge, Wallace set up a large telescope mounted horizontally at exactly the same height. Half-way between the two bridges he erected a long vertical pole with two red discs on it. The upper disc was the same 13 feet 3 inches above the water, the lower disc four feet lower. If the water surface was truly flat, anyone glancing through the telescope would see the upper red disc and the black mark on the far bridge in an exact line. Wallace had calculated that due to the earth's curvature and allowing for refraction, the lower red disc would in fact appear in line with the far bridge.

When two observers, one for Hampden and one nominated by Wallace, looked through the big telescope, they agreed that the view was exactly as Wallace had predicted: the top disc appeared significantly higher than the mark on the brick bridge. But to Wallace's astonishment, Hampden's observer claimed that this proved the water was perfectly flat. His mentor John Hampden refused even to look through the telescope. Carpenter's statement, he said, was proof enough for him.

Wallace suggested an umpire be appointed and Hampden agreed that Mr Walsh, the editor of *The Field*, was the right person.

Walsh quickly decided in Wallace's favour, but Hampden became obsessed with a personal hatred for Walsh and particularly for Wallace and his worthless 'globular theory'. He began writing letters to Wallace's friends, denouncing him as a fraud and swindler. He sent similar letters of denunciation to the learned societies of which Wallace was a member, as well as to the shopkeepers who supplied the Wallace household. He posted hate mail to Wallace's wife, Annie. He kept up these attacks against Wallace for almost 16 years, even retrieving his money on the dubious legal grounds that when he first claimed it back, the cash was still with Walsh the stakeholder, so the bet had not gone through. In vain Wallace tried to have Hampden restrained by the courts or fined. His tormentor declared a false bankruptcy, spent a few weeks in jail and returned to the attack. As late as 1885, Hampden appeared at the Royal Geographical Society's Exhibition distributing pamphlets stating that Moses had decreed the earth was flat, and that opponents to the idea were 'pagan mystics'.

Even this episode failed to dent Wallace's positive view of humanity. He said that he regretted turning Hampden away when the half-mad 'Flat Earther' turned up unexpectedly at his front door. He would have done better, he felt, to have invited him in.

The long-drawn-out fracas with Hampden cost Wallace dearly, in cash as well as patience. He wasted hundreds of pounds in legal actions, just when his savings were being eroded by his unfortunate habit of moving house every two or three years. Perhaps this nomad trait was inherited from his father and enhanced by his wandering lifestyle in Indonesia, where he had made more than 80 moves from one research site to the next. For whatever reason, Wallace found it difficult to stay still. He built or converted house after house, and always produced a plausible reason for the change. First, it was to be near a new museum of art and natural history at Bethnal Green, which the government was funding. Wallace had applied for the job of director, and expected to get it. He wrote an article setting out very advanced views on how the museum should be run for the public benefit and scientific research, and how it should be displayed in a simple, uncluttered way. He also wanted seats placed so that visitors could view the exhibits in comfort. Disappointingly, the government postponed an appointment indefinitely.

So he was off, 20 miles down the Thames to Grays where he bought a building site and hired a builder to put up a large, comfortable house. The builder cheated him, and the house was sold four years later. The next house, at Dorking, lasted two years, and after that it was on to Croydon to be near good schools for his two children who had reached kindergarten age.

Like his father, too, Wallace was finding that a bachelor's income was not enough for a family man. To mingle with scientific luminaries or be the president of learned societies brought intellectual stimulus and prestige, but no money.

So Wallace tried everything to make ends meet. He wrote articles for the *Encyclopedia Britannica*; he marked examination papers for the Indian Civil Service; he applied for the job of superintendent of Epping Forest, again with ideas far ahead of his time; he wanted a large part of the forest set aside as a Nature Reserve, with the trees planted according to the regions they came from so that visitors could see the flora of different continents. The Corporation of London thought the idea too expensive, and gave the job to someone else. To make matters worse, Wallace had been persuaded by old friends and spiritualist colleagues to shift much of his investments into other foreign railway companies, Welsh slate quarries and English lead mines. Almost without exception these failed during the slump of 1875 – 85, and he lost nearly all his hard-earned capital.

By the time he was 55, the strain of money-grubbing was beginning to tell. Wallace seemed to have shrunk from his six-foot, one-inch height, and had the first signs of a stoop. A full set of white whiskers and head of hair gave him a patriarchal look. But this was only the outward appearance. He was still firing off lively articles on evolution, birds and spiritualism. He had written a highly acclaimed book on his pioneer subject, *The Geographical Distribution of Animals*, and another on tropical nature. He also continued to be an outspoken Owenite. The Welsh social reformer had died while Wallace was in the East, but Wallace remained true to his teachings and he used the final paragraphs of *The Malay Archipelago* to launch a broadside at Victorian economic exploitation of the masses. Their misery was '*absolutely greater* than has ever existed before', he declaimed. The armies of the new poor had to bear the sight of the riches and luxuries flaunted by the few, and 'this is not a result to boast of, or to be satisfied with'. Wallace wanted more attention paid to the training and development of sympathetic feelings and moral faculties in the general populace, or 'we shall never . . . attain to any real or important superiority over the better class of savages'. This, he concluded resoundingly, 'is the lesson I have been taught by observations of uncivilised man'.

When the social philosopher John Stuart Mill read the final pages of *The Malay Archipelago*, he was so impressed with Wallace's upbeat descriptions of how native societies were organised that he wrote to Wallace asking to meet him. There were no such invitations from the missionary organisations which were springing up to sponsor the evangelisation of what they considered to be benighted lands. Wallace had referred only briefly to the Christian missionary effort he had seen in south-east Asia, and was not always complimentary. He admitted that the missionaries 'have much to be proud of' in Minahasa in Sulawesi, where the natives were now 'the best clothed, the best housed, the best fed, and the best educated' in the archipelago. But he could not resist describing a missionary-educated schoolmaster of Minahasa as 'a great man, preaching and teaching for three hours at a stretch much in the style of an English ranter. This was pretty cold work to his auditors, however warming to himself, and I am inclined to think that these native teachers, having acquired facility of speaking, and an endless supply of religious platitudes to talk about, ride their hobby rather hard, without much consideration for their flock.'

Judged to be a learned maverick and beset by financial worries, Wallace cheerfully continued on his own way. In 1881 he accepted the post of President of the newly formed Land Nationalisation Society, whose central credo was that the private ownership of land was inherently wrong, and that government should act as a ground landlord renting out to tenants. It was not an idea likely to appeal to plutocrats like Darwin or his neighbour, the scientist-banker John Lubbock, who owned 3,000 acres near Down House. They knew about Wallace's financial troubles, and they probably felt that he was his own worst enemy when it came to presenting a case for a salaried job. To help him out, Darwin considered employing him as an editorial assistant at 7s an hour, but then had a better idea. With a group of influential friends he petitioned the government to provide Wallace with a pension from the Civil List in recognition of his services to natural history. Prime Minister Gladstone granted the request and Wallace was finally secure, in a modest way. He was to receive £200 a year.

This was Darwin's legacy to Wallace, and it helped to make up for the 'delicate arrangement' at the Linnean Society twenty years earlier. The pension was conjured up by much the same method: a small group of highly placed scientists got together and brought pressure to bear. This time it was for Wallace's benefit.

When Darwin died the following year, his prestige was so great that the funeral was a national event. His friends insisted it took place in Westminster Abbey, and not in Down village as had been planned by the family. Two Dukes and a Lord were chosen as the pallbearers, along with the American ambassador and four representatives of English Science including Hooker. By an oversight Wallace, the outsider, was not included. Then someone noticed the error. He was hastily contacted and agreed to join the cortège.

Wallace was to survive Darwin by an astonishing 30 years, dying at the age of 90 in the year before the outbreak of the First World War. For most of the time he lived modestly with his wife and children, finally settled in Dorset and a happy man. As the years passed, he accumulated more and more honours — medals, honorary doctorates, and eventually the Order of Merit. He accepted the honours gracefully, with a twinkle in his eye reminding Oxford University, as they gave him a degree, that he had left school at the age of 14. Nothing would stop him from voicing his opinions even if they ran directly counter to public opinion, such as his contrary idea that mass vaccination did more harm than good. He was part gadfly, part guru. He was consulted on whether there was life on Mars — he thought it was highly unlikely — and he wrote yet more books on economics, social questions and evolution, as well as an autobiography succinctly entitled *My Life*. Nor would he abandon his optimistic view of life. Commissioned to write a history of recent science, it was typical that he called it *This Wonderful Century*. Asked whether he, not Darwin, had first discovered the theory of evolution by natural selection, he always maintained that Darwin should have the credit and had done by far the greater work.

In his final years Wallace came to look like a genial leprechaun, happily pottering about his garden and still firmly convinced that all people were basically decent and honest. He looked forward to each new day just as much as he had done during his travels in Indonesia which, he came to realise, had been the defining period of his life. When he composed the final blithe pages of his autobiography he sounded no different from the man who, after his first day on Kei Besar in the Spice Islands, wrote: 'This has been a day of thorough enjoyment.'

Epilogue

HOW would Alfred Wallace have revised his impressions of the Spice Islands if he had travelled with us during those four months? With his unquenchable optimism, he would have stressed the positive side of what we saw. Right at the outset, for example, he would have been astonished how much improved was Haar village on Kai Besar from the miserable cluster of a few squalid huts he had visited in the middle of the previous century. Present-day Haar was cleaner, more substantial and thriving. Similarly, the little hamlet of Kaboei, where we had seen the Red Birds of Paradise, was a much more agreeable home for its inhabitants than the typical Waigeo villages of Wallace's day. He had found people living dangerously close to the borderline of starvation, whereas we met a community which was well-housed and well-fed. Most families still lived in exactly the same sort of small thatched huts raised on stilts which Wallace had converted into his cramped quarters. But now the buildings were in good repair, and we saw not the slightest evidence that food was short. Vegetables were available, fish were plentiful in the bay and, thanks to their sensible harvesting of the Red Birds of Paradise, albeit illegal, the people of Kaboei had a neat small church and enough spare cash to buy themselves cooking pots, clothing and kerosene lamps to make life more convenient.

In both Haar and Kaboei, these improvements in the living standards of the people had been made without damaging the environment. We had walked to Haar through a forest filled with spectacular birds and butterflies; we saw no evidence that the woodland was being destroyed wantonly, or that its creatures were being hunted into oblivion. Around Kaboei the jungle had scarcely been touched. There were vast tracts of pristine wilderness, and a great variety of bird-life. Quite apart from the fact that there now seemed to be more Red Birds of Paradise than in Wallace's day, Budi counted no fewer than 82 bird species during our visit to Kaboei.

These were the best examples of unspoiled environment and improved living conditions we met, and they were all the more striking because they were both sustained with little formal effort at conservation. Kaboei lay within the huge western Waigeo Nature Reserve, but we never saw nor even heard of any field enforcement of environmental protection laws. The Nature Reserve, if it had any effect at all merely provided benign neglect to reinforce the advantages of isolation and having a very small population. The forest around Haar was more interesting because this was not even a notional Nature Reserve. Also, the population was much larger. Yet it appeared that traditional care for the environment had done as much to preserve it as any modern protection policy.

Positive impressions were distributed from one end of our journey to the other. Warbal, where our boat was built, had been delightful. Its clean sandy streets and relaxed pace gave its boatbuilding community an enviable quality of life. The Banda islands were probably as tranquil as when Bin Saleh Baadilla, the bird-skin trader, had lived there. The highlands of Minahasa in Sulawesi were still a fertile patchwork of rice fields, vegetable gardens and fruit orchards. Among the hundreds of horse-drawn carts taking the produce to market, we saw not one single malnourished animal between the shafts.

The black spots were the cities. All too often when we entered a major population centre, we wished we were elsewhere. Ambon, Dobbo, Sorong, Manado — all had the same depressing combination of severe overcrowding, shoddy housing, broken drains, ugly electric cables hanging down, and frequent noisy traffic jams. Only Ternate seemed to have developed with style and good planning. Here industry was confined to the south of the city; neat residential suburbs stretched away to the north; and traffic was banned from the city centre, except for delivery vehicles and traditional horse-drawn traps. Wallace would still have preferred to set up his base camp in pleasant Ternate rather than Manado or Ambon. He would have compared their slums with the equivalent in Victorian England, and I found it ironic that what Wallace had left behind in London or Liverpool 140 years ago, we found in the overcrowded cities of the twentieth-century Moluccas.

Yet in these cities, too, Wallace would have pointed to a huge improvement. He was a champion of public education, and the progress in the Spice Islands was perhaps the greatest and most positive change he could have wished. Primary education was virtually universal. Gaggles of schoolchildren in their uniforms were one of the abiding memories of the islands, whether in the town centres or along the rural roads. In the most remote village of a dozen palm-thatched cabins we found a Primary schoolteacher, despite the fact that there was no proper school building and very few books. Literacy was on a scale Wallace could not have imagined in his era, and he would have thoroughly approved.

How he would have judged the blending of the different peoples and the erosion of their regional cultures is less certain, for Wallace relished the wonderful variety he found among the inhabitants of the Moluccas. He had a good eye and ear for how dress, language, domestic architecture and custom differed from one locality to the next. He would have been disappointed to find just how much these differences have now been smoothed away. For our modern expedition, there was the benefit that it was easier to communicate now that nearly everyone spoke a common language. For Wallace, it was much more awkward as he struggled to make himself understood among tribes who spoke only local dialects. Yet, without doubt, some of the cultural richness had been lost. The Spice Islands were no longer the human kaleidoscope he had encountered.

The most important human trait, however, remained. Time and again Wallace makes the point that he never felt threatened or in danger among the people he visited. Even in the most remote village on Aru, he would turn in 'under my mosquito net, to sleep with a sense of perfect security'. The same was true of our own experience. The patience, openness and courtesy of the people we met was remarkable. We were given the same relaxed and friendly response whether we dropped anchor off a remote village and went ashore to fill water containers from the village well, or were asking a street vendor in Mandao where he obtained his stock of edible bats. An evasive or surly answer would have been understandable, but we met with an open, often disarmingly frank reply.

'I have a horror of small boats,' Alfred Wallace concluded. So he would probably have declined an invitation to travel aboard our slender prahu kalulis. Our Kei Island vessel was not big enough for him, being smaller than the boats he travelled in, with the possible exception of his 'small prau' which he used for his trip to Waigeo. Yet, as it had turned out, our prahu had been a major success of the expedition. After we had learned how to handle the strange rectangular sails, we made rapid progress whenever there was even a breath of a favourable wind to send us on our way. Passage-making in the Spice Islands turned out to be a real pleasure. No one felt cold in those balmy temperatures; we never experienced a bad gale; and navigation was no problem at all. One searched the horizon for a convenient landmark, and steered by it until the next island came in view. The risk to the seafarer was not too much wind, but too little. Wallace's worst experiences had been when he was becalmed, and then swept away by hostile currents. We were spared that indignity by the help of our little outboard engine, and it also meant that we never had to wait out a prolonged calm. But the strength of the sea currents was a surprise, even so. The power of the ebb and flow of the tides was funnelled by narrow channels between the islands, or disturbed by coral reefs so that there were overfalls and tidal races. Sailing through the Spice Islands meant watching the water as much as the sky.

Wallace always played down the dangers of travel. The Indonesian archipelago, he said, was no more dangerous than London. The risk of being attacked by a crazed dagger-wielding native, run amok, was no greater than being bitten by a mad dog in the street or being struck down by a toppling chimney in a London gale. As for the animal world, he was never stung by a scorpion nor bitten by a snake in all his time in Indonesia, even when pulling aside thick undergrowth while searching for beetles. The closest he had come to snake-bite was in the cabin of a large kora kora canoe, where he was settling down to go to sleep when he put his hand on a venomous snake coiled up in the luggage. With the help of the other passengers he killed the reptile with a chopping knife, and 'thinking it very unlikely that two snakes had got aboard at the same time, I turned in and went to sleep'. However, he did admit to having vague apprehensions of touching another snake so that he lay 'wonderfully still' all that night.

Then, as now, the real risks of travel in the Spice Islands were the unseen dangers of disease and ill-health. It is remarkable that Wallace's health was not permanently ruined, and that he eventually lived so long. He swallowed repeated doses of quinine against malaria, yet he still suffered from regular bouts of fever, 'brow ague' and — worst of all — the twin scourges of septic boils and ulcerating insect bites. In our travels, all of us including Yanis suffered from fevers of one sort or another, while Bobby had to be sent home due to his malaria. During the preparations we also experienced two cases of dengue fever. This was despite our precautions of inoculations, regular anti-malarial pills and scrupulous attention to filtering all the water we used for cooking and drinking. We had our own doctor, Joe, who had to stitch up a bad coral wound sustained by Paul Harris, our visiting photographer. There was no comparison with the risks that Wallace took. He had to doctor his own sores and wounds, and there was no one to attend to major injuries.

For every year that Wallace had been in the Moluccas, we had spent a little more than a month. So our impressions were inevitably hasty, though we did manage to cover the great majority of the ground where Wallace had done his significant pioneering work. Concentrating on Wallace's route, we ignored areas where other environmental protection programmes were in progress. In northern Sulawesi, for example, there were much larger Nature Reserves than in Tangkoko. On one of them there was an ongoing programme to breed maleos in captivity, to replace those strange blue-helmeted birds which had been eaten from the beaches of Tangkoko. But these other Reserves were outside the scope of our expedition, and we also had to keep in mind that our impressions were only gathered from a tiny sliver of the rim of Indonesia.

Birds of Paradise had been the focus for Wallace's quest as a collector, and in a sense they were the same for us. They symbolised for him all that was most remarkable and rare in the wildlife of the Moluccas. What would happen to them when their beauty became better known? he had asked. After three years in the Spice Islands, he had come to the opinion that their true numbers and variety were being concealed by the native hunters. He had been able to collect specimens of only five of the 14 species then known, whereas twenty years earlier twice that number of species could be purchased on the coast in a few weeks, and without all the inland exploration and effort that Wallace had made. The reason for the decline, he believed, was that the agents for the Sultan of Tidore had been too demanding. Recently they had been asking for lesser-known species that were hard work to trap, and then paying very little for them. The natives of the interior preferred to say that the birds were extremely rare, and handed over the more common varieties.

Wallace was wrong. The lesser-known species were not only difficult to catch, they were also few in numbers and confined to remote areas of New Guinea which he did not reach. 140 years later, we did not have the opportunity to see anything like the full range of Birds of Paradise. Our route in Wallace's wake led us to the habitats of just four species that he had found. The fifth was in Dorey in Irian Jaya, which we did not visit. So if the Birds of Paradise were also the symbol for our own quest to see what had happened to the natural world Wallace had described, then our verdict was mixed. We had seen just one Greater Bird of Paradise in the Baun Nature Reserve of Aru, and been told that the second species, the King Bird of Paradise, was also breeding there. But we left Baun with an uneasy feeling that all was not well with the Reserve itself, which seemed too heavily dependent on the support of foreign environmental groups. If their assistance faded, so too might the Reserve.

At the other end of the scale, the Red Birds of Paradise of Waigeo were flourishing because they were so isolated and of real economic value to the local people. In the middle came the surviving populations of Wallace's Standard Wings. We may have seen more of these extraordinary creatures than he did — he collected only seven, it will be remembered. Yet on Bacan, where he had done his collecting, not a single bird remained. Much of the island's woodlands had been cleared to make fields and market gardens, and their habitat was gone. Wallace's Standard Wing had probably vanished from Bacan before the bird-hunting professionals of Sidangoli had got to work. The focus had now shifted to Halmahera. The 'Sanctuary' for Standard Wings at Batu Putih was in its death throes. The noise of passing trucks, destruction of habitat and thoughtless tourism spelled the end of the bird colony there. Other colonies existed in the hinterland — some may yet be discovered — and we had seen the flock of Standard Wings displaying at dawn and dusk in the rainforest behind Labi Labi. So there was every chance that Wallace's own species of Bird of Paradise would continue to exist, if the proper steps were taken to protect them.

The manner of that protection contained a paradox. The most competent environmental protection we had seen was that of the Rangers of Tangkoko. They had the energy and commitment, but they lacked any real authority. By contrast, the employees of the Forestry Department responsible for wildlife protection had the legal authority but lacked the commitment, and they were so poorly equipped that they were denied the means. Culturally they disliked confrontation with poachers and other transgressors — and worse, their poverty meant that they were vulnerable to bribery. The result could be as dismaying as the slaughter of the turtles on the beach at Enue Island, and the mass pillage of their nests.

If Wallace had been with us, his worst shock would not have been in the teeming city streets nor in the forests. It would have been when he looked over the side of our little prahu as we sailed into Ambon harbour. The exquisite underwater coral garden which he had described with such enthusiasm was irretrievably gone. Instead of crystal-clear water, the bay of Ambon was a loathsome brown stew of pollution, where torn plastic rubbish floated in slicks of scum and oil. Wallace would have been appalled. For many, many miles we had sailed across sparkling, clean seas. On long passages we had never seen a hint of bilge oil from a ship, and man-made rubbish was rare. The usual flotsam was the waterlogged trunk of a palm tree bobbing and turning gently in the current. But Ambon's filthy harbour was a warning, and it was repeated at the very end of our trip when we sailed into Manado's small harbour. That, too, was squalid beyond belief. A foul-smelling, yellow-brown stain seeped from the land, carrying with it a burden of urban garbage. Almost incredibly, the stain was spreading out across Manado Bay towards one of the great assets of the region: Bunaken Island. It was a world-famous tourist attraction, particularly

Underwater scene

for divers exploring the magnificent coral reef. The metal skeletons of a dozen new hotels were rising on the edge of Manado Bay, ready to accommodate the expected rush of tourists. But Manado offered no municipal sewage. Unless action was swiftly taken, each new hotel would probably dispose sewage directly into the bay, and pollute the tourist resource itself.

If Wallace had known that the threat to the environment lay just as much under water as above it, he would have approved that we handed over *Alfred Wallace* to Coral Cay Conservation in Manado. Dedicated to preserving the underwater biology of the coral reefs, this group planned to use the prahu as a support boat in their Sulawesi programme.

Without a boat, we had no floating home, and our team began to go their separate ways. Julia left for England, where she would prepare a final information sheet to be sent to the schools where she and Budi had given talks. The total audience had been more than 5,000 children in 119 schools. The information sheet would tell the children about the outcome of our trip. Budi stayed on in Manado, finding himself a temporary post with the conservation department before he went back to Kalimantan. It took him almost a week to write up his notes on all the birds he had identified during our trip; the list came to 239 species. The saddest person was Yanis who, more than any of us, had made *Alfred Wallace* the focus of his life. He had looked after the vessel inside and out, scrubbing the bilges or ducking down and swimming alongside to clean off the light coating of weed that grew on the hull. When we went ashore to visit the forest, he preferred to stay on board as watchman, or would establish himself on the beach gazing out over his charge. He had been devoted and utterly loyal for the entire journey, though he must have felt slightly redundant as the rest of us learned to handle the sails and take over the running of the boat. His good humour had never faltered. Now he was like a schoolboy at the end of the happiest and most important term of his school life. In his pocket he had his ticket home to Kei, and his wages for the trip; with a bonus, it meant that he was very well off by island standards. Yet he was distinctly forlorn when he came to say goodbye. The expedition would be only a memory, something to tell over and over again to the people back home on Warbal.

Joe, Leonard, Trondur and I ate a final, farewell meal together in honour of Alfred Wallace. From his journal it was clear that Alfred Wallace had a culinary curiosity and he was always trying unusual dishes, whether dried sea slug or a scrawny cockatoo. So we ate a Minahasa meal, and chose a café serving only local food which offered three main dishes — dog, bat and rat, boiled in coconut oil and heavily spiced. We tried them all. The rat was acrid and unpleasant. Dog tasted a little like beef. We agreed with Wallace that bat was the best. He said it tasted like hare, but did not warn us that it was ladled on to your plate, leathery wings and all.

When all the others except Budi had gone their separate ways, I too left. At the airport I was detained at the immigration desk, because the tourist visa in my passport had expired. I was escorted to see a senior immigration officer. In his office I apologised, and explained how the bureaucrats in Jakarta had never managed to keep up with us. Our official research visas had not been ready when the monsoon winds changed, and we had been forced to start our voyage. Since that time no one had asked to see a visa, and it had been impossible to return to Jakarta to obtain the proper one. The senior immigration officer was courteous. There was

411

a fine to pay. I counted out the money and laid it on his desk. Then he asked me to tell him about the voyage, and I began to explain about Wallace. But he already knew about the Victorian traveller to his country, and about the Wallace Line. He listened to the outline of my story and then, as the departure of my flight was called, reached across and pushed the money for the fine back to me. 'Take it,' he said rather wistfully, 'I am glad that Wallace brought you and your team to parts of Indonesia that I have never seen, and that you enjoyed your journey so much.'

Further Reading

Wallace's *The Malay Archipelago* has been re-published in paperback by Oxford University Press (1986), and his correspondence was collected by James Marchant as *Alfred Wallace: Letters & Reminiscences*, 2 vols (London, 1916). The main source for his life story is, of course, his autobiography, *My Life* (London, 1905), and there have been two biographies: *Darwin's Moon* by Amabel Williams-Ellis (London, 1966) and *Biologist Philosopher* by Wilma George (London, 1964). The episode of the joint proposal of the theory of evolution by natural selection at the Linnean Society is considered in greater detail by J. L. Brooks in *Just before the Origin* (New York, 1984) and Arnold C. Brackman in *A Delicate Arrangement* (New York, 1980).

Acknowledgements

It took two years to plan and prepare the Spice Islands Voyage, and it is well known that most small private expeditions depend heavily on the generosity of sponsors. Perhaps less familiar is the great variety of ways in which people are willing to help — in our case, providing such different items as satellite communications equipment and reels of flax thread for stitching sails. Equally vital are the letters of introduction, the local advice, and the readiness to assist a visitor who arrives with a proposal that has nothing to do with the day-to-day business of making a living in a country where life is already demanding enough. Nor does the help end when the expedition gets under way. In the field, many acts of kindness helped us to a successful conclusion of our journey. It would be

415

impossible to make a complete list, but a glance at the range of generosity — commercial, official and, above all, private — gives some idea of the debt of gratitude. To all of those who helped the Spice Islands Voyage — many, many thanks.

In Europe: Aquaman Ltd (Max Malavasi) for waterproof cases; Barbour Campbell Threads (Eric Barfoot); Fuji Film; Henderson Ltd for Whale Pumps; Henry Lloyd for sea clothing; Lumic Ltd (George Durrant) for an Ampair wind charger; Lyon Equipment for waterproof kitbags & rucksacks; Dr Campbell Mackenzie for medical equipment; Colin Mudie for naval architect's expertise; Navico Ltd for a handheld VHF radio; North Sails for recycled cloth; Ricoh Europe BV (Takashi Nakamura) for fax machines for the education programme; RTE Irish Television (Tony O'Connor) for the loan of mini-digital video equipment; Telesonic Marine for help with chandlery; Trimble Navigation UK (Julian Grant) for a Galaxy Sat-C transceiver and an Ensign GPS; Vango Ltd for tents and sleeping bags; University of Limerick for organising the outreach education programme; and the Department of Education and IBM Ireland (also for providing a 755CD Thinkpad) for sponsoring it.

In Indonesia: Admiral I. N. Sudomo (ret), Chairman of the Supreme Advisory Council, Republic of Indonesia; HE Minister of Education Prof. Dr Ing. Wardiman Djojonegoro; Professor Ibnu Sutowo and the Wallacea Development Institute (Prof. Samaun Samadikin, Dr Sumadi,

Adnan Karamoy, Endie Singgih); British Embassy Partnership Scheme support for the in-country educational programme; ARCO Indonesia (Leon Codron); Birdlife International; British Gas Indonesia; Bouraq Airlines; Garuda Indonesia; Todd Hooe in Kei; Ita da Lima, Jeff and Diana Clifford in Ambon; Catherine and Heinz Lorenz of *Rolling Home*; Maxus (Mike Andersen); Murex (Dr Hani Batuna) in Manado for looking after our prahu; PT. Newmont Minahasa Raya for ground transport in Sulawesi Utara; Syamsuddin Muhammad, Ternate; Tangkoko Rangers (Yunus, Saskar, Yuri, Simsun, Fecky, Raymond, Desman); and Wetlands International.

Special thanks are due to our leading financial sponsor, BP Indonesia (Adrian Bond, Charles Proctor) and to IBM/PT Usaha Sistim Informasi Jaya who underwrote the cost of our satellite communications link for the outreach schools programme. In particular, I would like to thank Rosihan Soebiakto & Deva Choesin of IBM Jakarta for giving up their free time and lending their skills to keep that satellite link running so smoothly.

Finally, the most valuable and practical help any far-ranging expedition could wish for came from DHL World Wide Systems who have so often assisted me in the past, thanks to the kindness of David Allen OBE. As usual his teams in the UK and Ireland were highly efficient and helpful, and this support was matched by the competence and enthusiasm of their colleagues in Indonesia in DHL/PT Birotika Semesta.

Generous help came at every level and region, from Rudi Pesik in the lead, to Stephen Fenwick, Richard Legoh, Soraya Rudianti in Jakarta to Jumsi (Ambon) Herman (Ternate) and to Nancy Maukar and her colleagues in Manado who looked after the return of all our equipment. To all of them — my grateful thanks.

One team member is mentioned in passing in the story of the voyage: Paul Harris. He joined the expedition in Ternate for the final sector of the trip and — as on an earlier journey with me in Mongolia — provided his usual excellent photo-coverage. Ever the professional, Paul put total effort into his photography, even to the point of sustaining a bad coral gash while taking a key shot of the *Alfred Wallace* from a rocky islet.

I would also like to thank Kathy MacKinnon, acknowledged authority on Indonesian wildlife, for her kindness in checking biological facts in the text — errors which remain are, of course, my own.

Tim Severin
Co. Cork
Ireland

418

Other titles in the
Charnwood Library Series:

PAY ANY PRICE
Ted Allbeury

After the Kennedy killings the heat was on
— on the Mafia, the KGB, the Cubans, and
the FBI . . .

MY SWEET AUDRINA
Virginia Andrews

She wanted to be loved as much as the
first Audrina, the sister who was perfect
and beautiful — and dead.

PRIDE AND PREJUDICE
Jane Austen

Mr. Bennet's five eligible daughters will never
inherit their father's money. The family fortunes
are destined to pass to a cousin. Should one
of the daughters marry him?

THE GLASS BLOWERS
Daphne Du Maurier

A novel about the author's forebears, the
Bussons, which gives an unusual glimpse
of the events that led up to the French
Revolution, and of the Revolution itself.

CHINESE ALICE
Pat Barr

The story of Alice Greenwood gives a complete picture of late 19th century China.

UNCUT JADE
Pat Barr

In this sequel to CHINESE ALICE, Alice Greenwood finds herself widowed and alone in a turbulent China.

THE GRAND BABYLON HOTEL
Arnold Bennett

A romantic thriller set in an exclusive London Hotel at the turn of the century.

SINGING SPEARS
E. V. Thompson

Daniel Retallick, son of Josh and Miriam (from CHASE THE WIND) was growing up to manhood. This novel portrays his prime in Central Africa.